I0792922

POSTCARD HISTORY SERIES

Pittsfield

On the Front Cover: Pittsfield's pride in its buildings is evident in this card from about 1911. Two large hotels, the elegant Berkshire Athenaeum with its library and museum, the imposing bank, and the brand-new US Post Office building all symbolized the prosperity of the Berkshire County seat. (Courtesy of the Berkshire County Historical Society.)

On the Back Cover: This novelty postcard, printed in Austria in 1906, shows Pittsfield's North Street "in the near future." A series of similar cards, each with a particular New England city's main street superimposed with flying machines and a monorail, was commissioned by Reichner Brothers of Boston. Although fanciful, this postcard surely tapped into the spirit of the early 20th century, when Pittsfield was rapidly expanding and all seemed possible. (Courtesy of the Berkshire County Historical Society.)

Postcard History Series

Pittsfield

The Berkshire County Historical Society

ARCADIA PUBLISHING

ISBN 978-1-4671-3472-9

Published by Arcadia Publishing
Charleston, South Carolina

Printed in the United States of America

Library of Congress Control Number: 2015942180

For all general information contact Arcadia Publishing at:
Telephone 843-853-2070
Fax 843-853-0044
E-mail sales@arcadiapublishing.com
For customer service and orders:
Toll-Free 1-888-313-2665

Visit us on the Internet at www.arcadiapublishing.com

To the archives volunteers of the Berkshire County Historical Society

Contents

Acknowledgments		6
Introduction		7
1.	North, South, East, and West Pittsfield	9
2.	Literary and Cultural Sites	25
3.	Places of Worship	37
4.	Education and Civic Life	49
5.	Health and Wellness	63
6.	Business and Industry	71
7.	Recreation	87
8.	Restaurants and Lodgings	105
9.	Disruptions and Disasters	121

ACKNOWLEDGMENTS

For over 50 years, the Berkshire County Historical Society has collected artifacts, photographs, and documents that illustrate the history of western Massachusetts. This fascinating work is made possible by the many volunteers who step forward to organize the collections and make them available to the public.

This book is part of our tradition of dedication, hard work, and camaraderie. Eileen Myers and Barbara Bell led the effort, with the able assistance of June Marketonis, Fay Henry, Maida Henriques, Norma Purdy, Peter Bergman, and Will Garrison.

Unless otherwise indicated, all images are courtesy of the Berkshire County Historical Society. This book would not have been possible without the many donors who have given their postcards to the society over the decades. In particular, Lee C. Drickamer gave vast numbers of postcards, just a few of which appear here.

Introduction

Pittsfield has long been the home of innovation. From its earliest days as Pontoosuck Plantation (incorporating a Mohican word meaning "haunt of the winter deer") through today, this region has inspired invention and creativity, bringing forth an amazing array of new ideas and products. Pittsfield innovators used Merino wool to create American broadcloth, which clothed soldiers and society ladies alike. William Stanley's invention of electrical transformers attracted General Electric to Pittsfield, and the company later expanded into plastics, including the invention of Lexan. Gordon McKay, of Pittsfield, invented a sewing machine to attach soles to leather shoes, fostering more industry.

It was not all industry. Berkshire County, with its natural beauty, attracted authors such as Henry Wadsworth Longfellow, Oliver Wendell Holmes, and Herman Melville. Throw into the mix a thousand other strands of creativity, innovation, hard work, and recreation, and an image emerges of a vital and interesting small city. This book contains glimpses of this history, seen in the ever-evolving medium of postcards.

Postcards were an innovation in communication in the 1840s, when notecards were mailed in pictorial envelopes. The world's oldest postcard was sent in 1840 to the writer Theodore Hook of London, England. The next innovation developed during the American Civil War, when drawings, paintings, and photographs were printed on one side of hard cardstock and the other side left for a message, although many people wrote over the images, obscuring them. On February 27, 1861, Congress passed an act that allowed privately printed cards, weighing one ounce or under, to be sent in the mail. That same year, John P. Charlton copyrighted the first postcard in America.

In 1870, Hymen L. Lipman began reissuing Charlton's postcard under a new name: Lipman's Postal Cards. The first government-produced postcard was issued on May 1, 1873. By law, the government postcards were the only postcards allowed to bear the term "postal card." Private publishers were allowed to print postcards, but they were more expensive to mail (2¢ instead of 1¢ for the government-issued cards).

A few years later, American publishers were allowed to print and sell cards bearing the inscription, "Private Mailing Card, Authorized by Act of Congress on May 19, 1898." These private mailing cards could be sent with 1¢ stamps, making this the most significant event to enhance the use of private postal cards. Messages were not allowed on the address side of the private mailing cards, as indicated by the words "This side is exclusively for the Address." If the front had an image, then a small space was left for a message.

An international postal agreement in 1907 led to a major change in the design of postcards. Cards could have messages on the left half of the address side, meaning the entire reverse side could have an image. This change ushered in the divided back period (1907–1915), also known as the Golden Age of Postcards due to the vast popularity of postcards during this time period.

Another type of postcard that began to be produced and popularly used during the divided back period and through the white border period is the real-photo postcard. Real-photo postcards were first produced using the Kodak "postcard camera." The postcard camera took a photograph and then printed a postcard-size negative of the image, complete with a divided back and place for postage. In chapter 9, the postcards produced by Pittsfield native Matthew H. Powell (1869–1922) fall into this category.

Most of the privately published pictorial cards sold in America were produced in Germany, where companies perfected the color lithograph process. But in Pittsfield, two companies offered to create cards privately for anyone who wished to supply personal photographs. The 1908 Pittsfield City Directory includes Manning's Photography Studio as a potential supplier and Eagle Printing and Binding as another. A series of baseball-oriented cards was created by the innovative local photographer Matthew Powell, who used early wide-angle lenses.

With the beginning of World War I, trade with Germany ceased, and American printers supplied most of the postcards in the United States. Since they did not have the same sophisticated technology as German printers, the quality of the cards fell, effectively ending the golden age. Also, printers saved ink during this time by not printing to the edge of the card, leaving a white border around the image. Postcards from the so-called white border period also had a description of the image on the message side, which retained the divided back.

Beginning in the 1930s, new printing processes allowed printers to produce postcards with high rag content, which gave them the appearance of being printed on linen, rather than paper. The most notable printer of this period was Curt Teich & Co. of Chicago, Illinois, which printed its first linen card in 1931 and whose postcards became popular around the world. Teich's process allowed for quicker production and brighter dyes to be used to color the images. Most postcards retained the white border, though some were printed to the edge of the card. The back remained divided and usually contained printed information about the image.

The production of linen postcards eventually gave way to photochrome postcards, a color-printing process that closely resemble photographs. However, linen cards continued to be produced for over a decade after the advent of photochrome postcards.

Modern photochrome-style postcards first appeared in 1939, when the Union Oil Company began to sell them in their western service stations. Production of the postcards slowed during World War II because of supply shortages, but after the war, they dominated the market. In the 1990s, the advent of e-cards and e-mail started the decline of the postcard's popularity. Today, postcards are typically purchased as souvenirs, rather than a quick way to communicate. They often can be purchased as connected groups of cards that fold and unfold. But just like those first cards printed and mailed 150 years ago, the newest cards illustrate the changing landscapes of Pittsfield.

The postcards in this book are drawn almost exclusively from the collection of the Berkshire County Historical Society at Herman Melville's Arrowhead, located in Pittsfield, Massachusetts. Although the collection is vast, it does not include every possible site in the city. Donations of other cards are always welcome.

One

North, South, East, and West Pittsfield

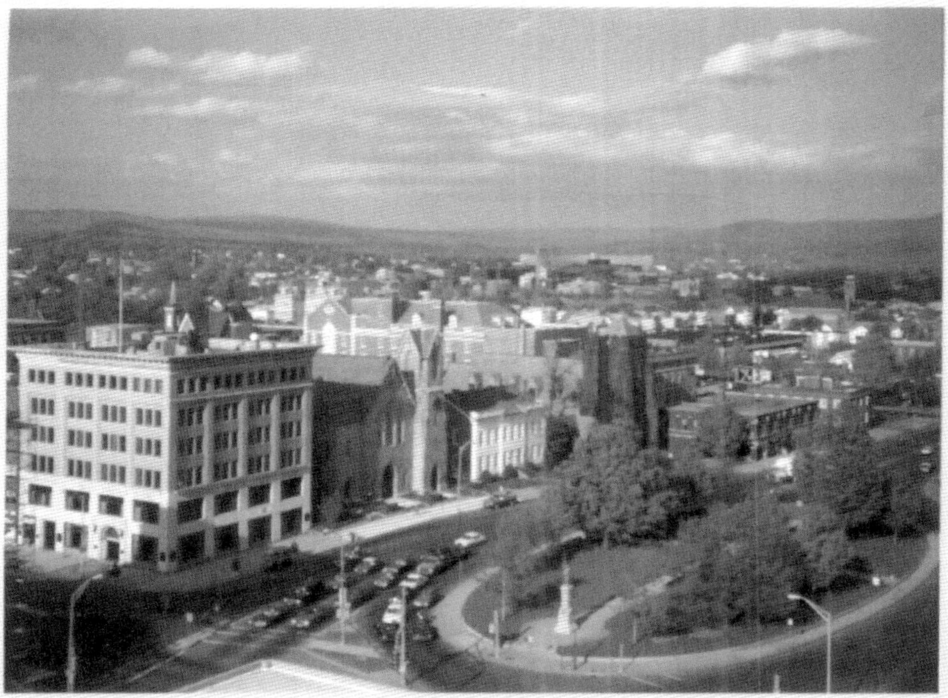

This image of Park Square from around 1975 illustrates the center of Pittsfield and its four main streets: North, South, East and West. In 1825, a citizens' committee fenced in the area and laid out the roads around it. The fence is gone, and the cars circle, but Park Square remains the heart of the city.

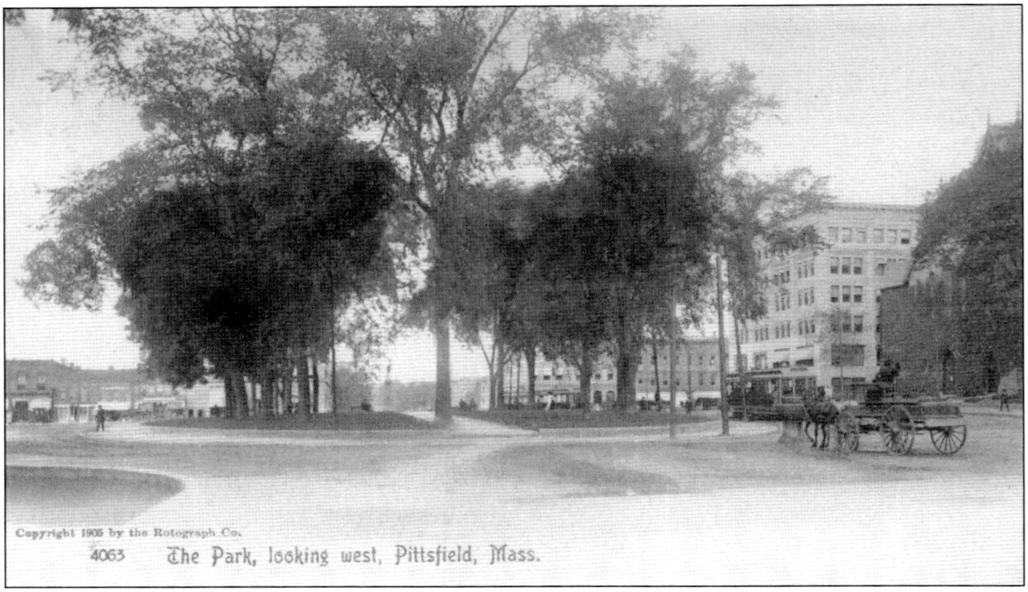

Local historian J.E.A. Smith noted in 1869, "The Park – hallowed of Pittsfield tradition – which forms the central gem of the village is shaded by an elliptical grove of handsome elms, in the center of which stood a veteran of the same species." The famous 113-foot-tall Pittsfield Elm, seen here, was removed in 1864. A memorial plaque and a disease-resistant young elm mark the site.

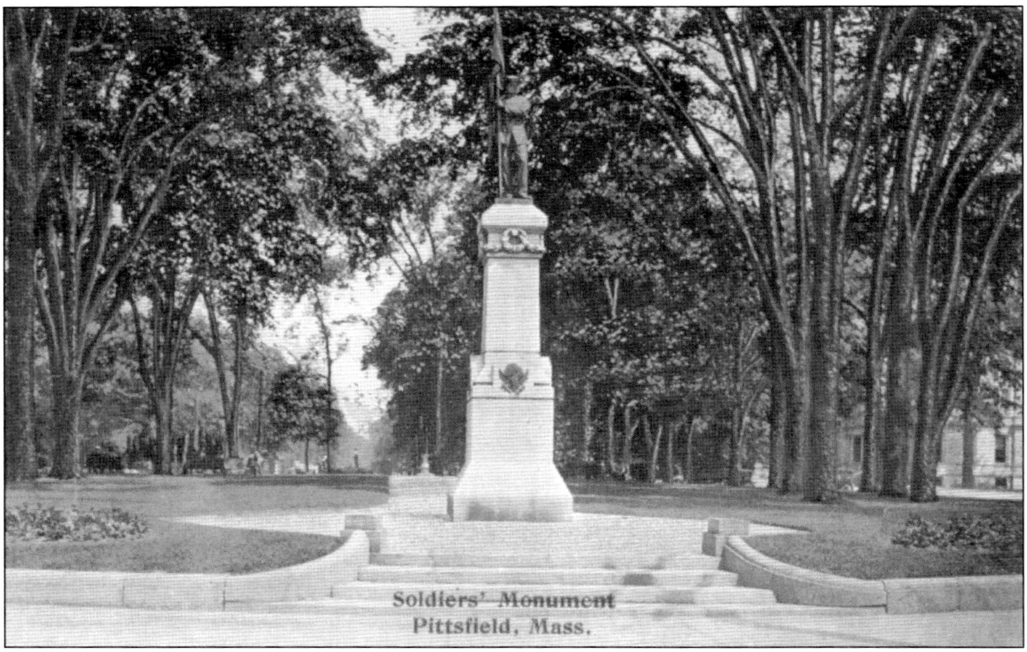

On September 24, 1872, a bronze Union army color sergeant statue was unveiled in Park Square. The statue, created by Launt Thomas of New York City, stands on a base inscribed with the names of 108 Pittsfield citizens who died in the Civil War and the words "For the dead a tribute, for the living a memory, for posterity an emblem of loyalty to the flag of their country."

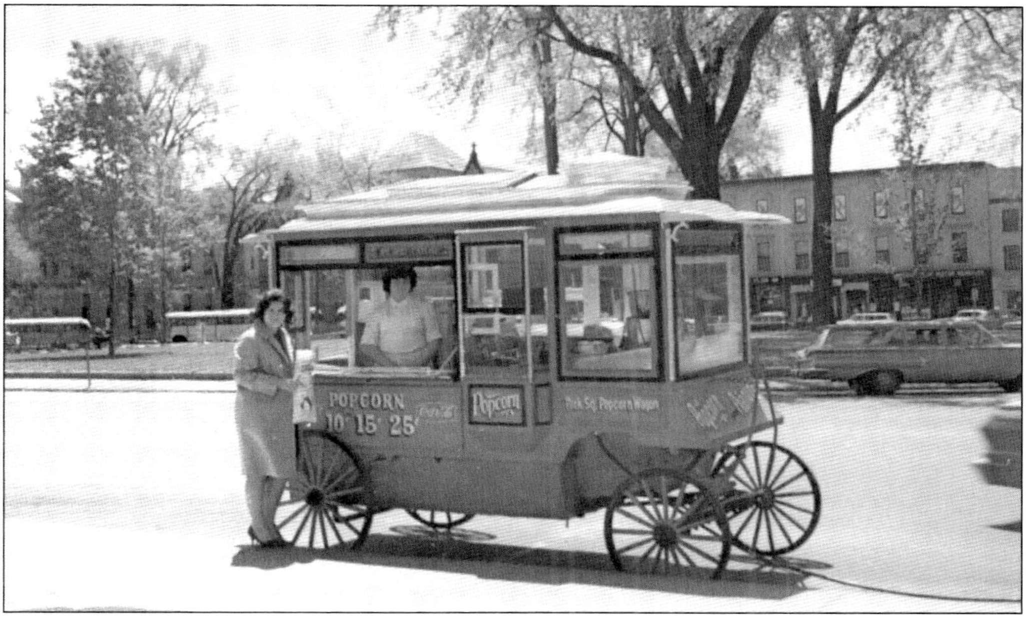

The Pop Corn Wagon has been a downtown landmark since Daniel McGinnis installed it on Park Square in 1910. It offered freshly made popcorn, 5¢ a bag, to people waiting for trolley cars. Later, it was run by Earl Borden. Today, it can be found at 99 North Street, operated by Goodwill through a partnership with Berkshire Bank Foundation. Its appearance each year is a welcome harbinger of spring.

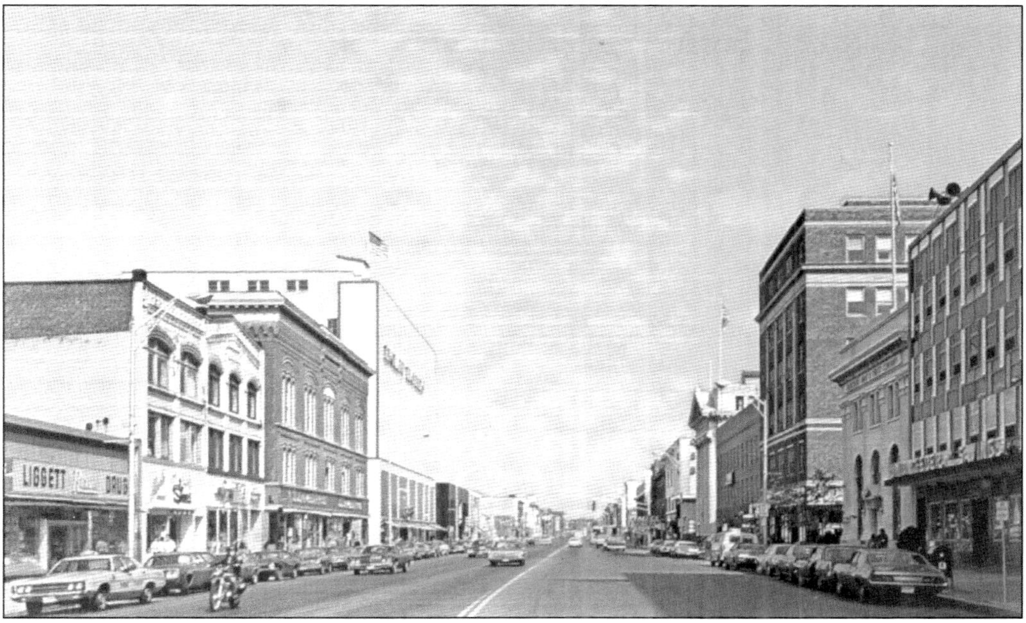

This view, looking north, shows North Street in the early 1970s. Businesses such as Liggett's Rexall Drug Store, Union Federal Savings Bank, J.J. Newberry's, England Brothers Department Store (with its 1966 facade), Holden & Stone Department Store, and the Palace Theater contributed to a prosperous downtown. It was still a wide street without islands.

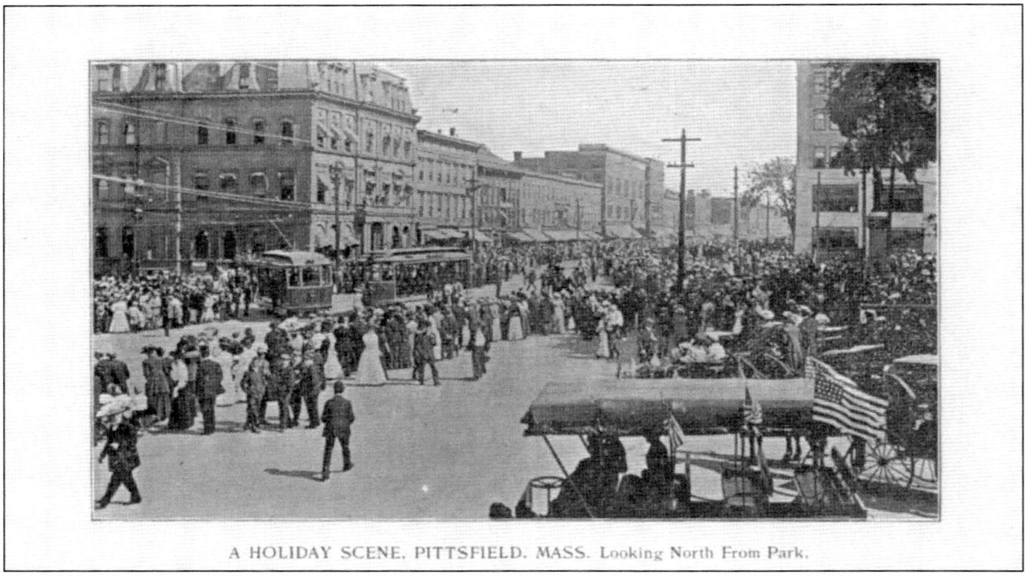

Pittsfield's Merchant Association organized a celebration on July 4, 1909, that brought 30,000 people downtown. This was a precursor to the huge celebrations that marked the 150th anniversary of the Gem City of the Berkshires two years later. For three days, July 2–4, 1911, there were speeches, pageants, and a parade watched by 50,000 spectators, who arrived by special excursion trains and trolleys.

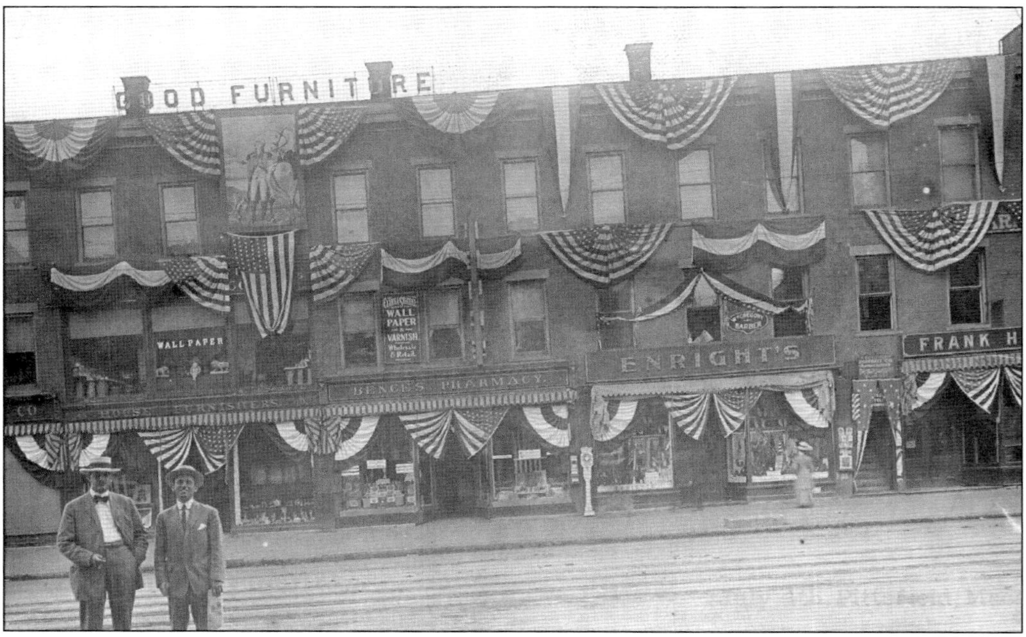

Pittsfield has a long history of decorating the buildings along North Street for parades and celebrations. Pictured here around 1918 are Frank Howard's Hardware Store, Enright's Shoe Store, and Bence's Pharmacy, all ready for one of Pittsfield's famous Independence Day parades.

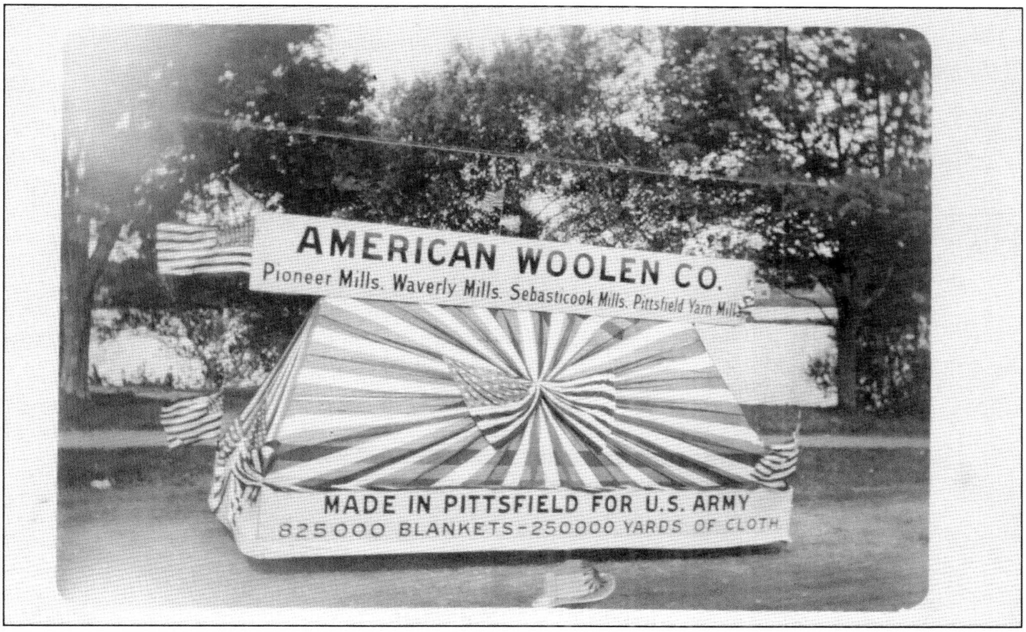

Pittsfield businesses have a long tradition of supporting civic and patriotic celebrations. The American Woolen Company float expresses pride in the fact that Pittsfield mills produced blankets and cloth for the US Army during World War I.

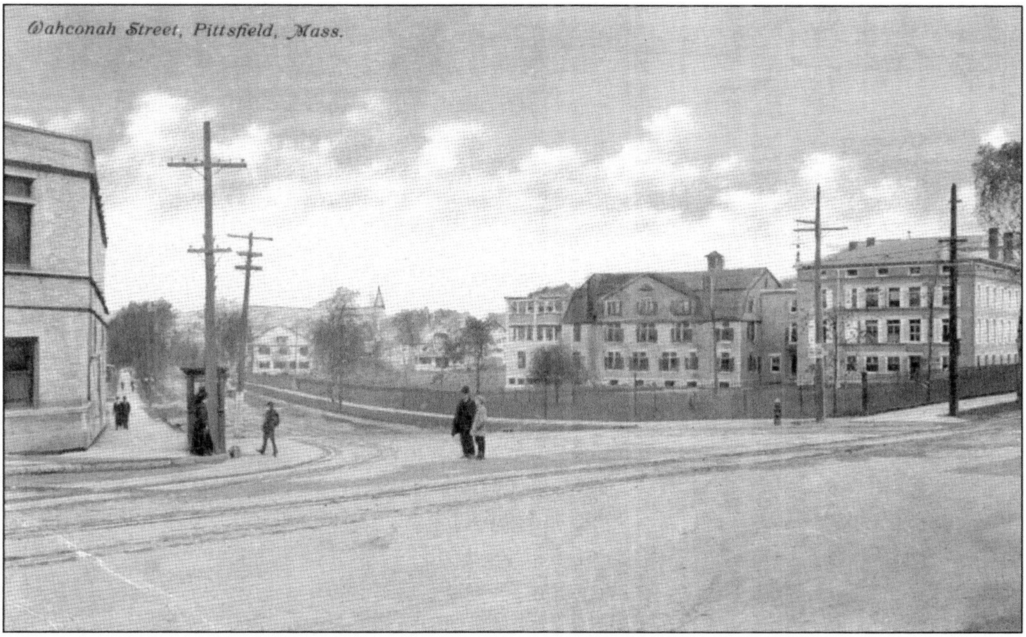

One of Pittsfield's hospitals, the House of Mercy, was at the intersection of Wahconah and North Streets. The small house just above the couple crossing the road was the graduate nurses home, and the steeple in the distances belongs to St. Charles Church. The House of Mercy became Pittsfield General Hospital in 1949 and is now Berkshire Medical Center, part of Berkshire Health Systems, the largest employer in Berkshire County.

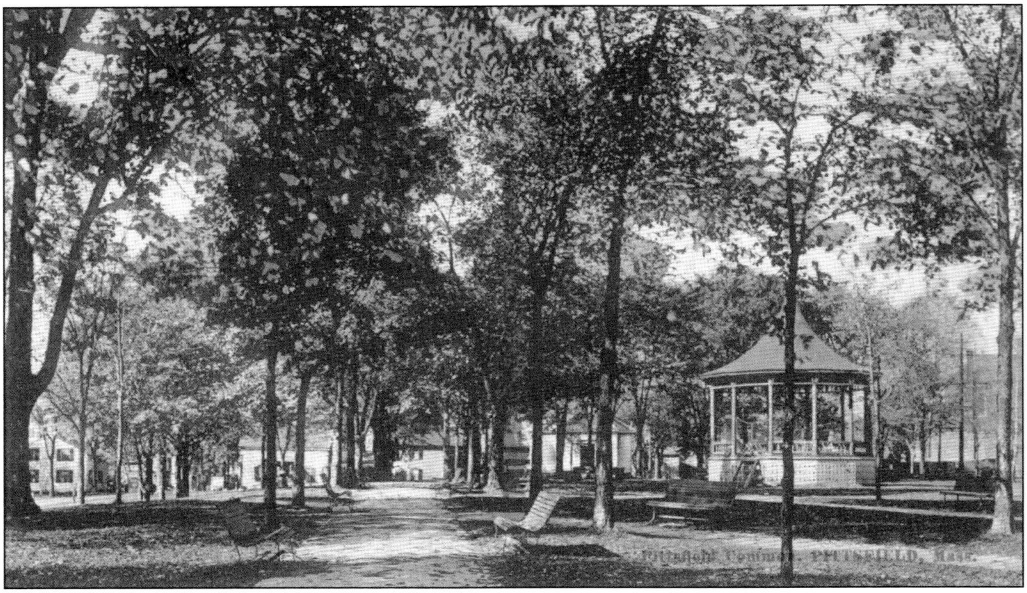

In 1764, Pittsfield's first cemetery, the Old Burial Ground, was located in the center of town between North, School, and Allen Streets. In the 1830s, the bodies and headstones were moved to the New Burial Ground, where the First Street Common is located today. All were moved again in the 1890s to the northern edge of Pittsfield Cemetery. This view of the common was taken in the early 1900s.

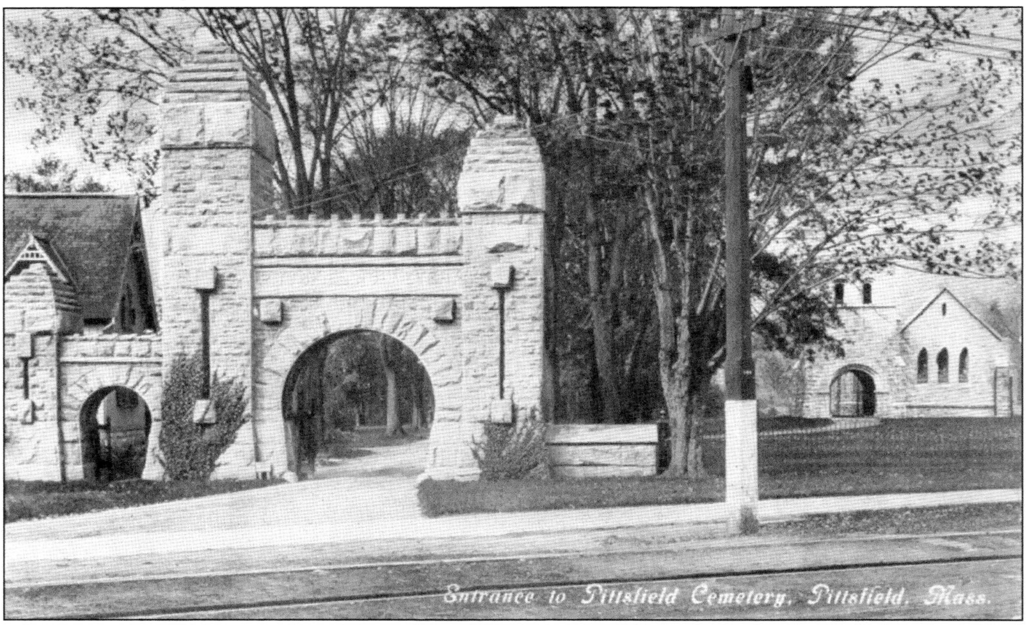

The 83-acre Pittsfield Rural Cemetery, at 203 Wahconah Street, was dedicated on September 9, 1850. In 1885, the estate of Thomas Allen (1813–1882) provided $5,000 for the elaborate stone gateway. The Martin Memorial Chapel (right) was dedicated October 17, 1900, by Mary Martin Clapp in memory of both her father and husband. In 2007, the cemetery, now 142 acres, was listed in the National Register of Historic Places.

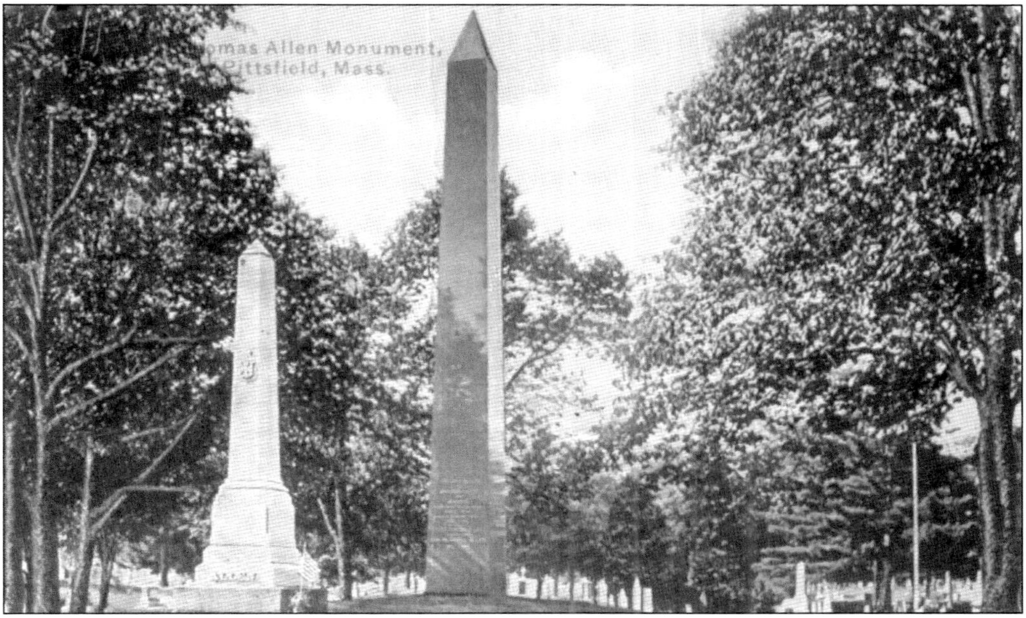

The Reverend Thomas Allen (1743–1810), nicknamed the "Fighting Parson" for his exploits during the Revolutionary War, is memorialized by the shorter obelisk (left). Allen was a dedicated public servant and the father of 12 children. His grandson Thomas Allen (1813–1882), a publisher and owner of several railroads and banks, lived in Missouri. The 1885 Allen Monument (right) was said to be the largest piece of polished red granite in the world.

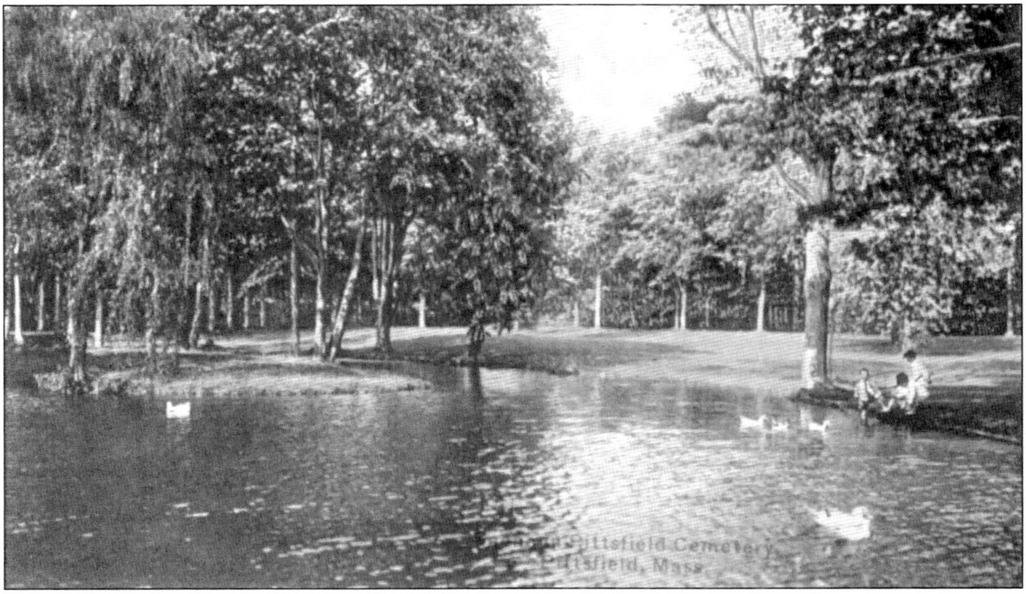

At one time, St. John's Lake divided the Fountain Lawn section of the Pittsfield Cemetery. When the cemetery was dedicated in 1850 before an audience of 4,000, the choir sang, "Where flows the stream from hidden urn, where by its banks the spring flowers wave; from scenes like these the heart may learn, fit lessons for the silent grave." The lake was drained later for use as burial sites.

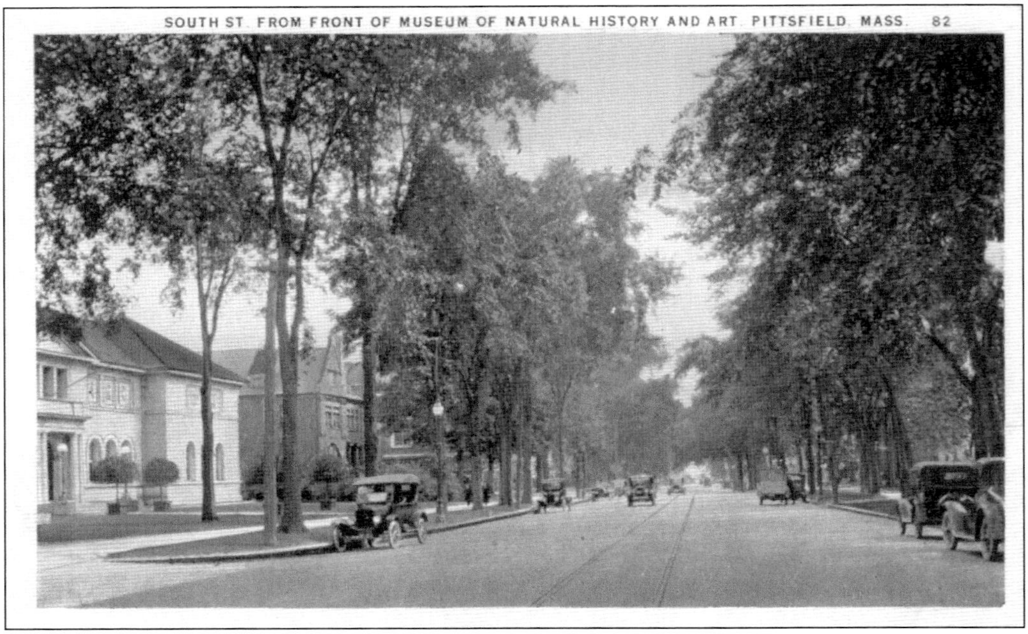

In 1920, South Street was a wide street with trolley tracks and lined with magnificent elm trees, civic buildings, and large houses. This view includes the Museum of Natural History and Art (now the Berkshire Museum) and the Berkshire Home for Aged Women (now Berkshire Place). Across the street, not visible, are the South Congregational Church and the Masonic temple.

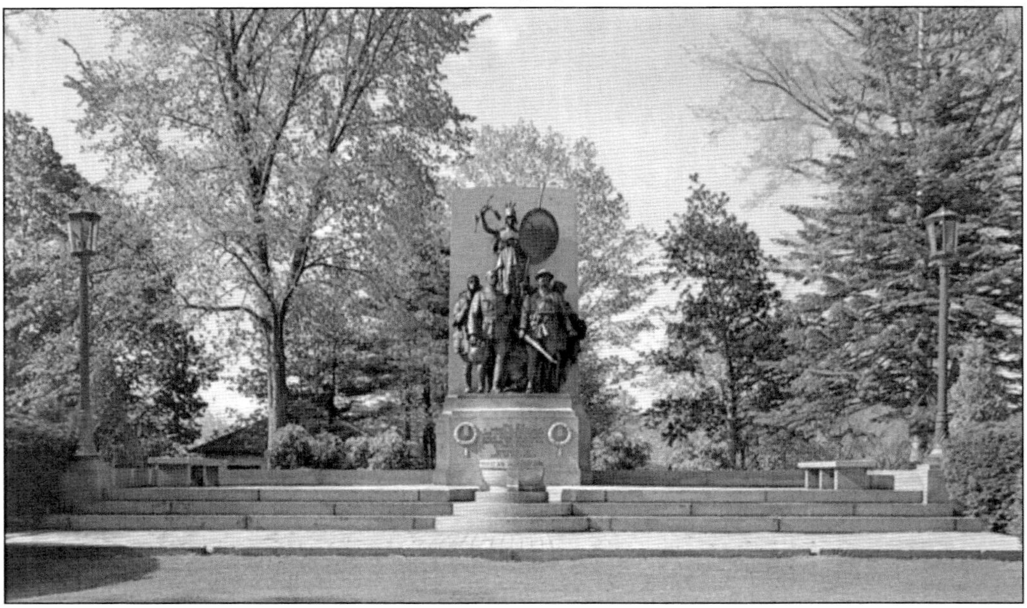

On July 8, 1926, Stockbridge sculptor Henry Augustus Lukeman presented the Soldiers' and Sailors' Memorial, located just off South Street, to Pittsfield mayor Fred Francis. US attorney general John Sargent gave a speech, and schoolchildren sang. The group of five figures represents soldiers who served in World War I; plaques were added for those who served in World War II, Korea, and Vietnam. The memorial was restored in 2010.

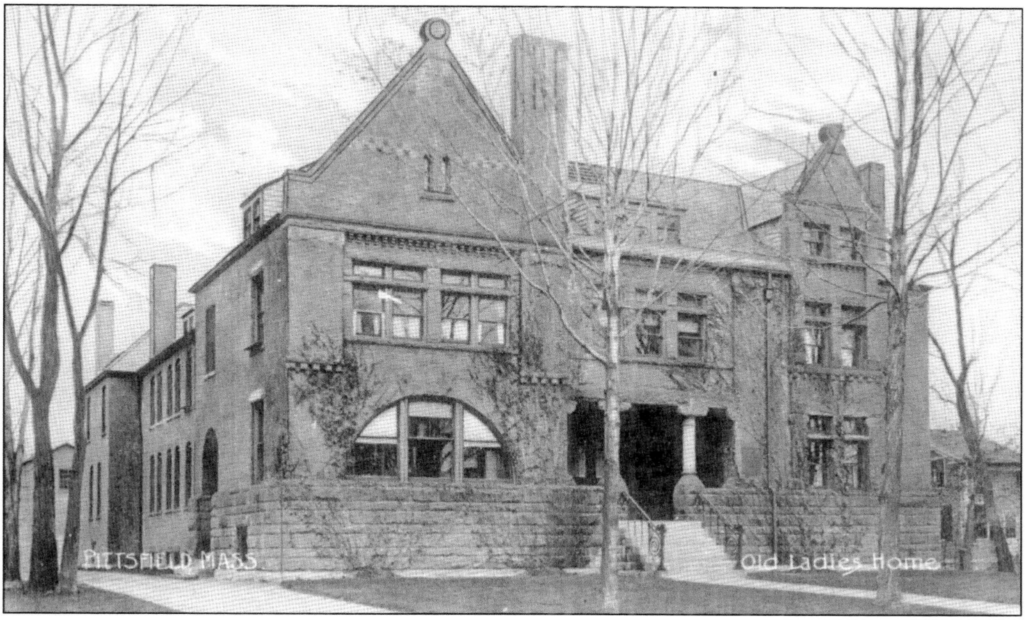

The Berkshire County Home for Aged Women was built in 1888 in memory of Zenas Crane. With the intent to enhance the comfort of aged women, it was one of few such institutions in the country. A board of women managers raised funds and set fees. In 1891, the entrance fee was $300. A fourth floor was added in 1925, and the name changed to Berkshire Place in 1960.

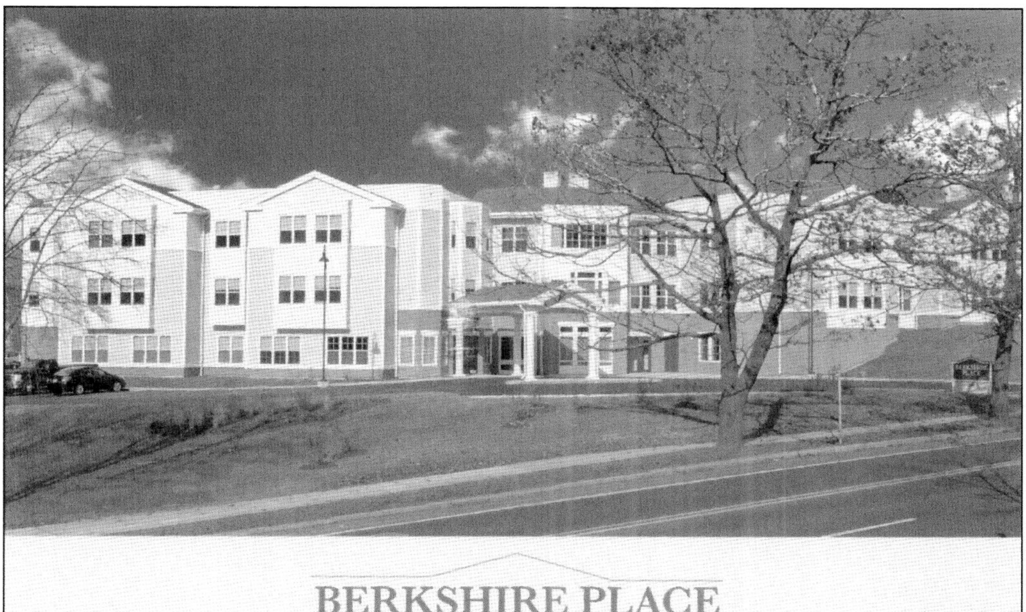

In 2014, Berkshire Place relocated to a new 54-bed facility half a mile south on South Street. St. Teresa's, one of six Pittsfield churches closed by the Diocese of Springfield in 2008, was razed. The now coed institution continues to enhance the comfort of its guests, providing more programs and personalized care than imagined by the founders in 1888.

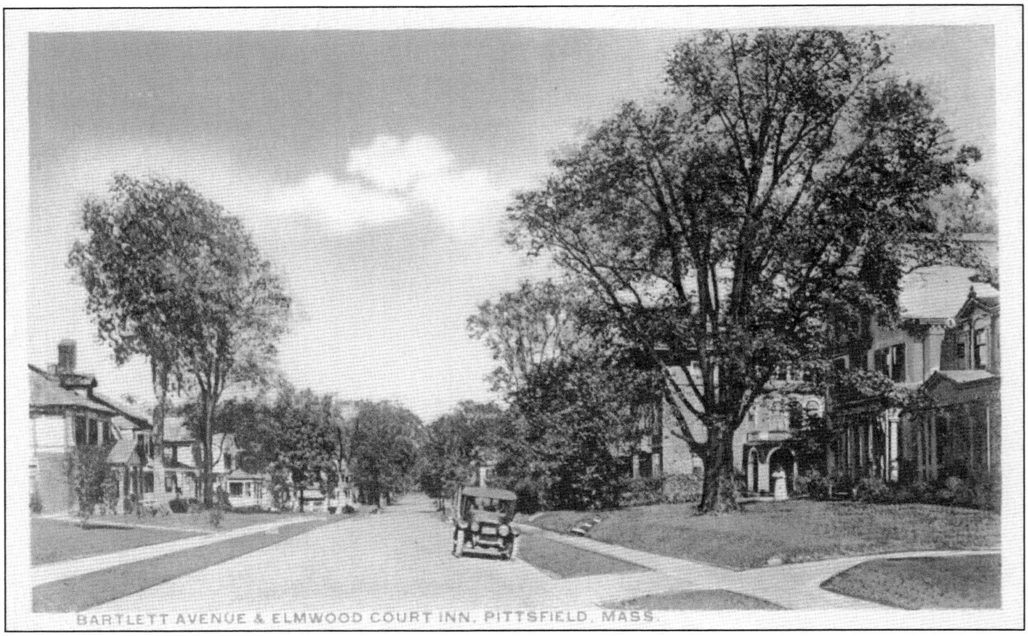

Bartlett Avenue runs north and south, parallel to South Street. Originally a street of grand homes, it is now a mix of residences and offices. Elmwood Court, occupying an entire block, was the home for entrepreneur Edward Learned and his large family for decades before it was first Miss Hall's School for girls, then an inn operated by Florence Learned. Eventually, it was divided into apartments before burning in 2011.

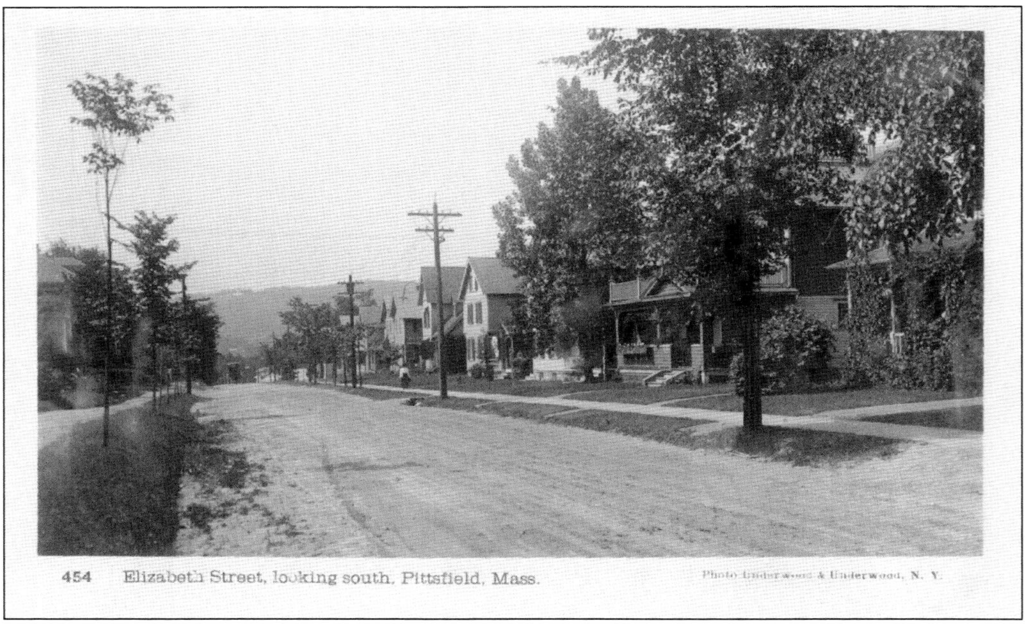

On the west side of town, running parallel to South Street and connecting West Housatonic Street and Bay State Road, is Elizabeth Street. Pictured here around 1920, the neighborhood was a typical solid middle-class neighborhood, representative of most of Pittsfield.

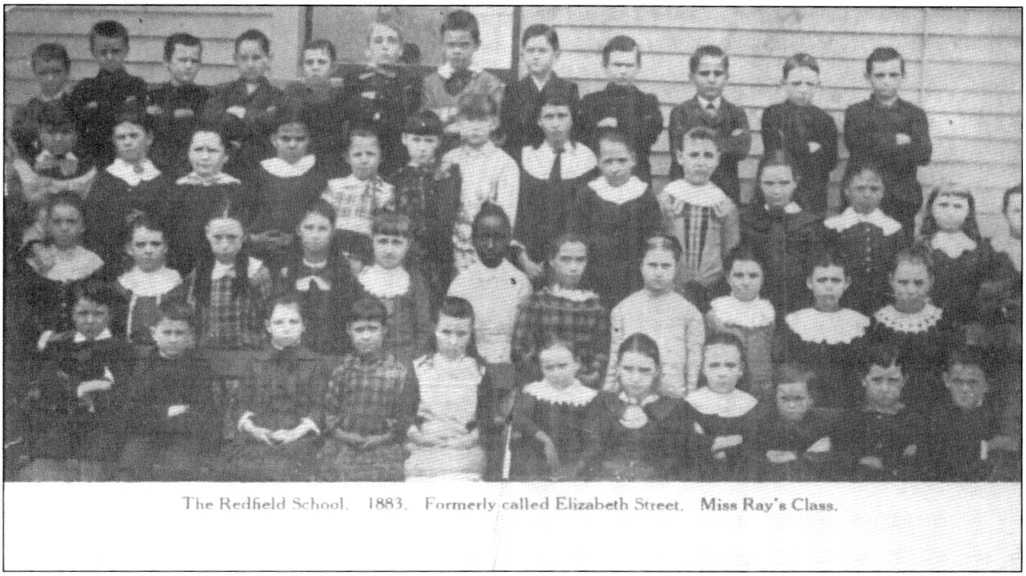

In 1883, Abbie Ray's class poses in front of the Elizabeth Street School, a modest clapboard building. As Pittsfield's population expanded, additional and larger schools were required. In 1896, this school was replaced by the new 350-student Redfield School at a cost of $40,000.

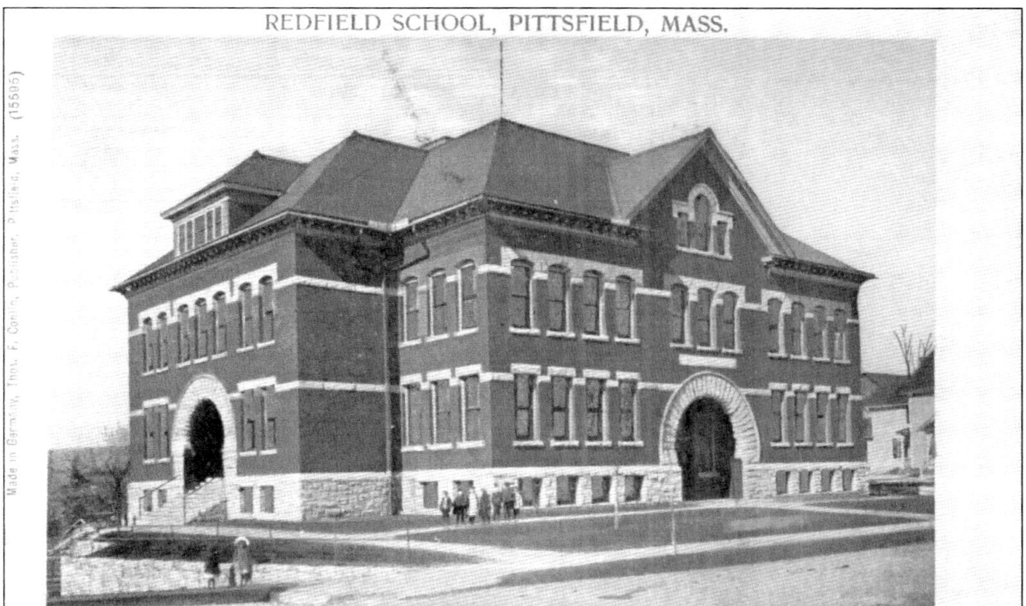

The Charles B. Redfield School on Elizabeth Street was named in honor of a distinguished Pittsfield citizen who championed the cause of creating a progressive education system. Redfield developed a new organizational plan to replace the old district school system. This impressive redbrick building now serves Berkshire Children & Families, one of the oldest social service agencies in Berkshire County.

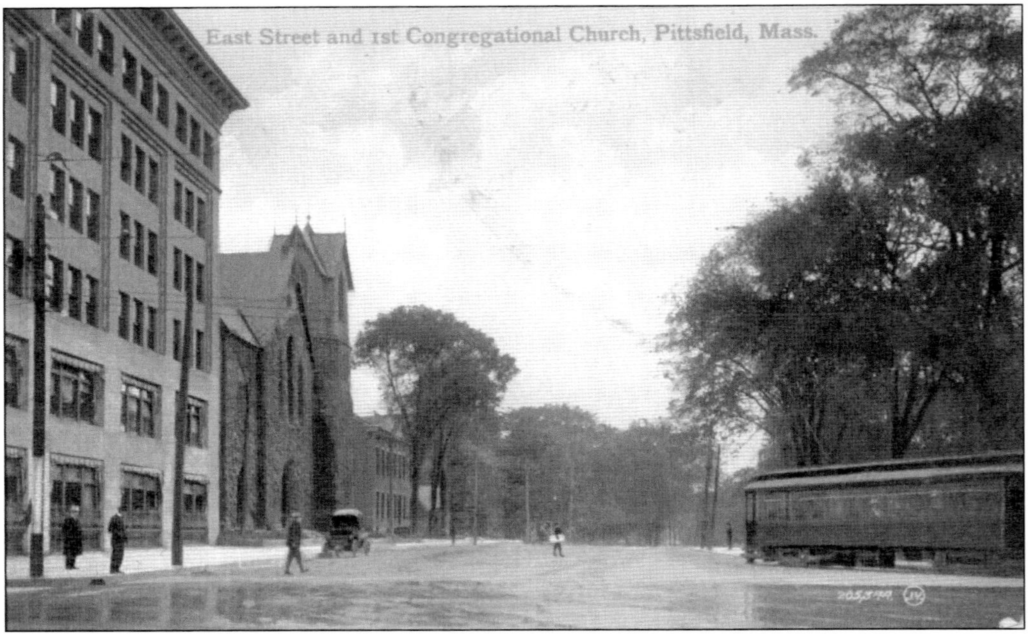

This c. 1908 view of East Street, looking east toward Dalton, shows the Berkshire Bank, the First Congregational Church, and Pittsfield City Hall. On the right are the grand elms of Park Square behind one of the Pittsfield trolley cars of the Berkshire Street Railway.

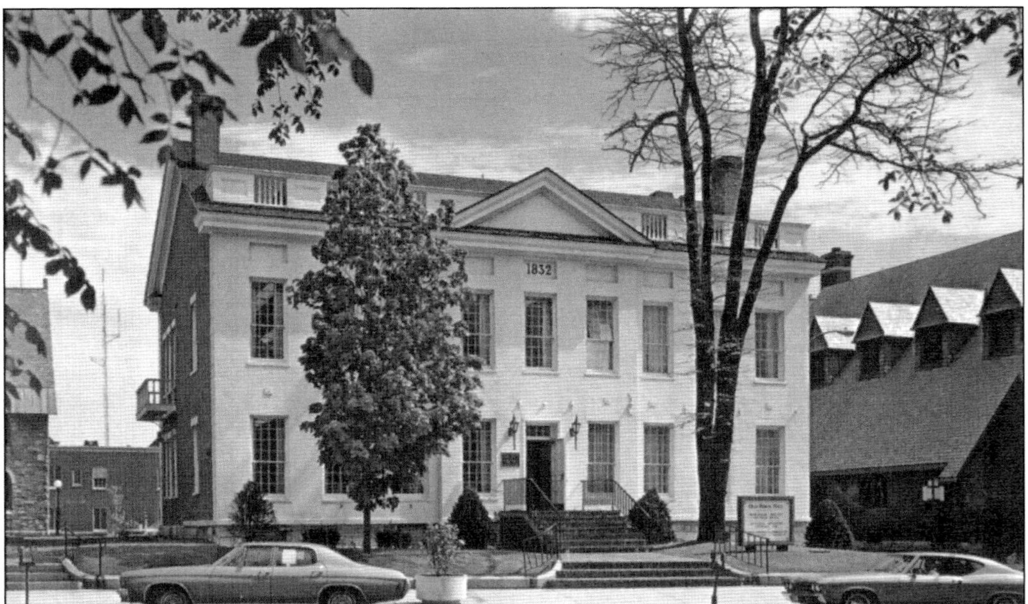

The Old Town Hall, at 32 East Street, was built in 1832 across from Park Square. From 1891, when Pittsfield became a city, to 1968, it was known as city hall. In an early victory for historical preservation advocates, it was restored by the Berkshire County Savings Bank in 1970 and placed in the National Register of Historic Places in 1972.

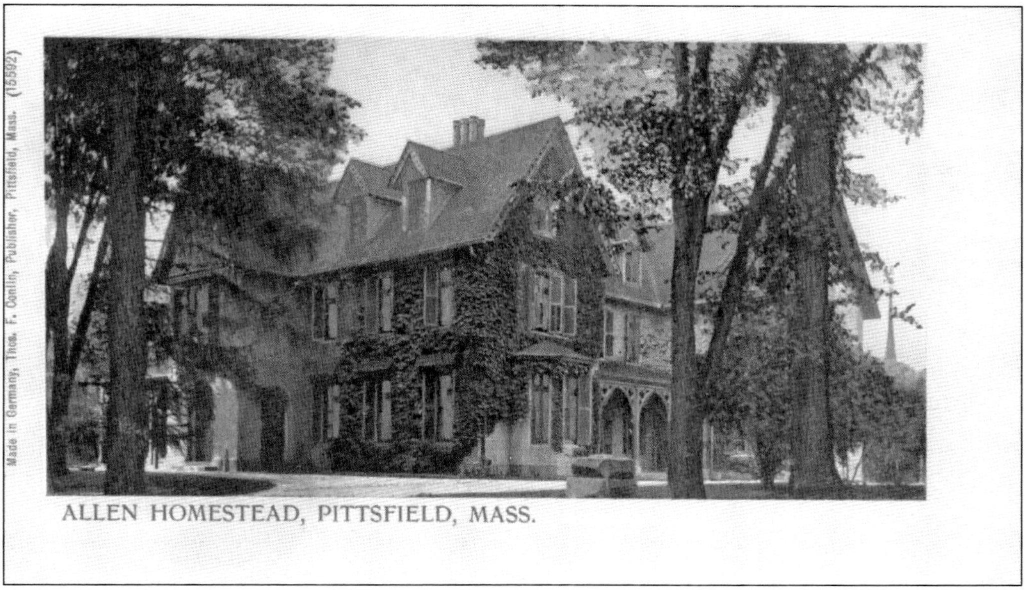

In 1858, Thomas Allen, a Missouri businessman and grandson of Pittsfield's "Fighting Parson," Rev. Thomas Allen, built a blue limestone mansion on the site of his grandfather's parsonage at East and First Streets. Allen and his family summered in Pittsfield until his death in 1882. Following his wife's death, the property was sold, and the house razed in 1913. The land was divided by Federal Street and Wendell Avenue Extension.

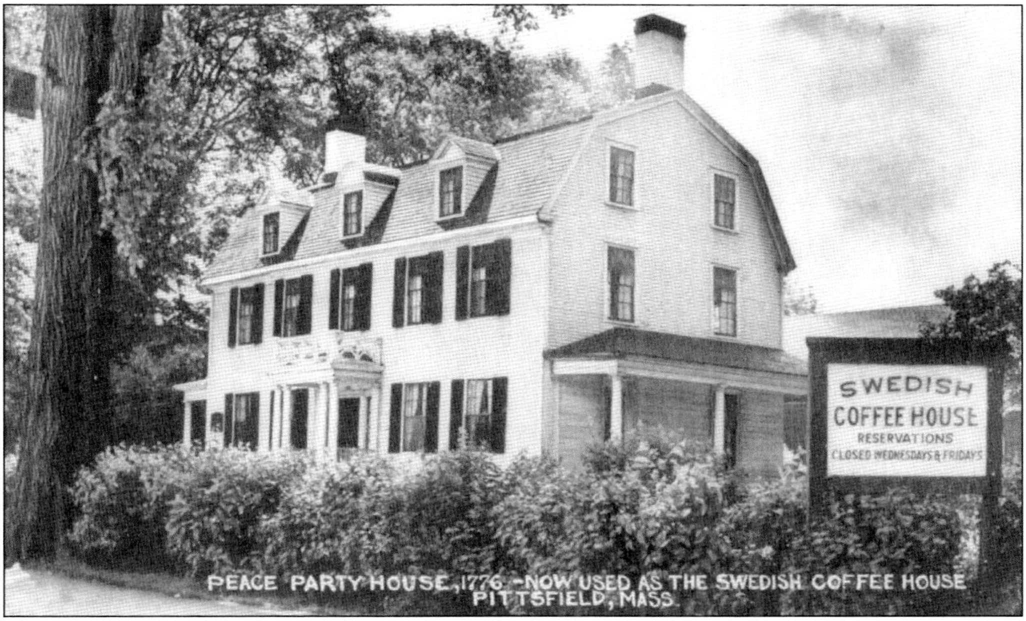

In 1776, Col. James Easton built this impressive home at the southwest corner of East Street and Wendell Avenue. The site of a celebration marking the end of the American Revolution, it was dubbed the Peace Party House. In 1869, the house was moved to the southeast corner of East Street and Wendell Avenue to make way for the new Berkshire County Courthouse. After serving several uses, it was demolished in 1957.

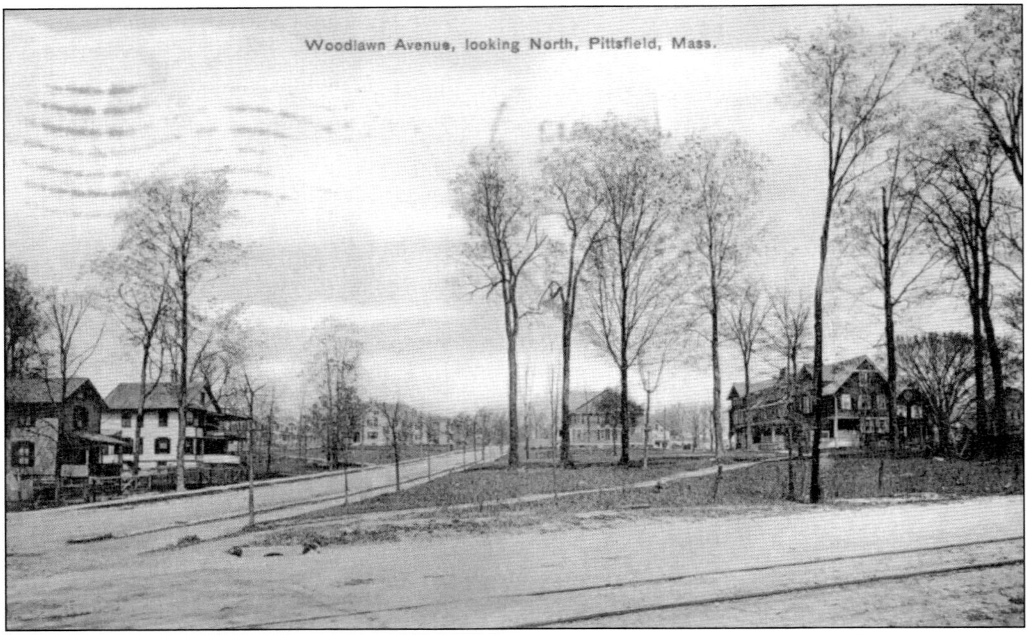

Woodlawn Avenue, running north and south across both Tyler Street and Dalton Avenue, is located between what was the main gate at the Pittsfield Works of General Electric and Springside Avenue. Much of the street is still residential, but the area south of the intersection, pictured around 1910, is awaiting redevelopment after the GE factories were demolished.

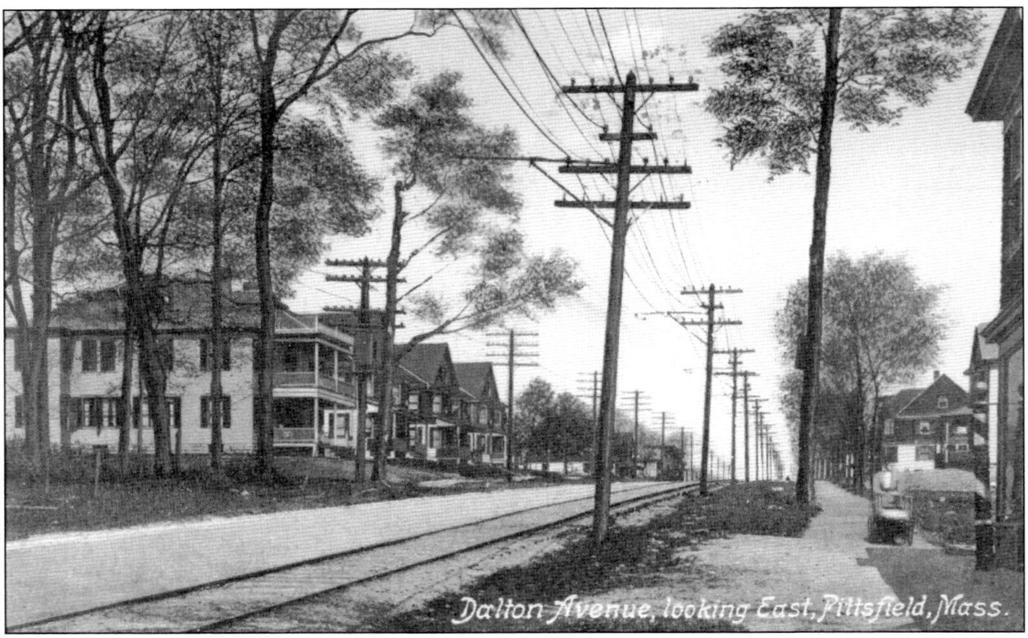

By the 1910s, Dalton Avenue was a main east-west artery connecting Pittsfield's businesses, residential neighborhoods, and farmlands. The trolley—its tracks seen here—carried passengers from downtown Pittsfield eastward to the Coltsville Station and on to Dalton.

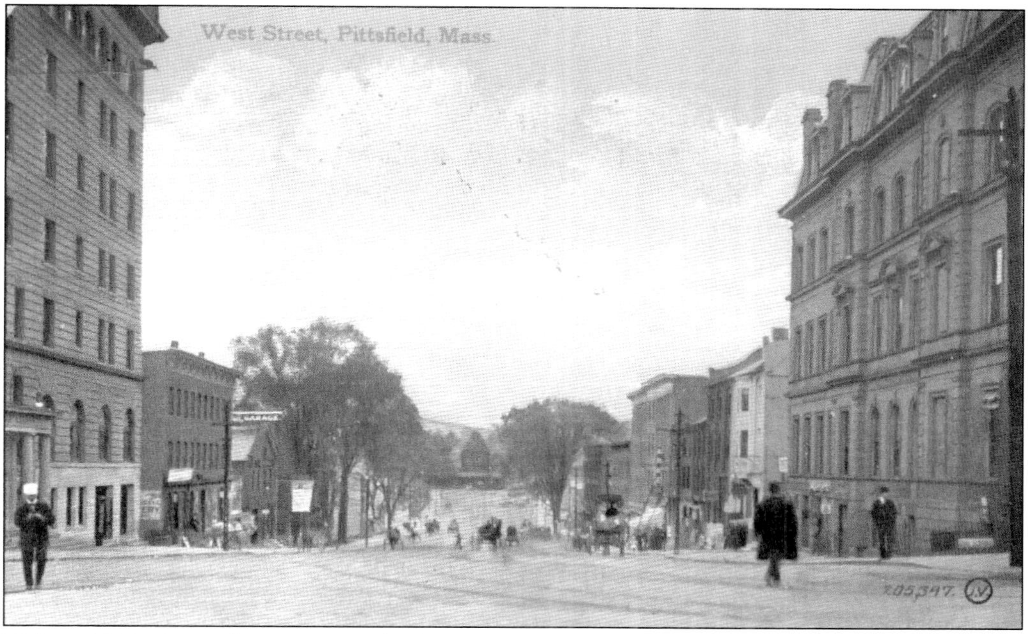

This c. 1908 view of West Street, looking west toward Union Station at the foot of the hill, shows the Wendell Hotel, the Wendell Livery, and an automobile garage (left). The Berkshire Life Insurance Company building (right foreground) is the only structure in this view remaining after the urban renewal of the 1960s and 1970s.

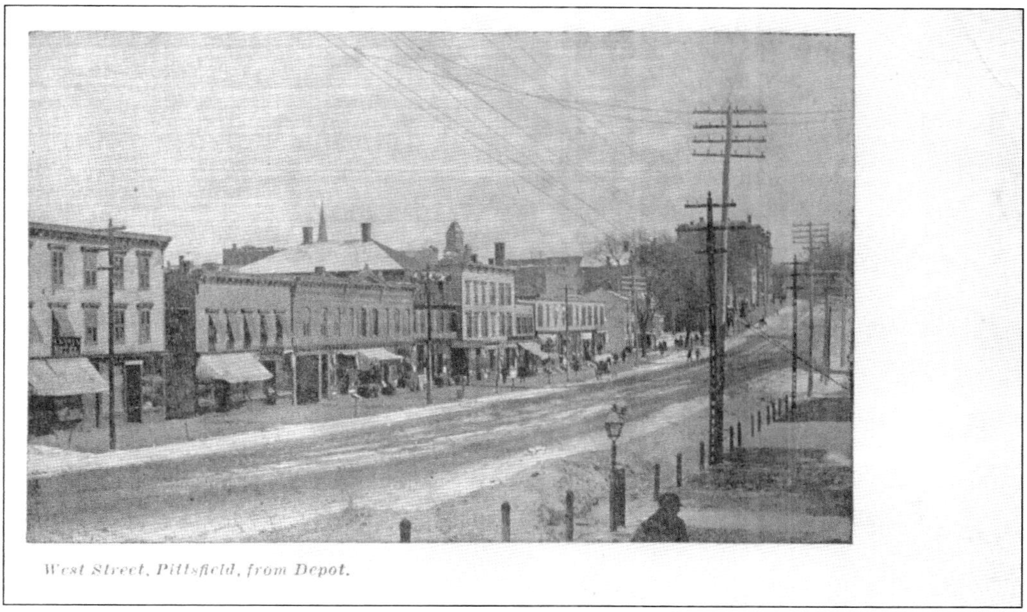

This c. 1900 view of West Street from Union Station looks east toward the Berkshire Life Insurance Company Building. Many businesses were related to the railroads, such as the United States Hotel and Thomas E. Hall & Company, whose services included freight and storage. The café at the Parker House served hungry travelers. Also on West Street were the Musgrove Knitting Company and the Robbins and Gamwell Coal Company.

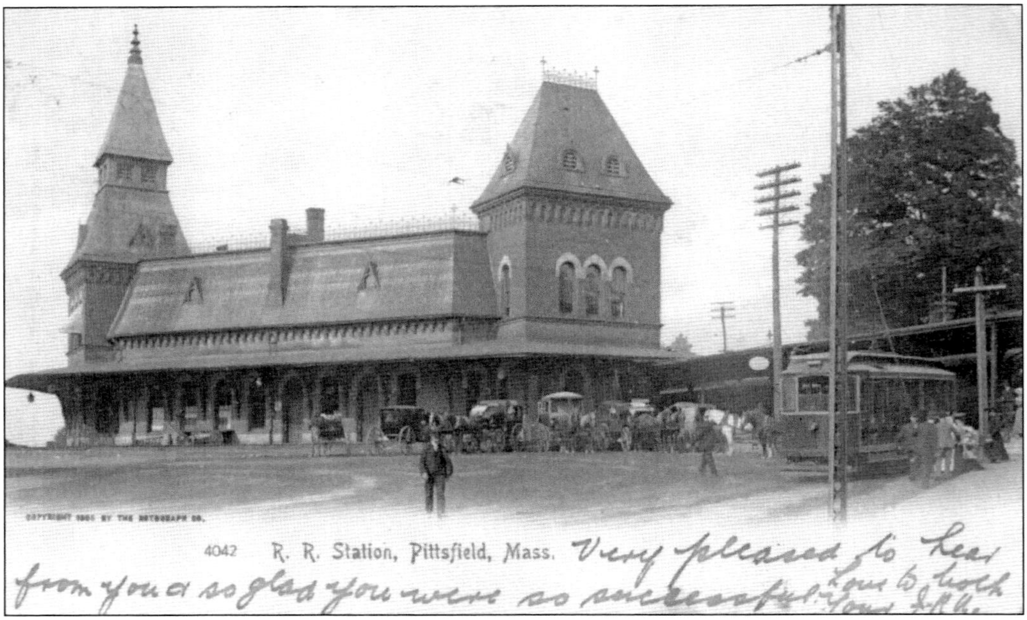

In 1866, the Boston and Albany Railroad and the Stockbridge and Pittsfield Railroad collaborated to build the large and ornate Pittsfield Depot. Now passengers and freight companies could easily switch between lines. Previously, travelers had to walk several blocks between stations.

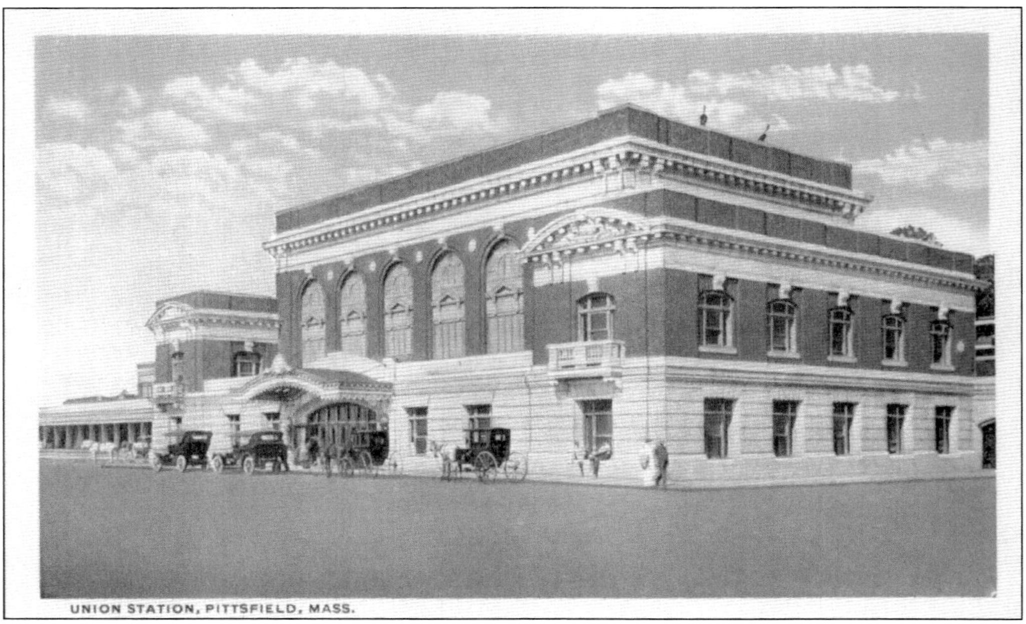

Union Station replaced the Pittsfield Depot in 1914. The Beaux-Arts–style building, with its marble walls, high domed ceiling, and chandeliers, cost $300,000. Travelers on the New York Central Railroad and the New York, New Haven, & Hartford Railroad enjoyed the grand station. Its demolition in 1968, in the name of urban renewal, sparked historical preservation efforts in Pittsfield. Not until 2004 was there again a railroad station in Pittsfield.

Two

Literary and Cultural Sites

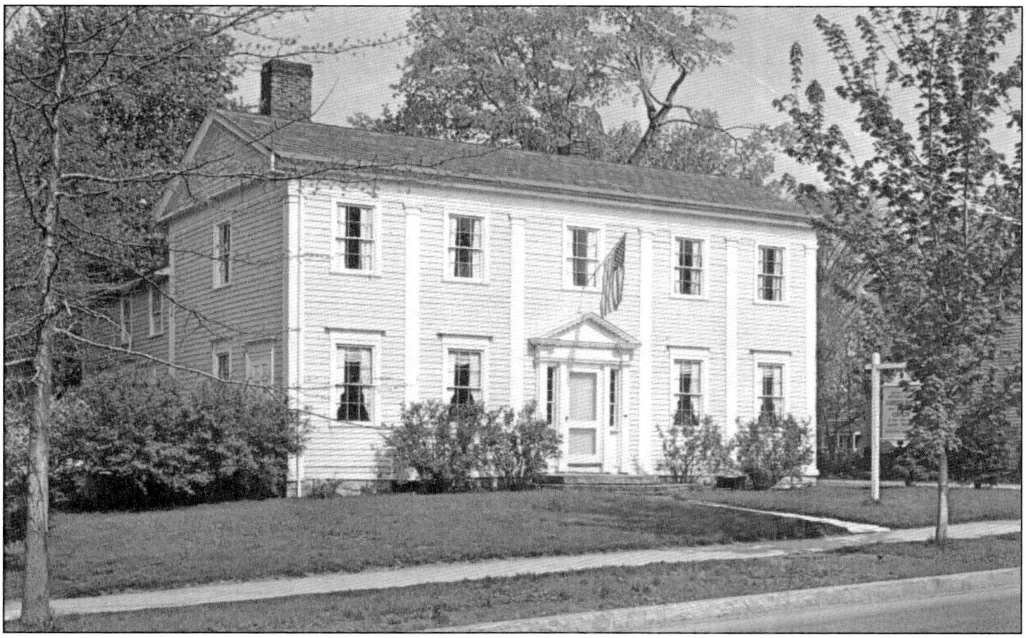

Pittsfield has always been a historic, literary, and theatrical center. In 1792, Maj. Butler Goodrich built a house on upper North Street. The house was sold to the Berkshire County Historical Society in 1963, when it was restored and used as a museum. The society sold it in 1975 in order to purchase Herman Melville's Arrowhead. The Goodrich House is now a boardinghouse.

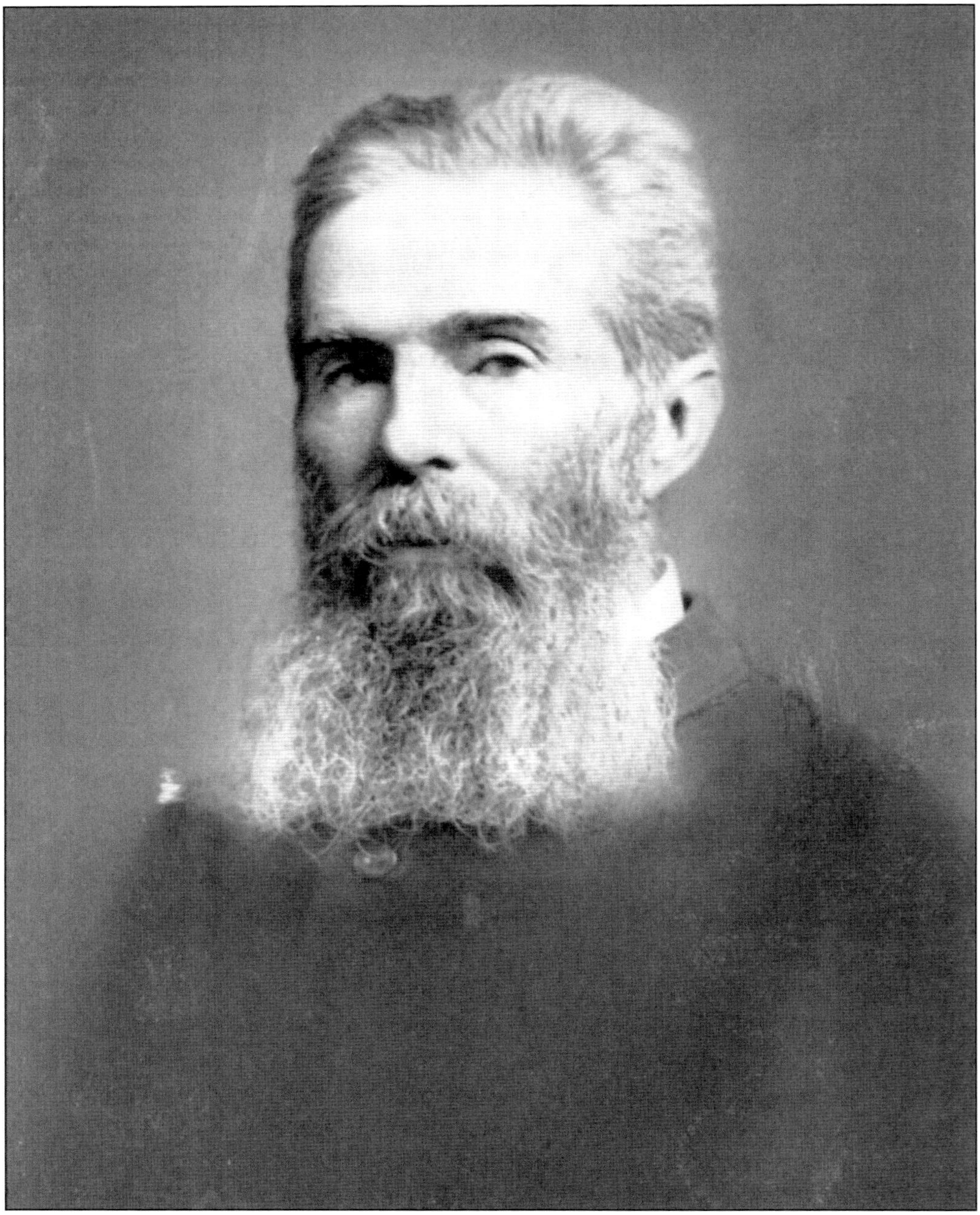

Herman Melville (1819–1891), born in New York City, had deep connections to Pittsfield. As a boy, he helped his uncle on his farm (now the Pittsfield Country Club) and returned to teach at one-room schools. In 1850, after adventures in the South Seas and marrying Elizabeth Shaw, Melville purchased his Pittsfield farm, Arrowhead. There he farmed and wrote *Moby-Dick* and other novels. But his writing did not provide his family sufficient income, so Melville returned to New York City. There he worked for 20 years as a customs inspector, his writings almost forgotten. By the 1920s, his work was rediscovered, and it is now considered some of the best writing in American literature. Arrowhead is open to the public.

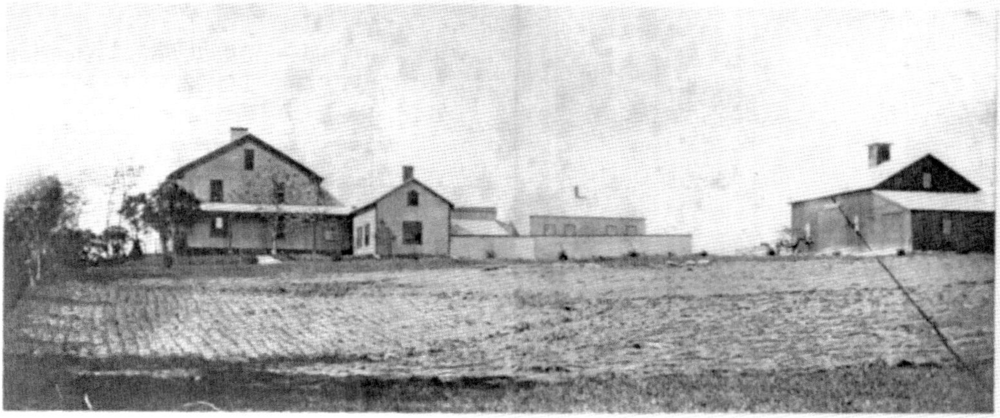

". . . . I have been building some shanties of houses (connected with the old one) and likewise some shanties of chapters & essays. I have been ploughing & sowing & raising & printing & praying, and now begin to come out upon a less bristling time, and to enjoy the calm prospect of things from a fair piazza at the north of the old farmhouse here." —Herman Melville

In a June 1851 letter to his friend Nathaniel Hawthorne, Melville detailed some of his work on Arrowhead: "I have been building some shanties of houses (connected with the old one) and likewise some shanties of chapters & essays. I have been ploughing & sowing & raising & printing & praying, and now begin to . . . enjoy the calm prospect of things from a fair piazza at the north of the old farmhouse here."

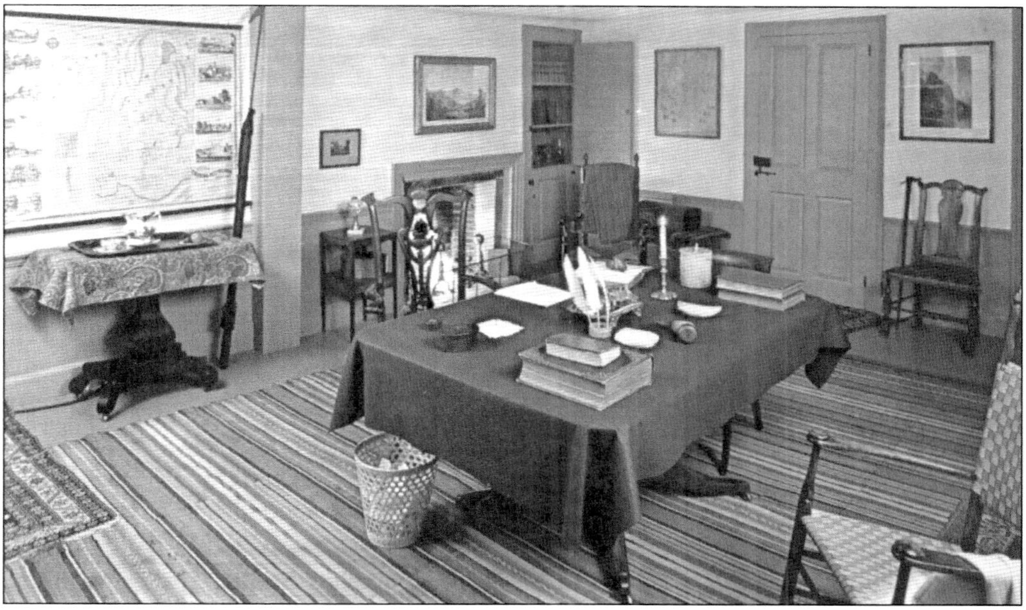

Each day during the winter of 1850–1851, Herman Melville locked himself into his upstairs study, furiously wrestling with the white whale on page after page to create, arguably, American literature's greatest novel. Gazing out the north window to the snow-covered fields, he often felt he was looking out the porthole of a ship on the Atlantic at Moby Dick, instead of his actual view—Mount Greylock, Massachusetts's tallest mountain.

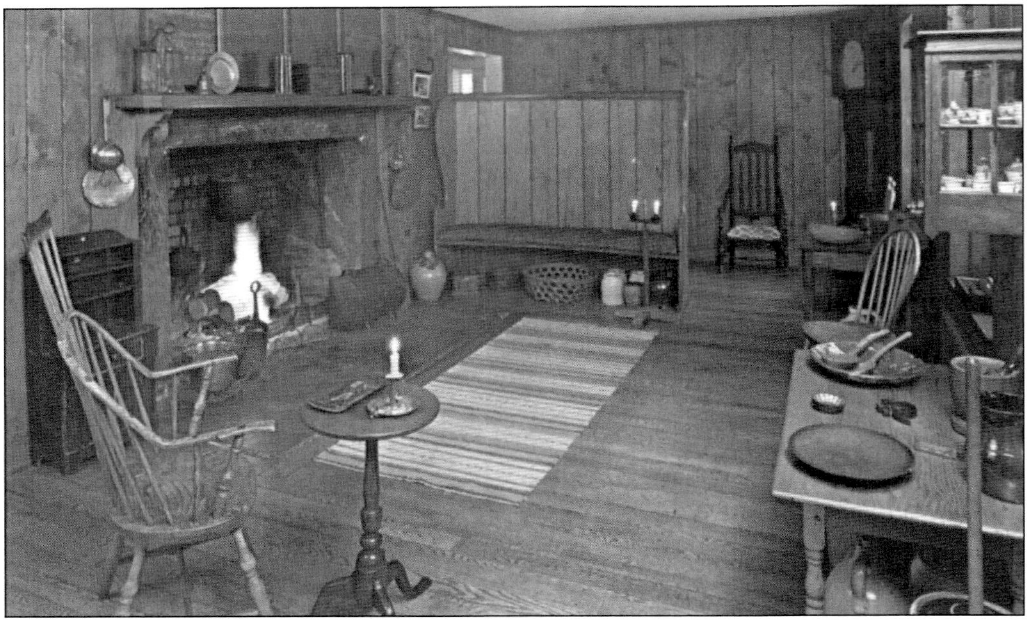

When the farmhouse at Arrowhead was built in the 1790s, it had a kitchen with an open hearth. In the 1850s, the Melvilles used it as their dining room. Herman's brother Allen, who purchased Arrowhead in 1863, had quotations from the short story "I and My Chimney" inscribed above the massive hearth, "I and my chimney, two grey-headed old smokers."

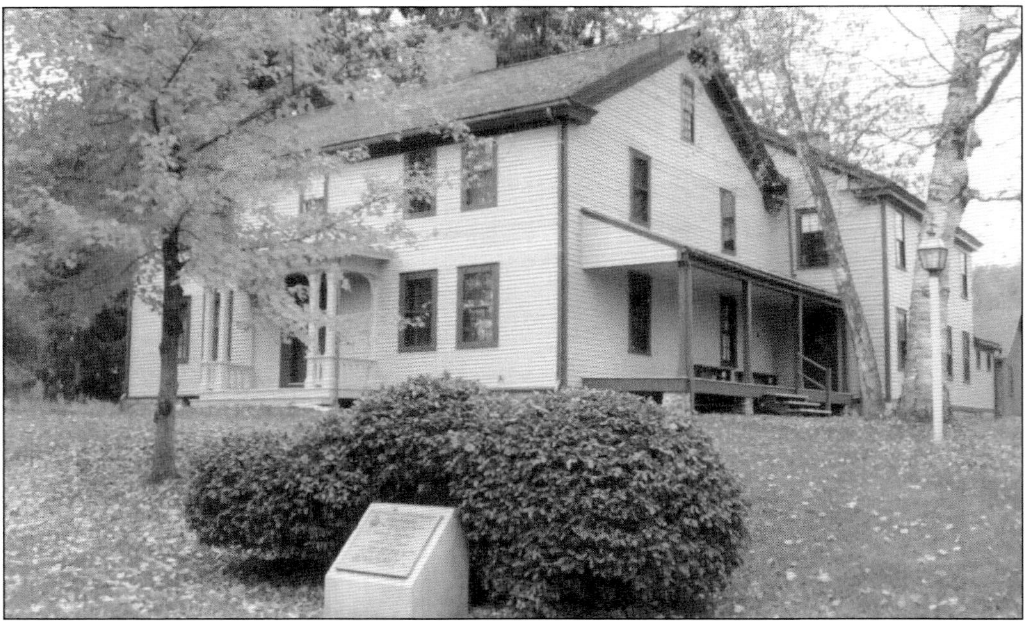

In September 1850, Herman Melville purchased an old farmhouse, barn, and 160 acres in southeastern Pittsfield. He named it Arrowhead after the artifacts he uncovered while plowing the fields. While at Arrowhead, Melville wrote *Moby-Dick*, three additional novels, and many short stories. Arrowhead was declared a National Historic Landmark in 1966. Today, it is owned by the Berkshire County Historical Society and open to the public.

Dr. Oliver Wendell Holmes Sr. (1809–1894) was a famous Boston physician, prolific writer, and Pittsfield summer resident. While known as a poet, he also wrote medical papers, essays, and novels. Holmes was often commissioned to write commemorative poems, such as a dedication for the new Pittsfield Cemetery in 1850. Schoolchildren across the country were required to memorize his poetry, particularly "Old Ironsides," about the USS *Constitution*.

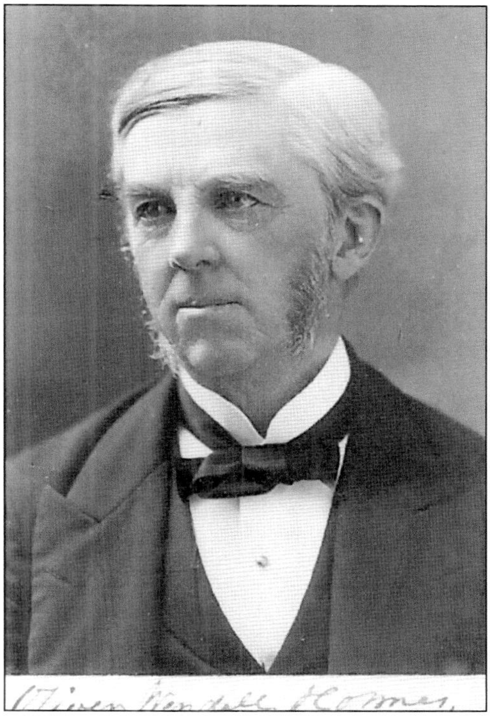

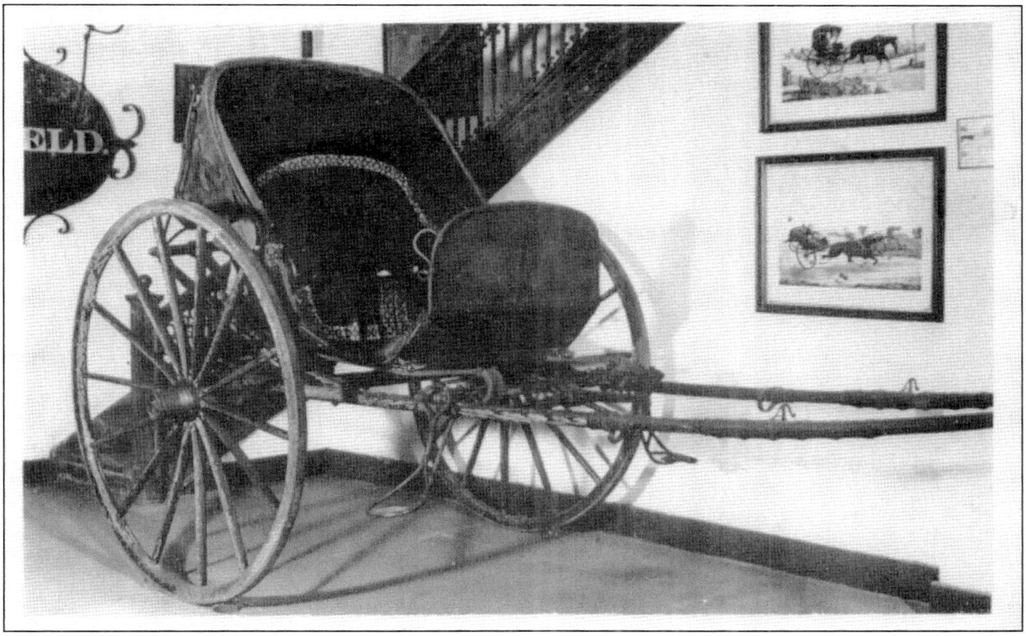

Oliver Wendell Holmes memorialized a one-horse shay in his satirical poem, "The Deacon's Masterpiece or The Wonderful One-Hoss Shay." The light, covered, two-wheeled carriage was crafted in Berkshire County in the 1700s. According to Holmes, "It was built in such a local way, it ran a hundred years to a day." The famous shay is part of the Berkshire Museum's extensive collections of history, science, and art.

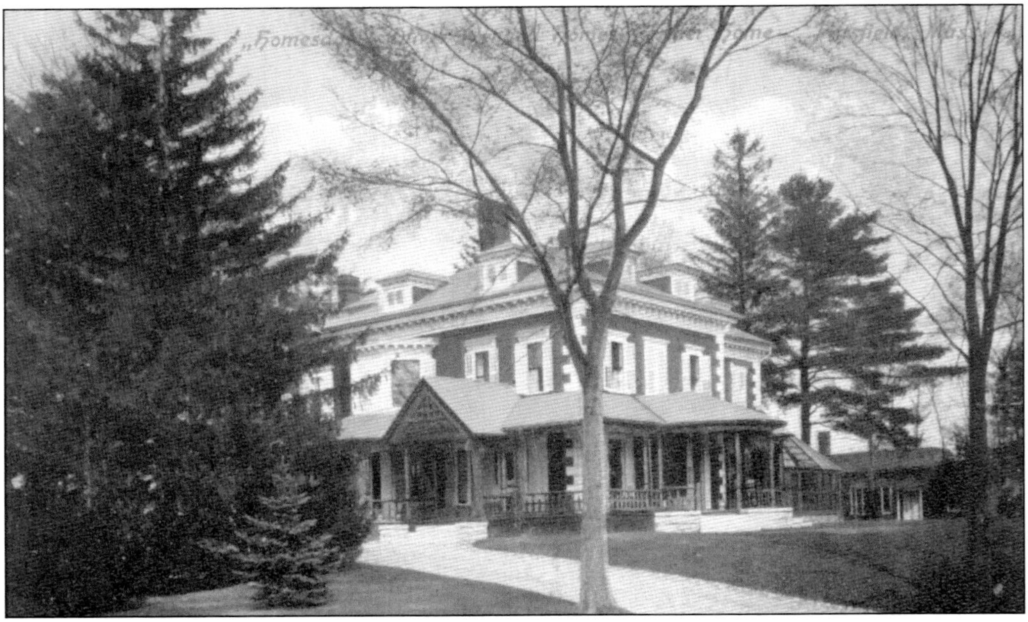

In 1848, Oliver Wendell Holmes Sr. inherited a 280-acre Pittsfield farm known as Canoe Meadows. He built a 15-room summer cottage near the Housatonic River, staying there "seven sweet summers, the happiest of my life." In 1877, New York City socialite Louise Pollock expanded it to a sumptuous villa, Holmesdale, seen here. In 1894, Middle Road was changed to Holmes Road by order of the City of Pittsfield.

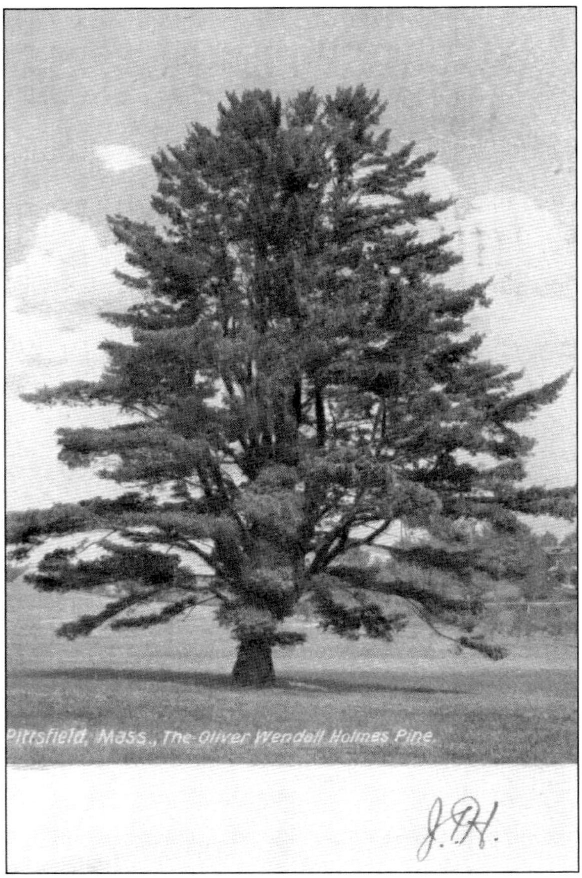

Catherine Drinker Bowen, in her book *Yankee from Olympus: Justice Holmes and His Family* (1944), wrote, "Before the house, a great single pine spread its branches . . . and the children had a secret place high in the branches of the big pine." This tree at Holmesdale was famous enough to be featured on numerous Pittsfield postcards.

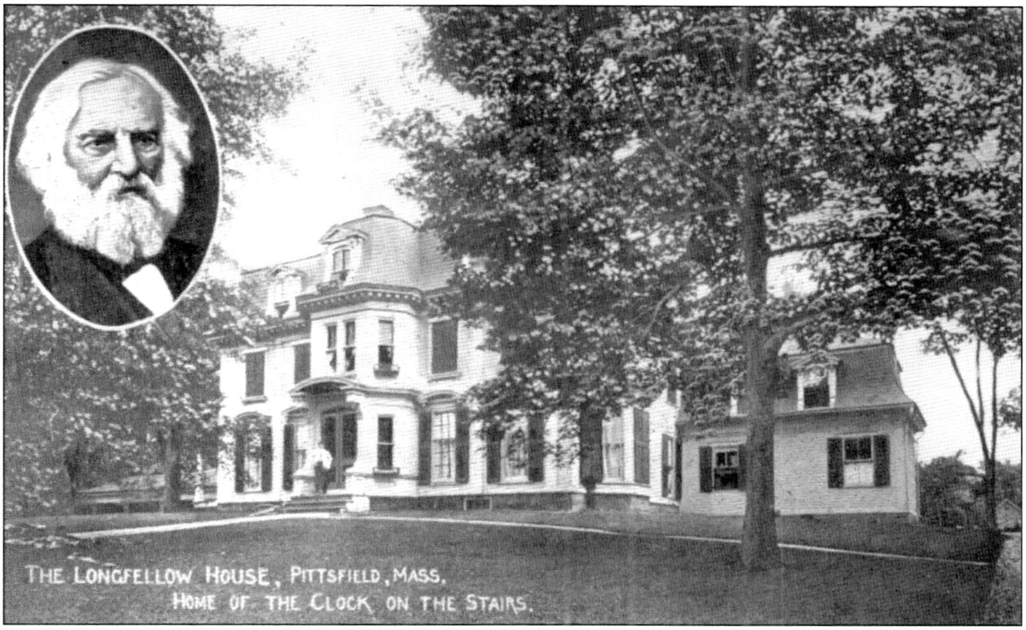

The Longfellow House, more properly known as the Gold-Appleton House, was built in 1790. Nathan Appleton's daughter Frances married Henry Wadsworth Longfellow in 1843. While visiting his wife's family, Longfellow wrote "The Old Clock on the Stairs," giving fame to the mansion at 8 East Street. It was razed in 1930 to build Pittsfield High School; a plaque in its entryway honors Longfellow and the poem.

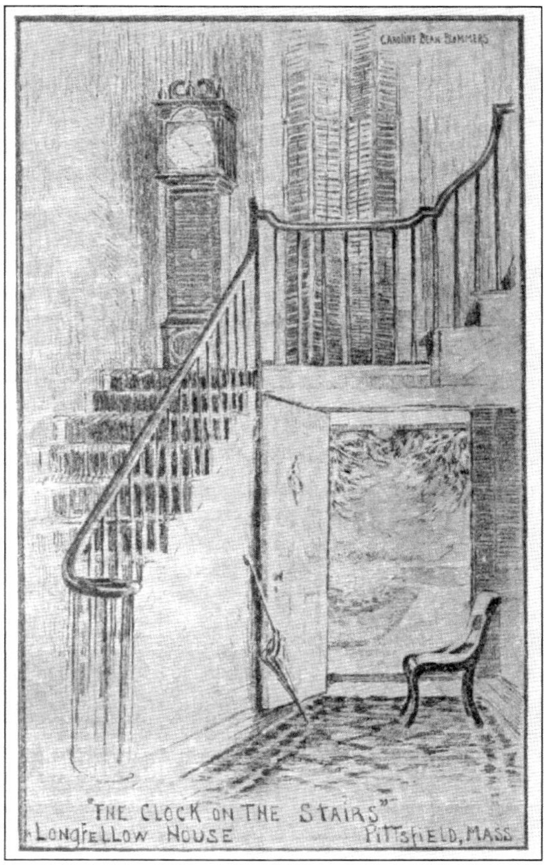

This 1917 postcard, created by Caroline B. Blommers of Pittsfield, honors Henry Wadsworth Longfellow's poem "The Old Clock on the Stairs." Frances Longfellow, who died in a tragic accident in 1861, inspired her husband to write this poem, published in 1866. "Halfway up the stairs it stands / And points and beckons with its hands . . . With sorrowful voice to all who pass, / Forever--never! / Never--forever!"

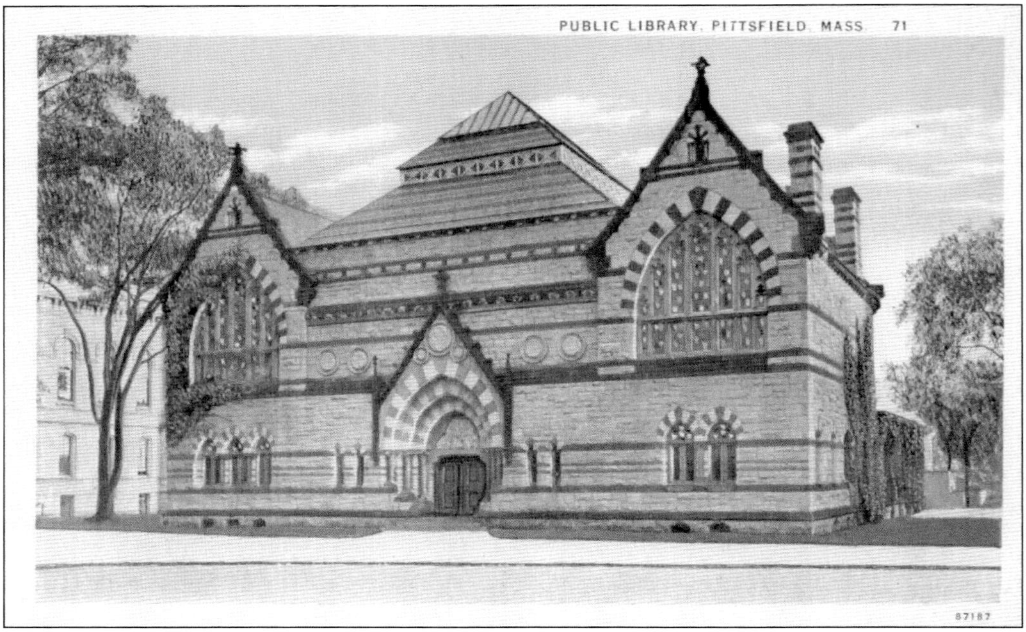

The Berkshire Athenaeum began as a private lending library and is now Pittsfield's public library. This beautiful Victorian Gothic building, constructed of blue limestone and red granite between 1874 and 1876, was a gift from Thomas Allen, a Pittsfield native, railroad magnate, and philanthropist. Since 1975, the building has housed the Berkshire County Registry of Deeds. The commonwealth had it restored in 2014–2015.

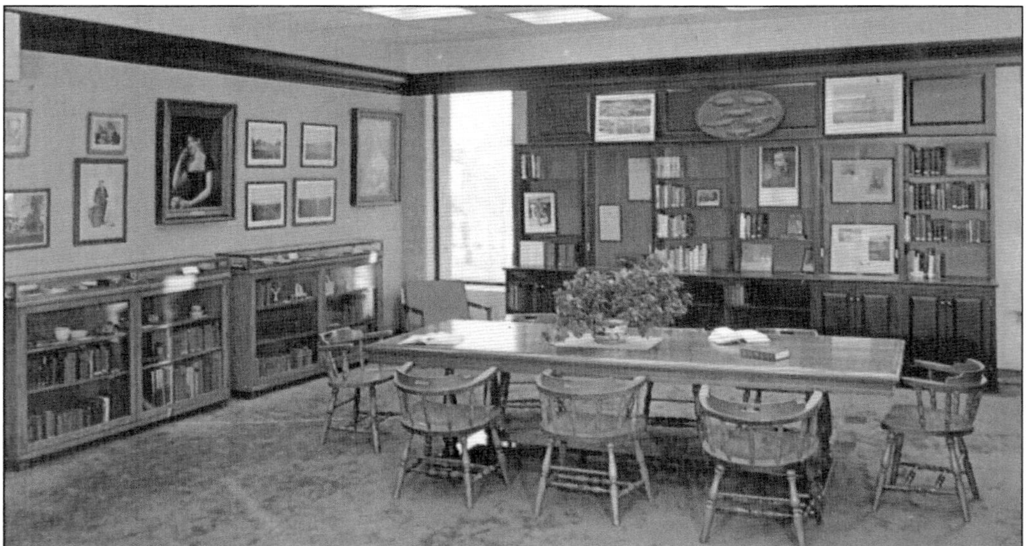

The Melville Memorial Room (established 1953) is shown at the new Berkshire Athenaeum, built in 1975. The room houses the world's largest collection of personal Melville memorabilia. Built on a large collection given by Harvard University professor Dr. Henry A. Murray, the Memorial Room gives students and scholars access to books, prints, manuscripts, furniture, and the bread box in which the manuscript of Melville's last novel, *Billy Budd*, was discovered.

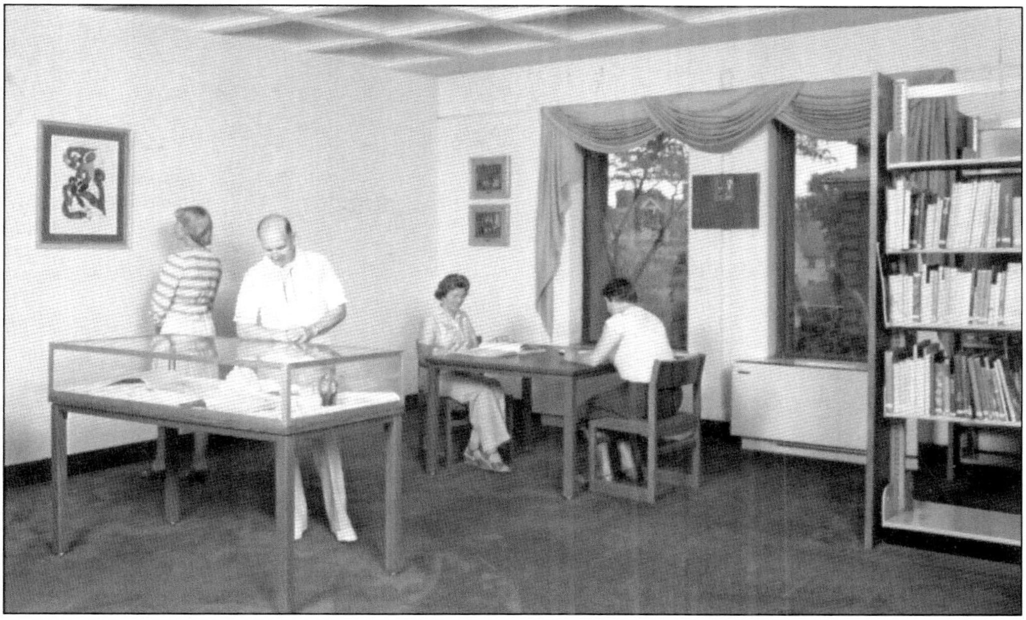

The Mary Rice Morgan Ballet Room at the Berkshire Athenaeum contains one of the finest collections of ballet memorabilia in the nation. The collection contains rare books, artifacts, and costumes, requiring strict security. These materials were collected (and donated to the Berkshire Athenaeum in 1977 in memory of his mother) by Leon Morgan of Chicago (1897–2002).

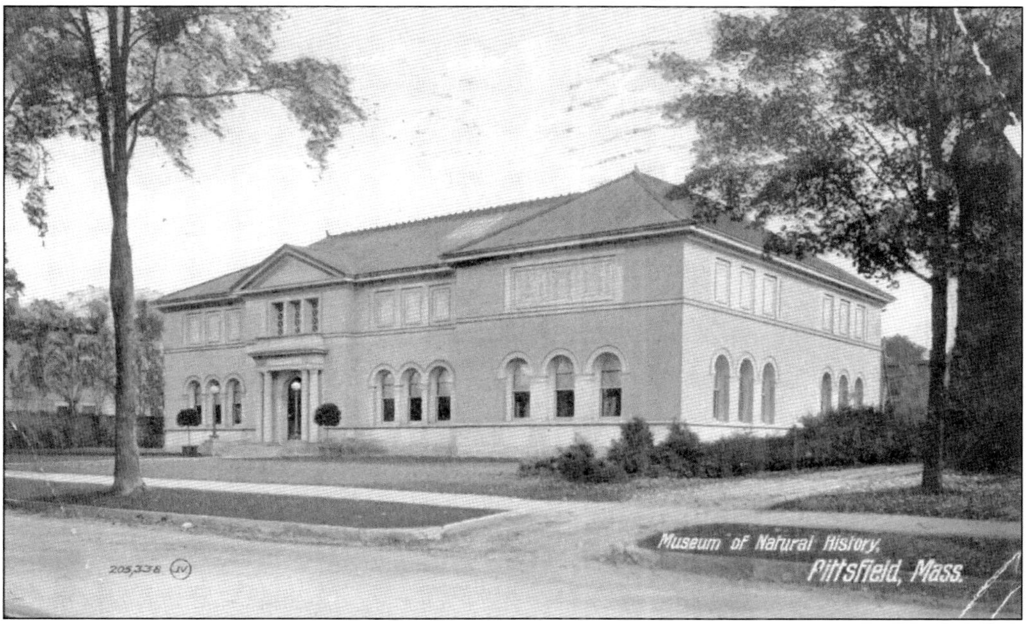

In 1902, Zenas Crane used part of the fortune earned making paper for US currency to create the Museum of National History. Located on South Street, it was designed by the Pittsfield architectural firm Harding & Seaver. Crane and others gave collections of art, science, and nature to educate and delight and provide access to the world for Berkshires residents. It is now known simply as the Berkshire Museum.

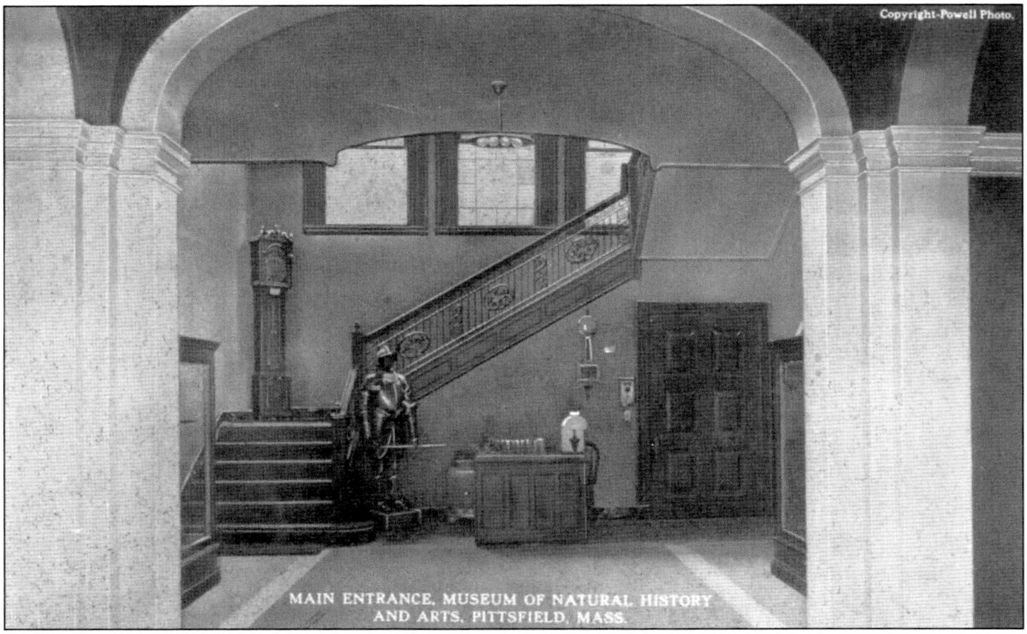

Pictured here around 1910 is the "Old Clock on the Stairs," made famous by poet Henry Wadsworth Longfellow. The clock was owned by Nathan Appleton, Longfellow's father-in-law. The entrance to the Berkshire Museum has changed tremendously over the decades.

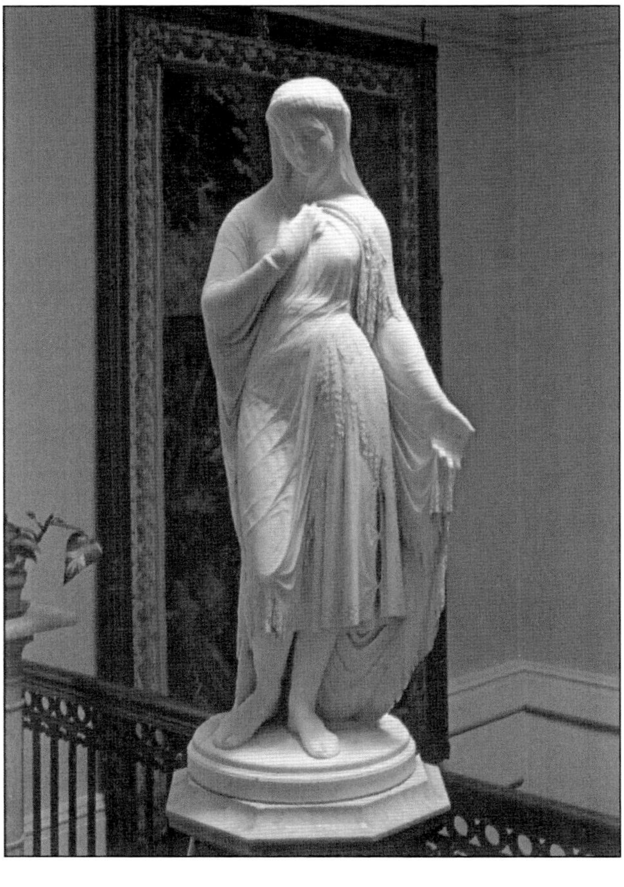

The Veiled Rebecca was given to the Berkshire Athenaeum in 1884 by the Clapp family. Since the Berkshire Museum separated from the Athenaeum in the early 20th century, this white marble statue has been on view at the museum. The sculptor was G.M. Benzoni of Rome, Italy.

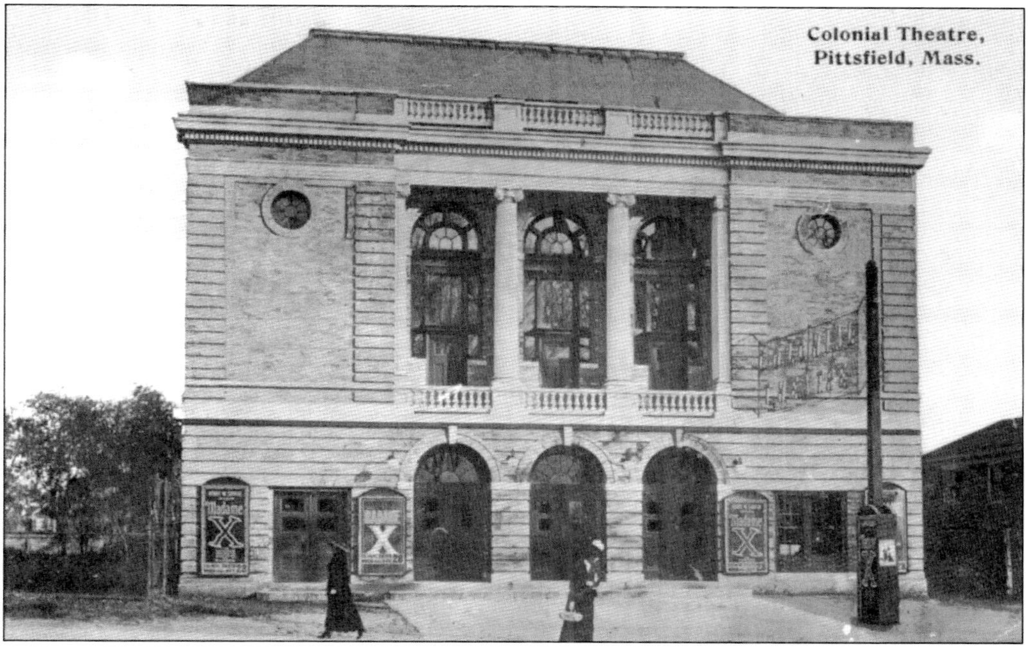

The Colonial Theatre opened its doors on September 28, 1903, after just 5.5 months of construction. In 1934, stage shows ended, and it was converted into a movie theater. The George Miller family opened an art-supply store there, preserving the interior behind temporary walls. In 2006, after years of effort by many people, including Hillary Clinton, the Colonial was restored to its former glory.

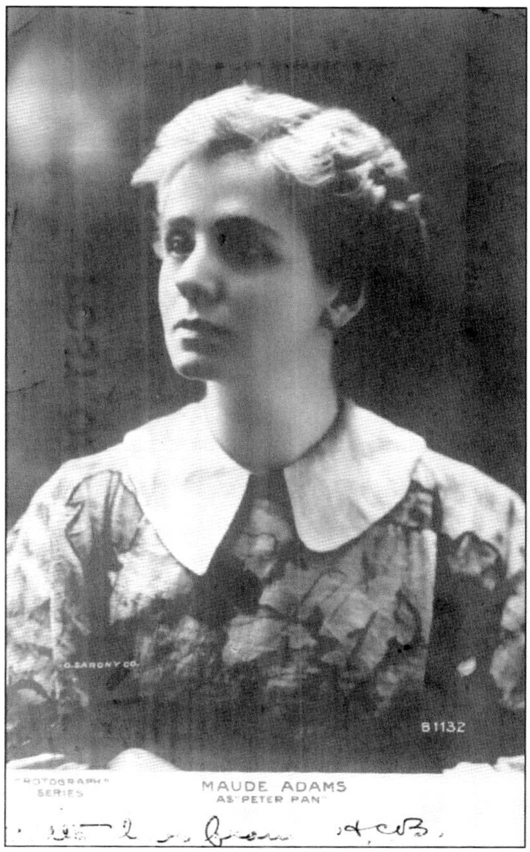

Actress Maude Adams (1872–1953) appeared at the Colonial Theatre four times, notably in the role of Peter Pan. She appeared on Broadway in more than 25 plays and appealed to a large audience, becoming the highest paid performer of her day, with a yearly income of more than $1 million. Others who appeared at the Colonial include Will Rogers and Sarah Bernhardt.

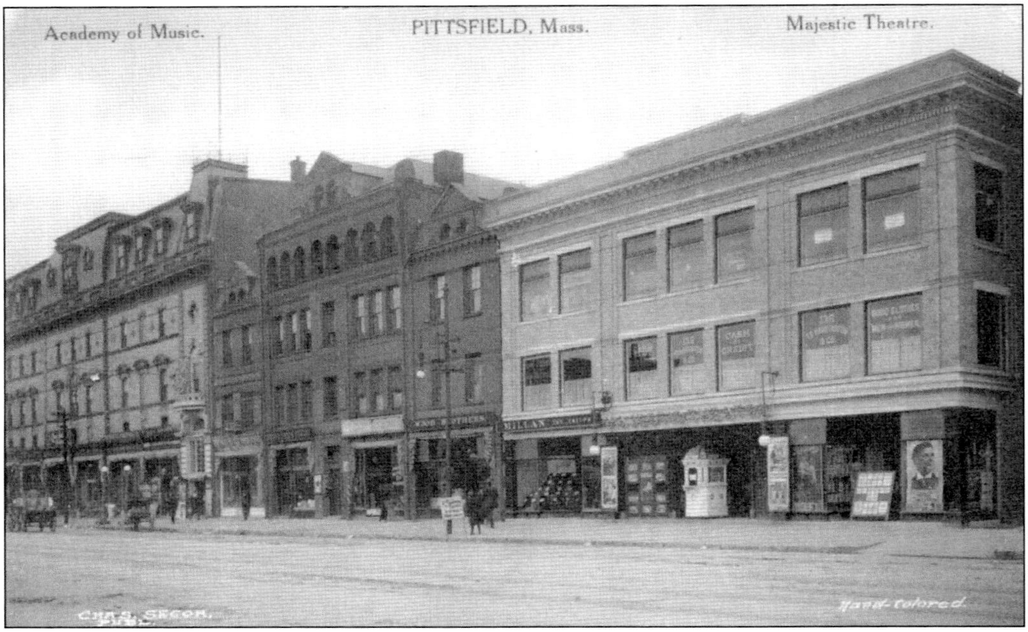

Two of Pittsfield's famous theaters are pictured here. The Academy of Music (left) was built in 1872, attracting famous performers of the day to its opera house–style stage until 1903. The Academy of Music burned in 1912. The Majestic Vaudeville Theater (right) opened its doors in 1910. As times changed, it became a movie house and eventually was renamed the Palace Theater. It was razed in 1993.

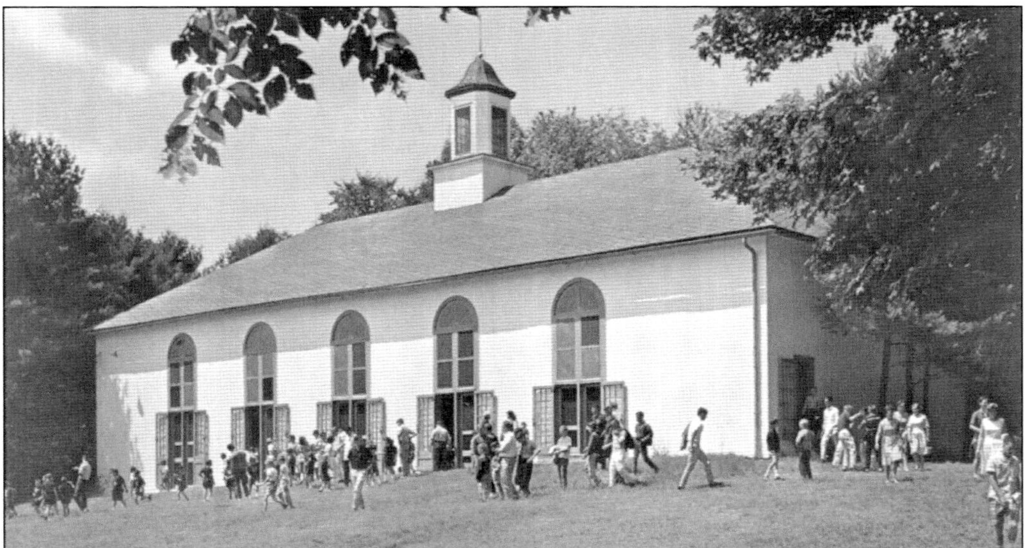

In 1916, Elizabeth Sprague Coolidge, a supporter of chamber music, established the Berkshire String Quartet to give concerts at her home on South Mountain. A performance hall, built in 1918 on the same property, used old church pews for seating. Cabins were provided for the convenience of the musicians. The tradition of holding concerts in the building, which is in the National Register of Historic Places, continues today.

Three

Places of Worship

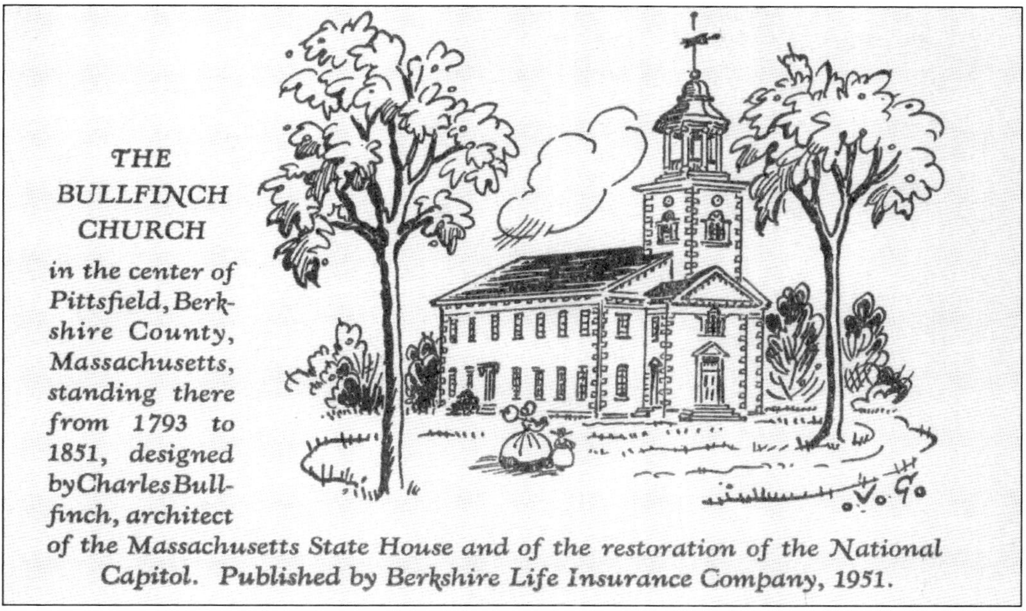

Each 18th-century New England town required a meetinghouse for government and worship. By 1789, when Pittsfield's population increased to 2,000, a larger Congregational church and meetinghouse was deemed necessary. Over the years, Pittsfield became a multifaceted religious community.

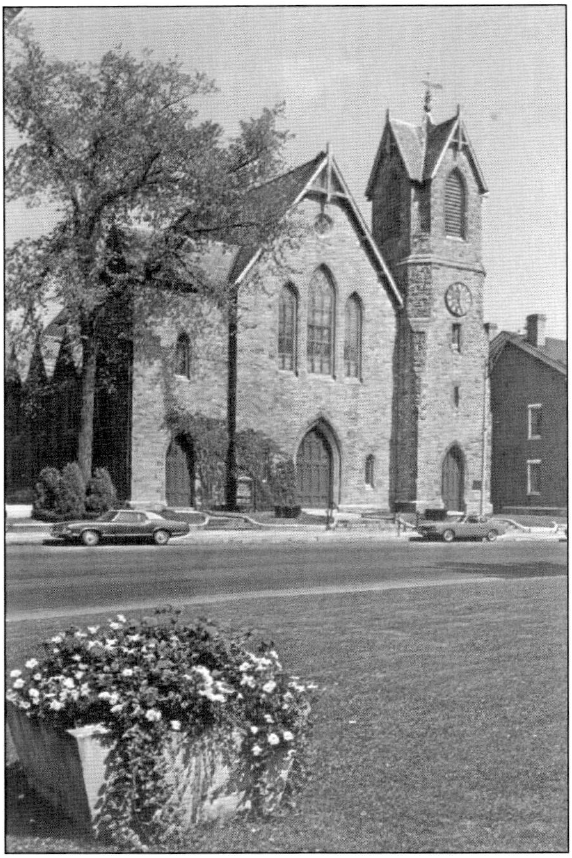

This elegant stone building used by First Church Congregational, on Park Square, replaced the Bullfinch Church. It was dedicated on July 6, 1853, and still stands here today. Two of the stained-glass memorial windows, dating to the 1880s, were designed by Louis Comfort Tiffany.

The first Roman Catholic masses in Pittsfield were held in 1835 at the home of Thomas Daly on Honasada Street (now near High Street). A church on Melville Street, built in 1849, served the Catholic community before St. Joseph's Church was constructed on North Street. The first Mass was celebrated there on Christmas Day 1866. St. Joseph's is one of the largest and most architecturally distinctive churches in western Massachusetts.

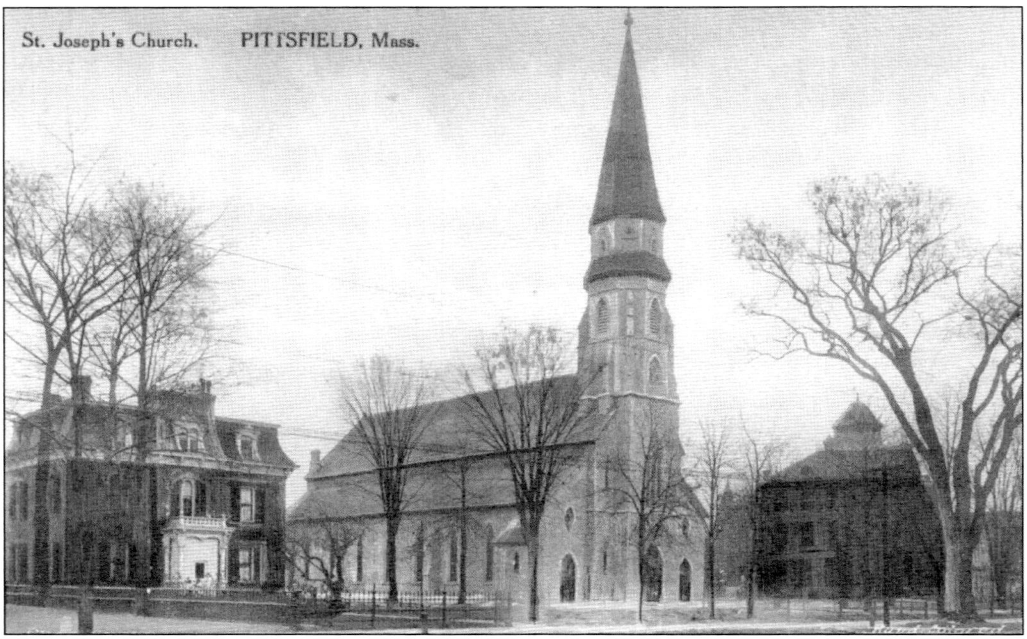

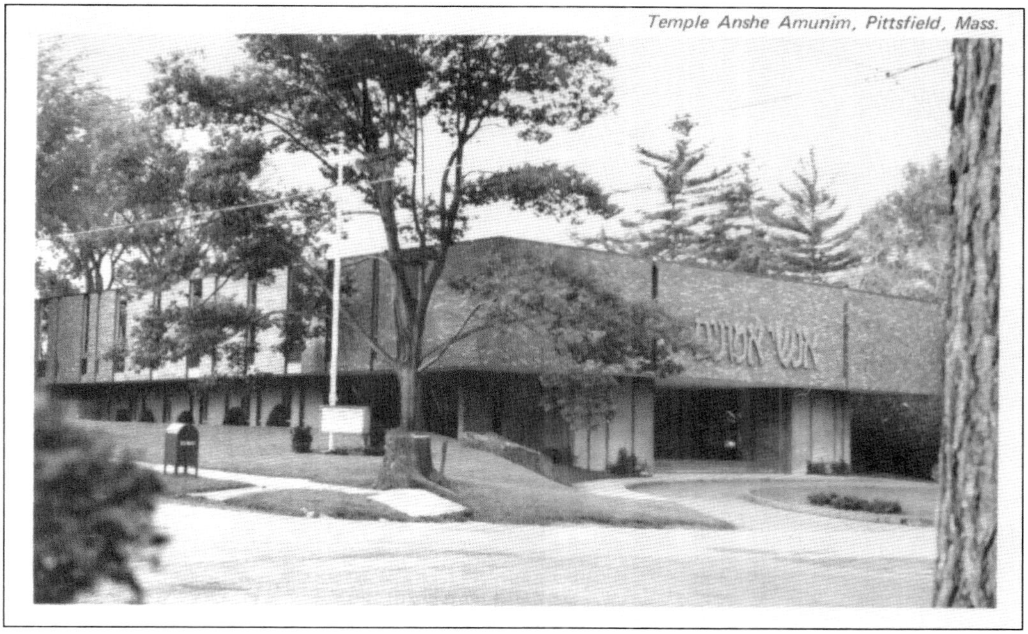

In 1869, the Society Anshe Amunim (Men of Faith) was organized by 25 Jewish families. Meetings were held in homes, then in rented quarters. In 1927, a church on the corner of Fenn and Willis Streets was purchased, renovated, and dedicated as a temple. The England-Blau family donated land in 1959 on Broad Street and Wendell Avenue. The building, with its sanctuary, social hall, and 10 classrooms, was dedicated in 1965.

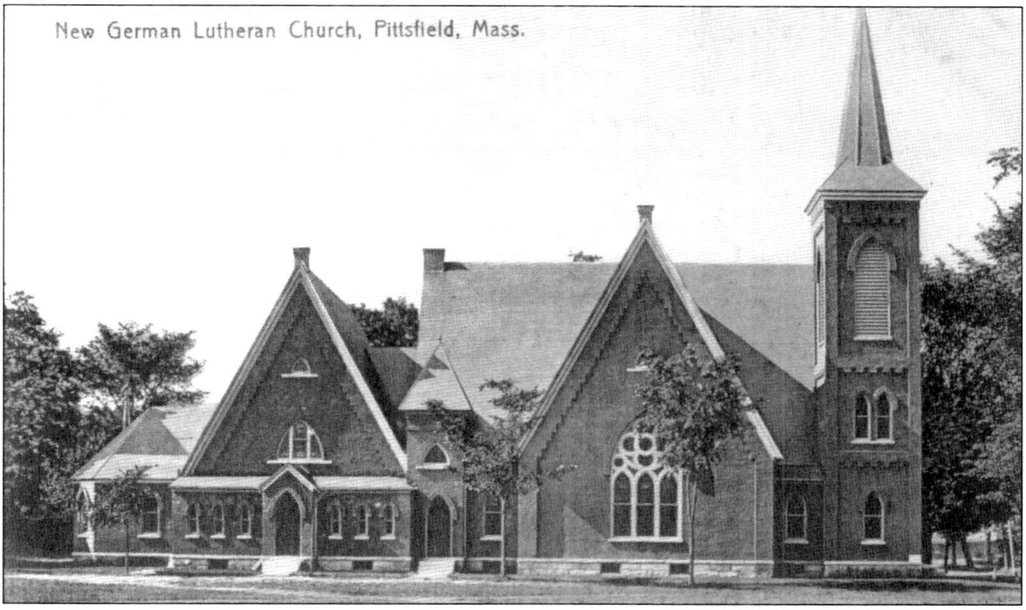

In 1858, about 400 German Protestants held their services in private homes. In September 1865, a portion of the old burying ground on the common was allocated to the Evangelical Lutheran congregation for their new church building. Today's Zion Lutheran Church continues on the same site at 74 First Street.

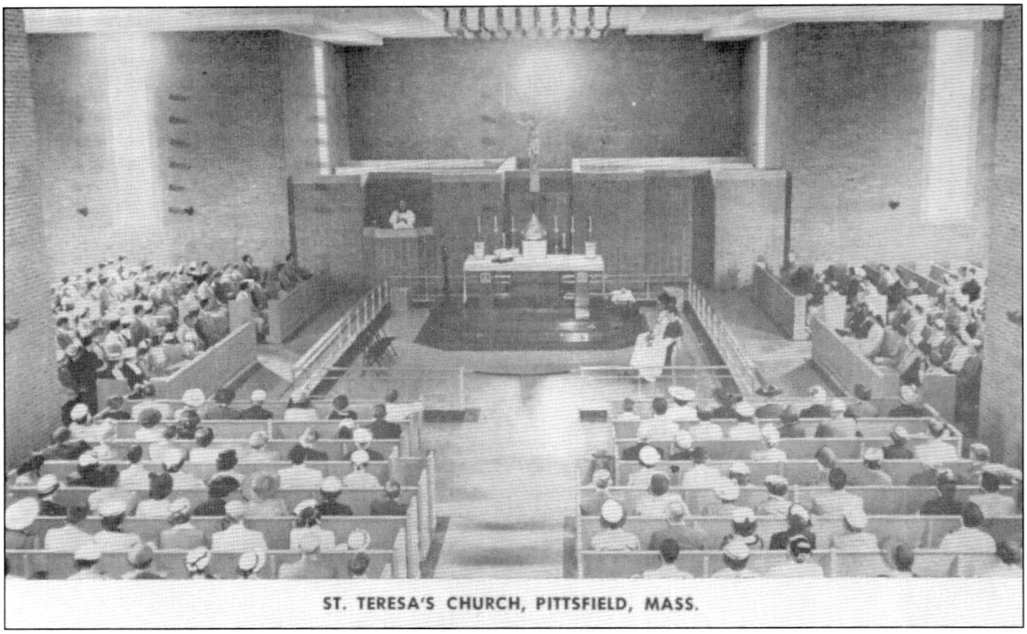

In 1926, the Springfield Diocese bought Dr. Timothy Child's 1860 Redfield estate on South Street for $30,000. The first marriage celebrated in the newly converted St. Teresa's Chapel was between Mary Leahy and Frank Gorman. By 1931, church membership had exceeded 1,000 parishioners, making the construction of a new church a necessity.

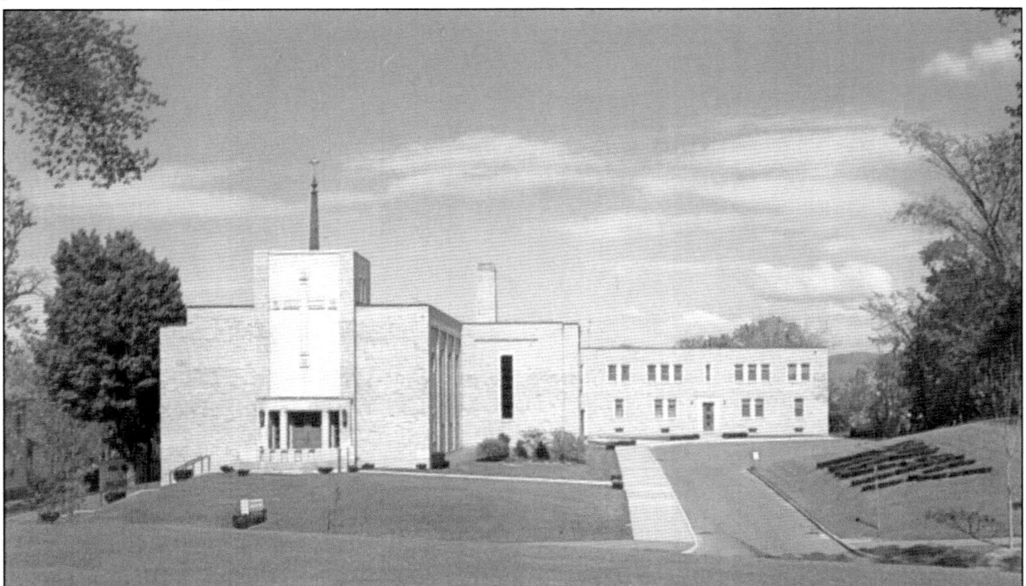

By 1949, funds had been raised to construct the 1950s-style brick church pictured here. Coincidently, the first couple to exchange marriage vows at the new altar was Rita Gorman and Robert Mackey. Rita was the daughter of Mary and Frank Gorman, mentioned above. St. Teresa's Catholic Church was closed in 2008 and razed in 2013.

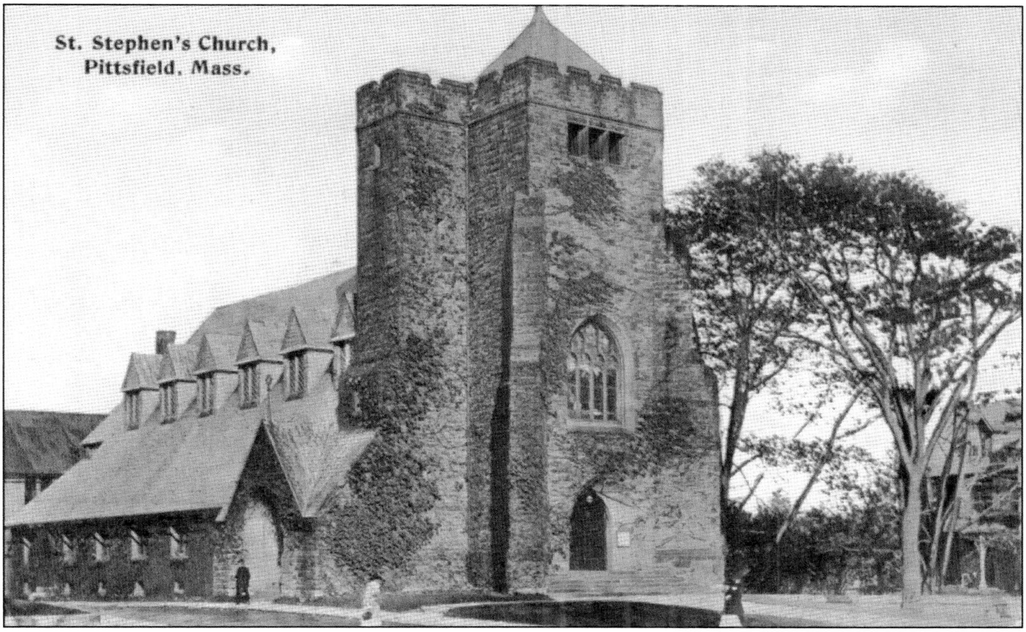

In 1830, Edward A. Newton organized a campaign to establish an Episcopal church in Pittsfield. The congregation's first church was built in 1832 and could seat 400 people. In 1889, it was replaced by a larger stone building with a Norman-style tower at the same location near Park Square. St. Stephen's Episcopal Church was expanded in 1916 and renovated in 1984.

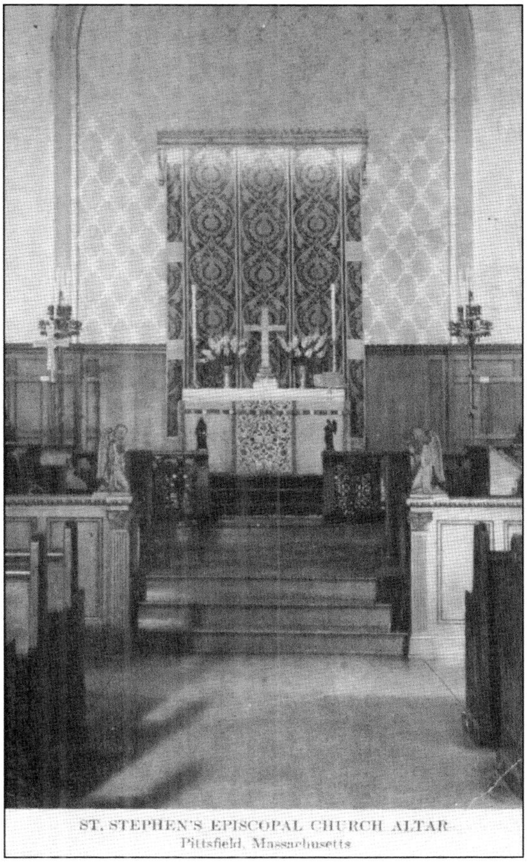

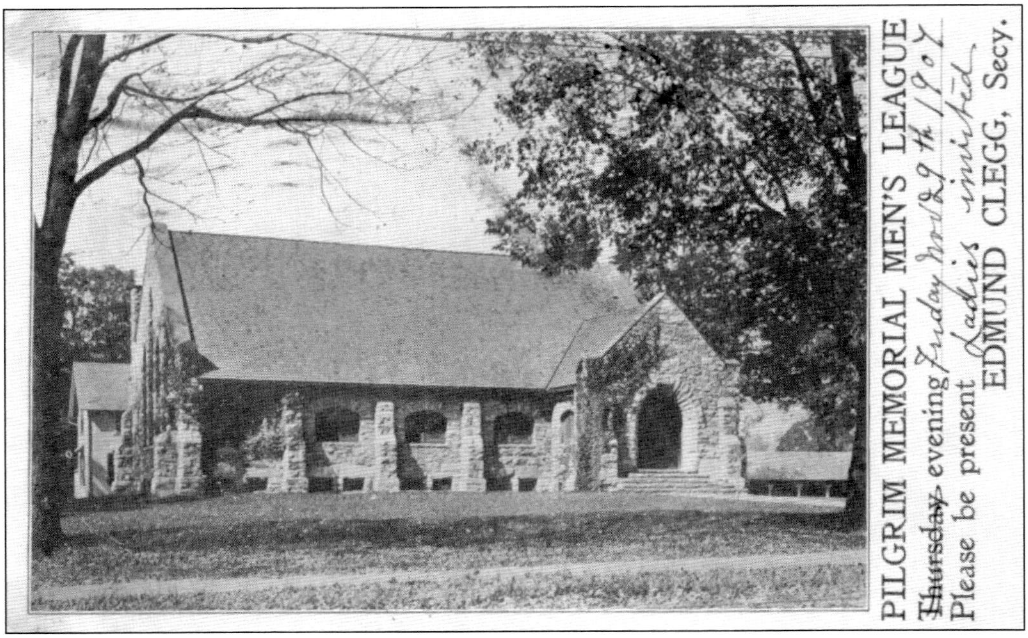

Pilgrim Memorial Church and Parish House are located at 249 Wahconah Street. Pilgrim Memorial began in 1863 as a Sunday school on Peck's Road, established by the First Congregational Church. In 1897, a group of 79 members of the congregation gathered to break ground for this new building, which was completed one year later. The parish house was built in 1927. The complex is listed in the National Register of Historic Places.

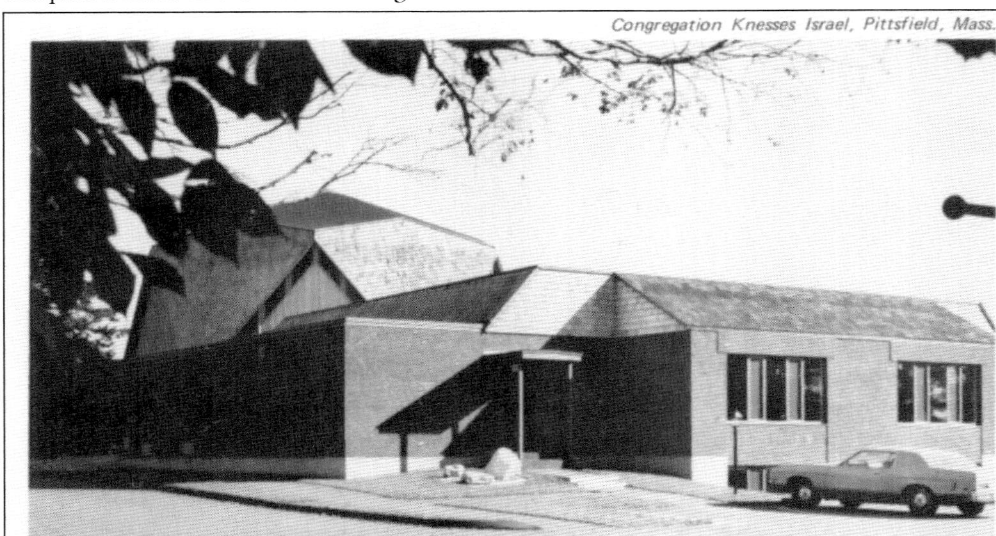

Knesset Israel, founded in 1893, constructed its synagogue at 16 Colt Road in the 1970s. Featured are a sanctuary, chapel, social hall, kosher kitchen, offices, and classrooms. Knesset Israel is a member of the United Synagogue of Conservative Judaism.

The First Baptist Church was formed in Pittsfield in 1772. Membership grew, and a larger church was built on North Street. Once again the congregation outgrew its building, and in 1850, a large new church was dedicated. It was remodeled and expanded in 1874. In 1926, the Baptists sold the property for $145,000 and moved to South Street. The Onota office building stands on the original North Street property.

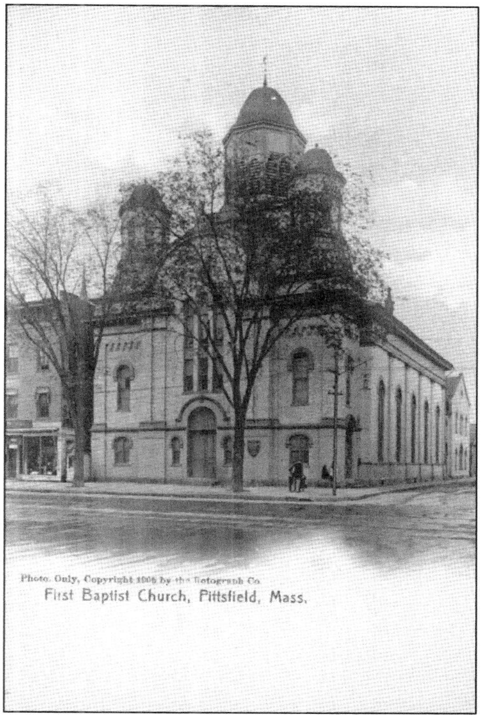

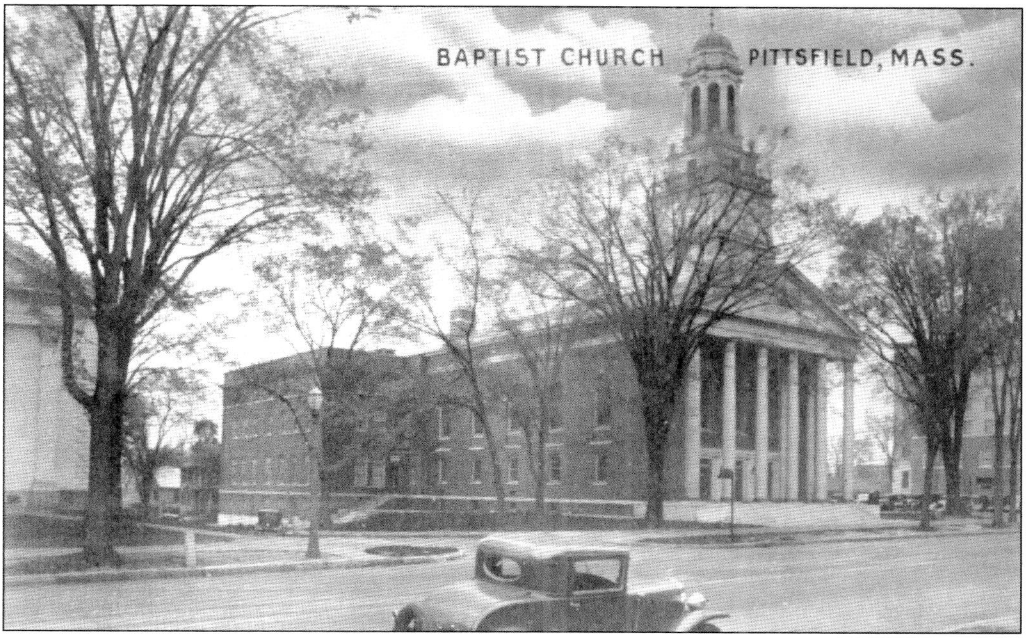

Today, the First Baptist Church is located at 88 South Street. After selling their North Street property in 1926, the congregation first built a school and parish house. Services were held there until the sanctuary, seating 800 people, was finished in 1930. The church established two missions within Pittsfield, one in the Morningside neighborhood and the other at the corner of Elm Street and Northumberland Road.

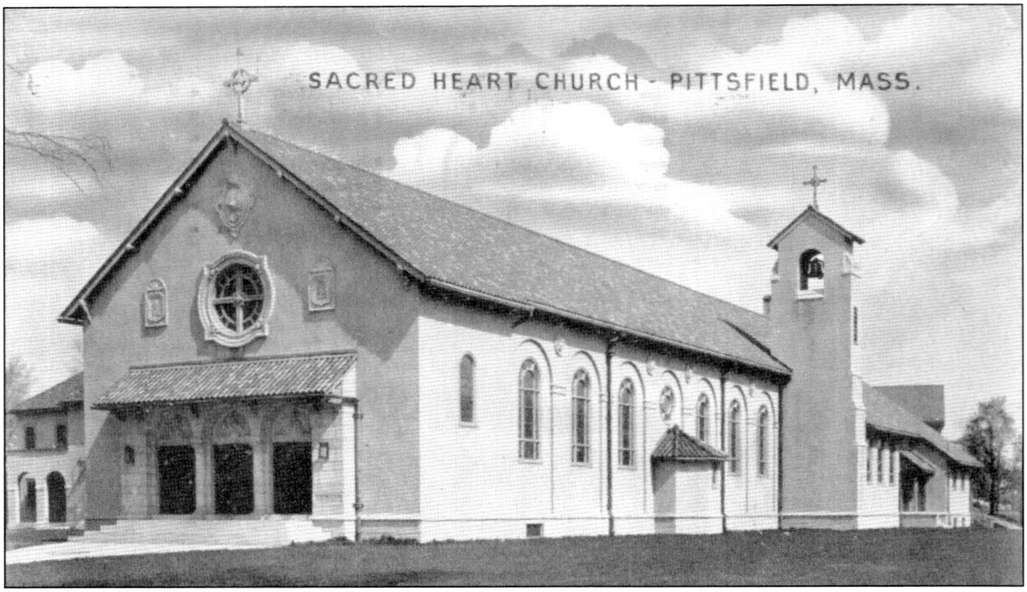

Sacred Heart Parish was formed in 1919, in response to the need for a Roman Catholic church in southeastern Pittsfield. First, a chapel was established in a house at 191 Elm Street, with the second story serving as a rectory. In 1923, when the parish had grown to 800 members and was debt free, a building fund was established to construct a new Spanish-style church, completed in the 1930s. It still serves the community today.

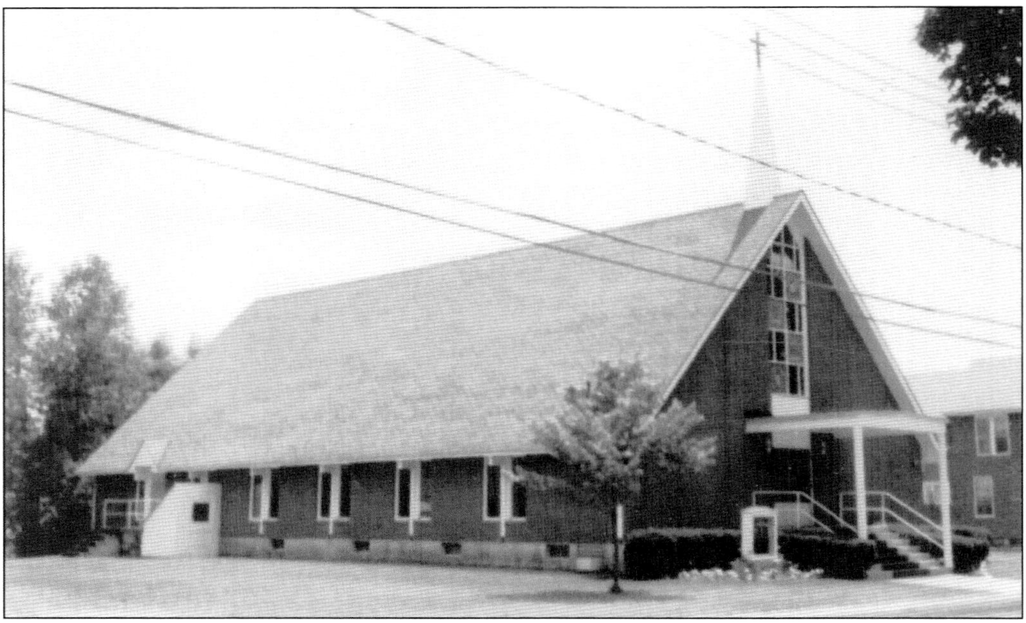

Seven members of Pittsfield's black community founded the Second Congregational Church in 1846. The Reverend Samuel Harrison was the first pastor and, except for serving as chaplain for the 54th Massachusetts Volunteer Infantry, he led the church for 50 years. In 1941, services were moved from First Street to a house on the corner of Columbus Avenue and Onota Street. The present church, seen here, is at 50 Onota Street.

In the 1840s, some parishioners left the overcrowded First Church Congregational to create South Congregational Church. A series of disasters tested their resolve. Just before the church was finished in 1850, it burned down. In 1859 and 1882, strong winds blew down the tall steeple, which was replaced by today's short steeple. The church remains active in the community, feeding hundreds of families a week at its food pantry.

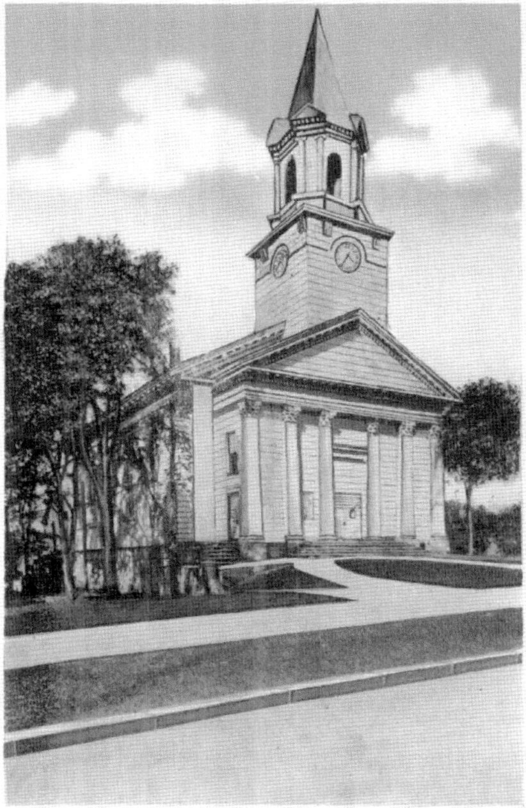

THE OLD SOUTH CHURCH, PITTSFIELD, MASS.

The many Polish immigrants who moved to Pittsfield in the early 20th century formed the Parish of Immaculate Conception of the Mother of God. After gathering in a temporary chapel in a house on Linden Street, the parish purchased the old Berkshire Street Railway trolley barn on Seymour Street, spending $60,000 to convert it to the Holy Family Church. It closed in 2008, but the famous Polish summer picnics continue.

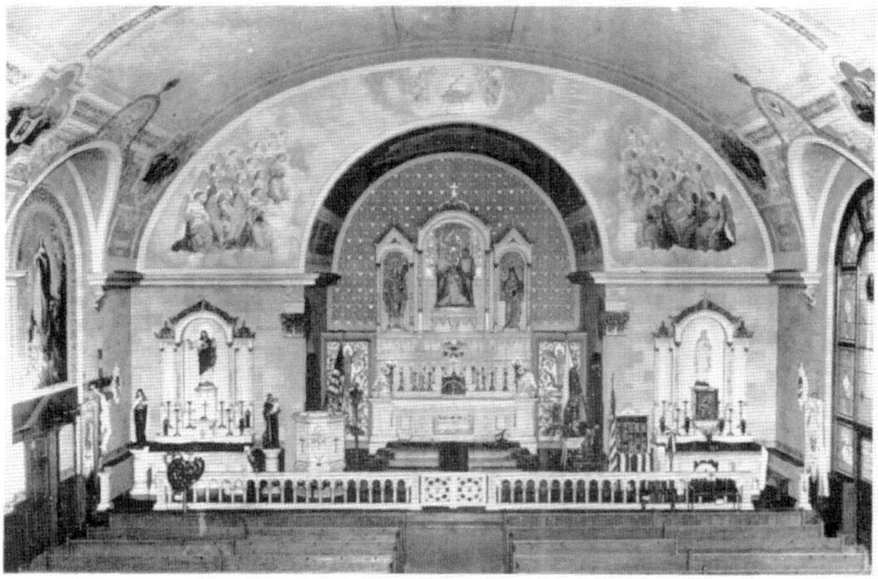

Sanctuary of the Holy Family Church, Pittsfield, Mass.

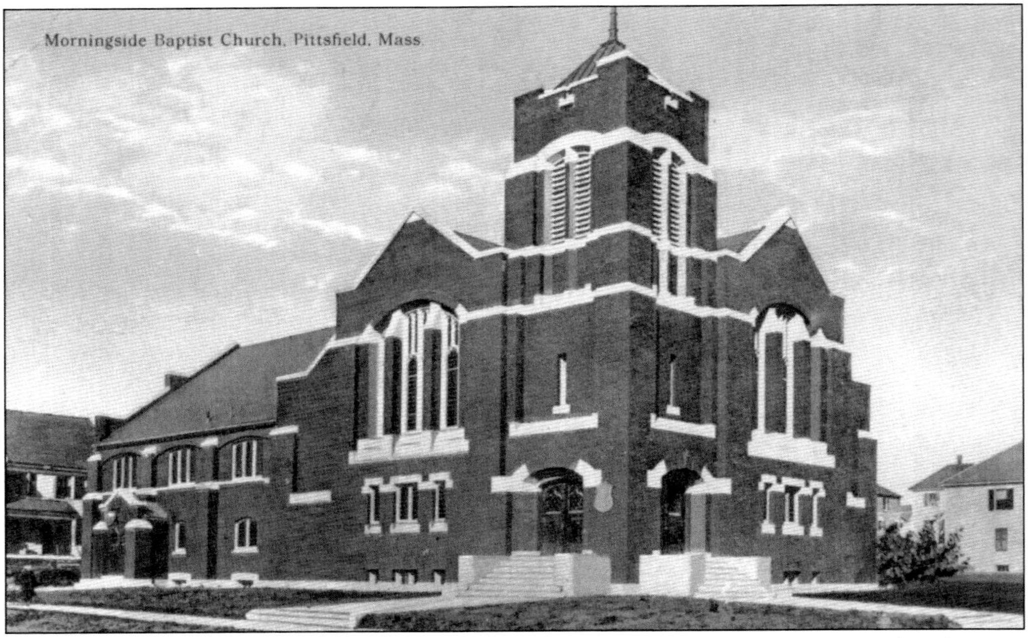

The Morningside Baptist Church was an outgrowth of a series of cottage prayer meetings. The church was organized April 29, 1896, with 118 members. The present church, at 475 Tyler Street, was dedicated on March 2, 1913.

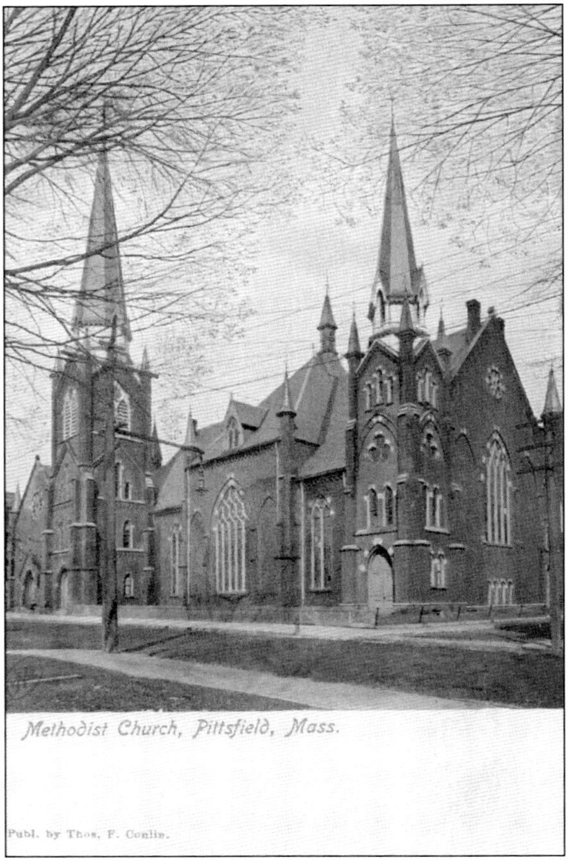

In 1798, Methodist parishioners built their first meetinghouse on West Street. The large Victorian building at 55 Fenn Street was constructed in 1874 by Pittsfield architects and contractors. In 1927, some 50 female parishioners wrote a letter to the pastor requesting a voice in the affairs of the church. Women have held board positions ever since. First United Methodist Church shares its building and resources with many community groups.

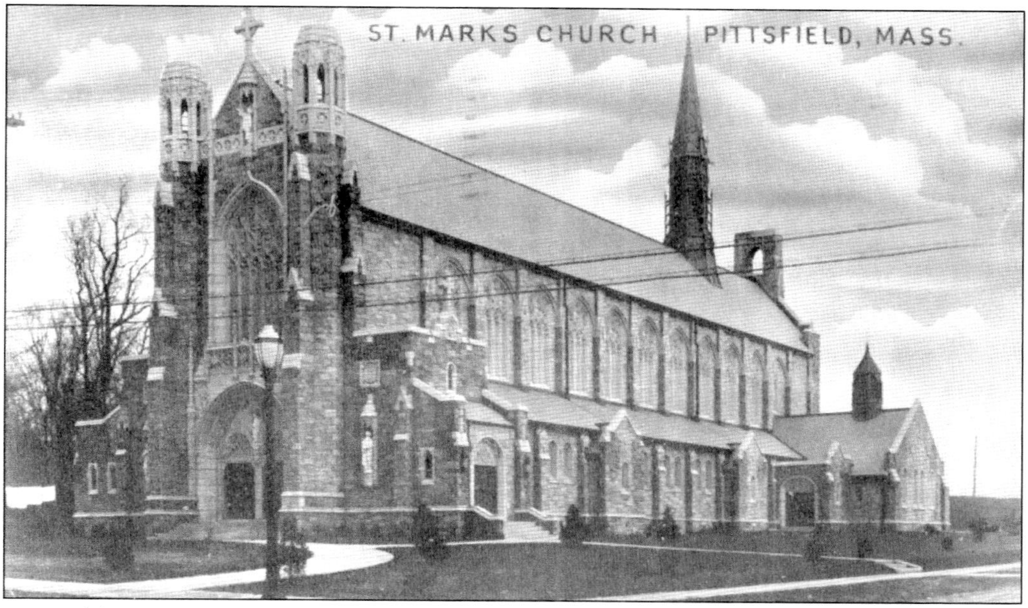

St. Mark's Parish was founded in 1913, with the first services held in a wooden chapel on the corner of Onota and West Streets. By 1929, the place of worship was outgrown, and the present large building was opened in 1932. It is of Gothic design, built of granite, with seating for 700 parishioners. In recent years, it has added services to support Pittsfield's Hispanic and West African communities.

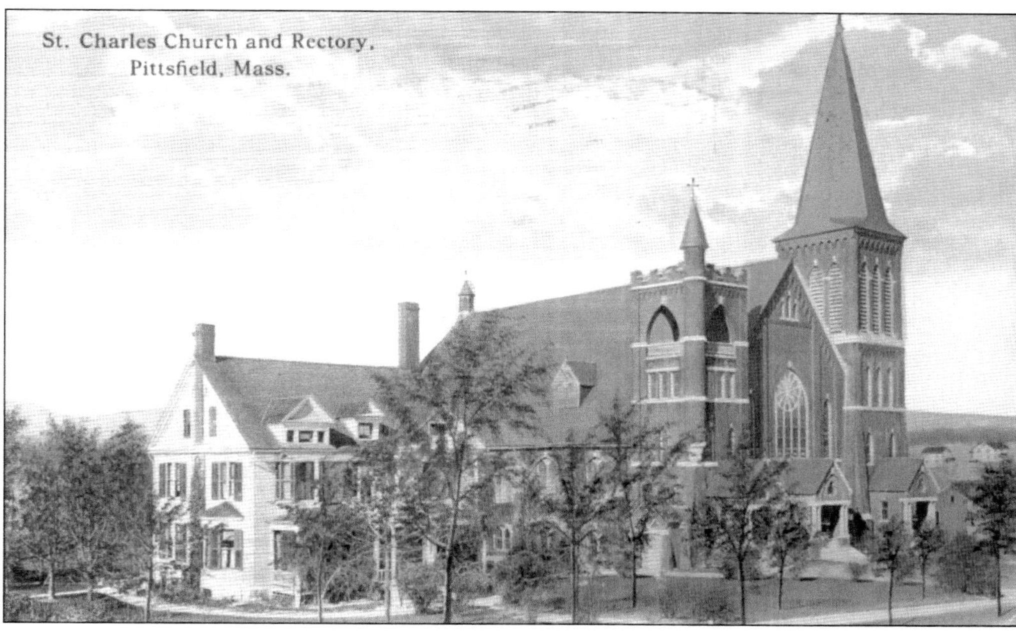

Ground was broken for St. Charles Borromeo Catholic Church in May 1894, and the cornerstone laid by Bishop Beavon on October 7 that same year. It was built by Pittsfield's many Irish parishioners. The stained-glass windows in the English Gothic–style church on Briggs Avenue contain 40 shades of green, reflecting the builders' immigrant heritage. It remains open today.

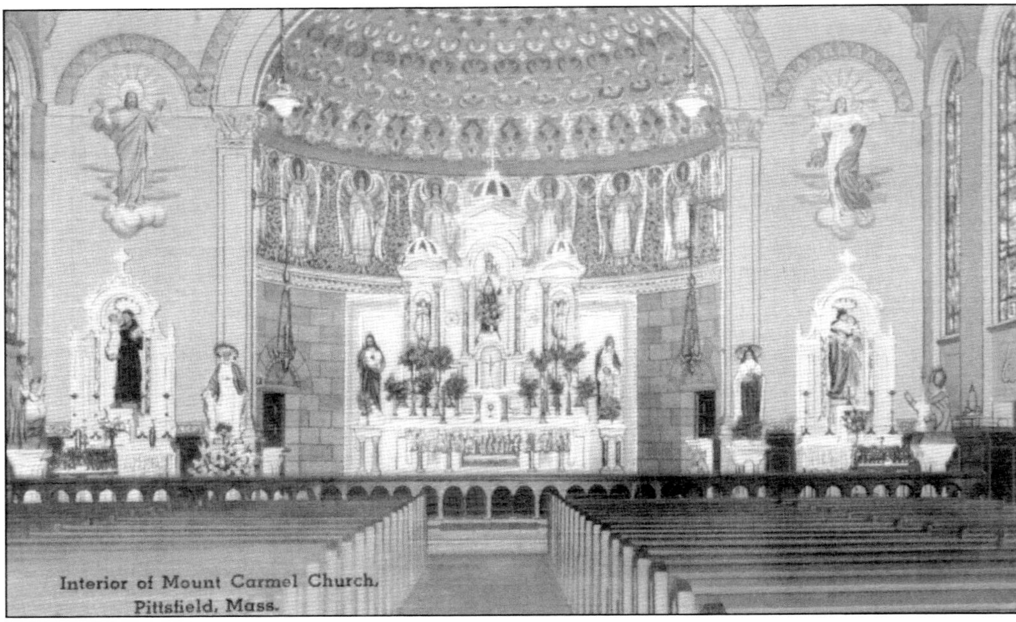

Mount Carmel Parish served the large numbers of Italian Americans in Pittsfield. In the late 19th century, without a building of its own, parishioners celebrated Mass at St. Joseph's. In 1910, the parish purchased a house on Fenn Street, converting it to a chapel and rectory. The Stigmatine Fathers were assigned to the parish in 1915, and a new building and school were finished in 1924. The church closed in 2008.

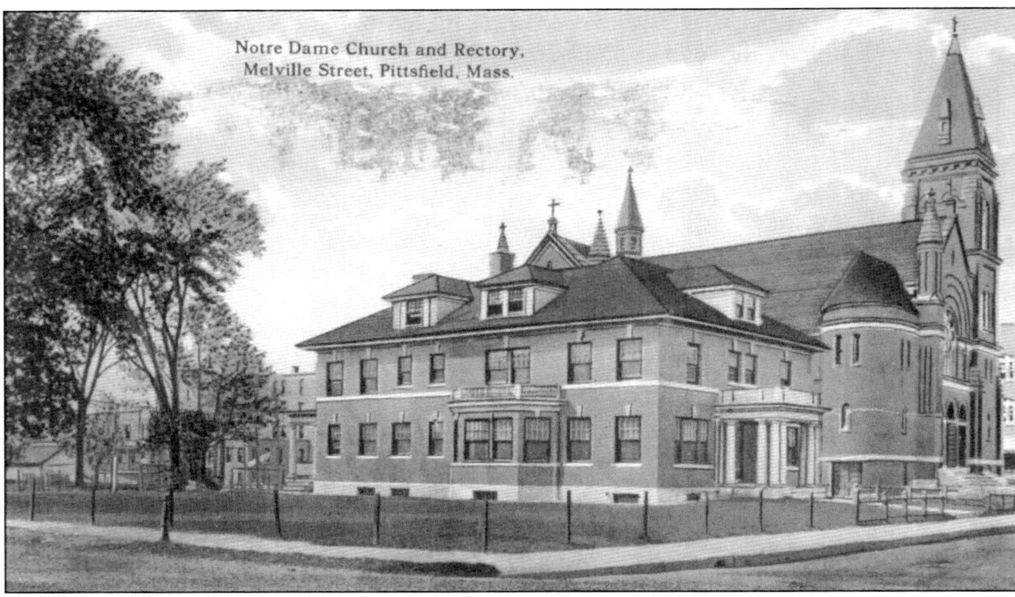

French members of Pittsfield's Catholic community first met at the old wooden church on Melville Street in 1867. In 1897, after two years of construction, their new church, Notre Dame de Bon Conseil, opened on the same site. At one time, there was a church school across Melville Street. The church, closed in 2008, is now the nonprofit Shire City Sanctuary, and the school building was converted to apartments.

Four

Education and Civic Life

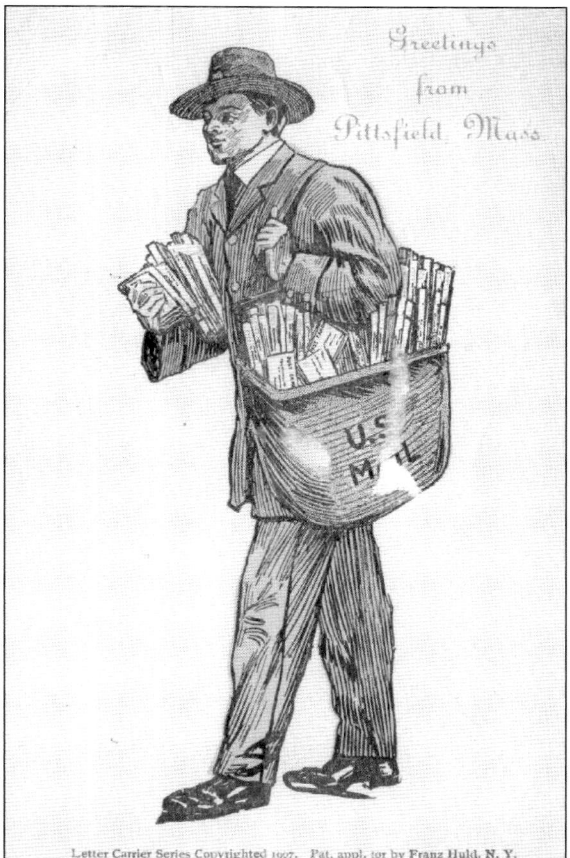

This dedicated mailman symbolizes the network of public services that remain the backbone of Pittsfield. The history of the post office in Pittsfield is its own saga worth telling. In 1906, a dispute erupted regarding the location of a much-needed new post office. Two vocal factions, the north-enders and the south-enders, lobbied the US Postmaster General to build near Madison Avenue (north) or near Park Square (south).

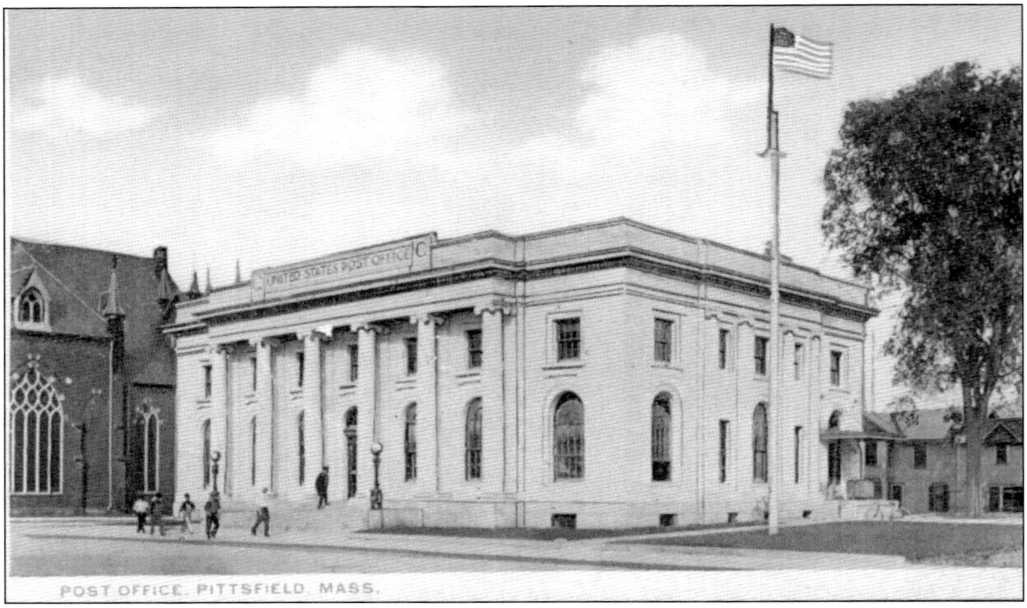

Pittsfield's first post office opened in Joshua Danforth's store on East Street in 1794. By 1858, it had relocated to North Street, until a fire in 1868 required a move to the Berkshire Life building at the corner of North and West Streets. In 1911, this impressive building opened on Allen Street. The federal post office is currently located on Fenn Street, and this marble building is now city hall.

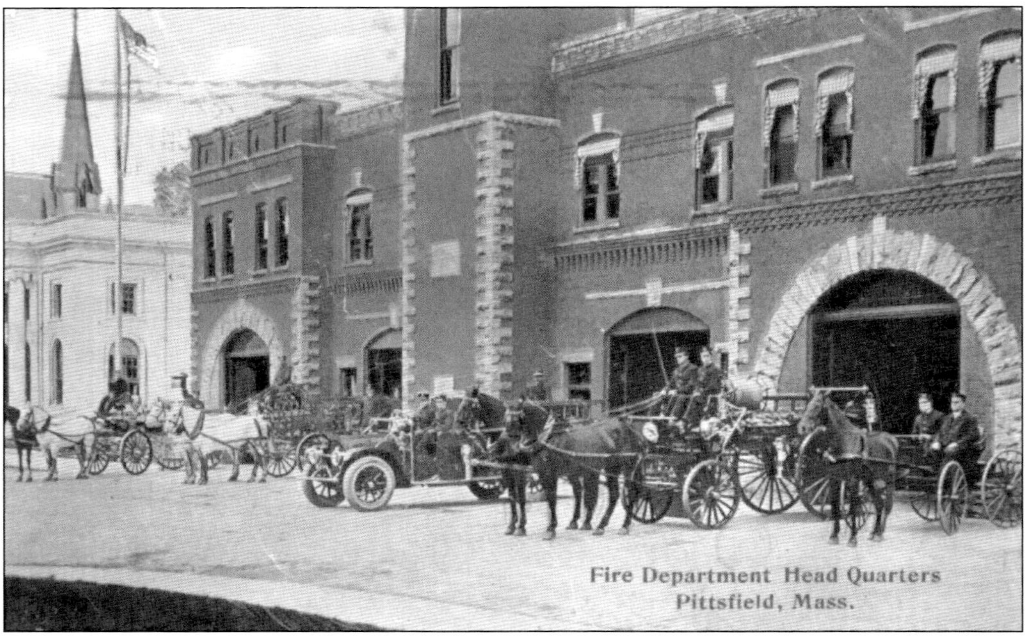

Central Fire Station, at 66 Allen Street, was built in 1895, possibly the first city station in the country stabling horses on location. In 1916, the horses were replaced by motorized fire engines. The station was used until 1976. It is now part of the Park Square Historic District and is used for offices. The 1911 post office is visible in the background.

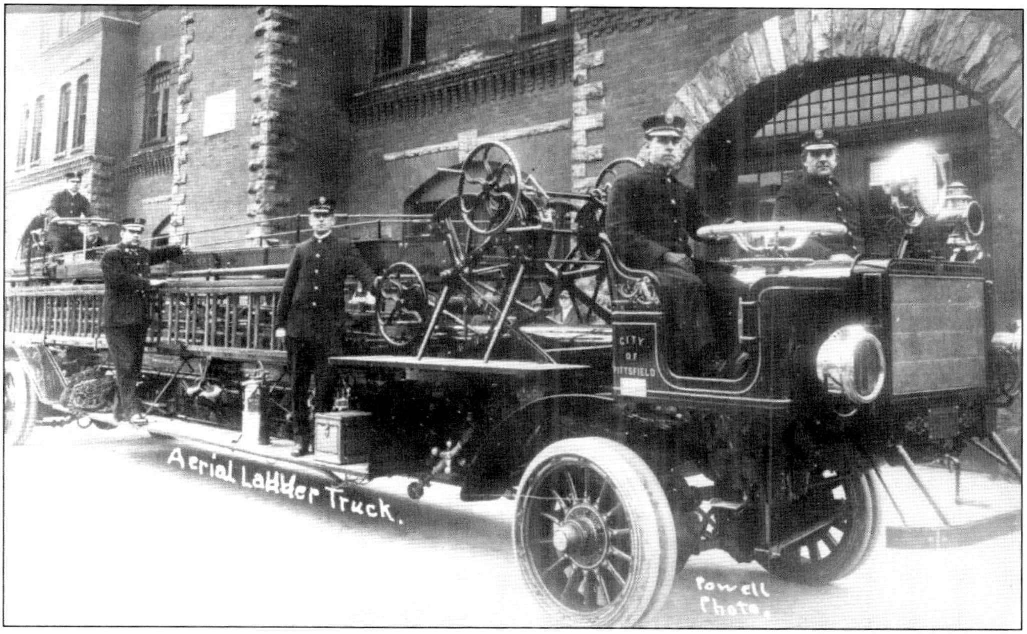

In 1912, the Pittsfield Fire Department acquired an aerial ladder truck. Driven by gas and electric motors, it allowed firefighters to reach the upper stories of Pittsfield's tall buildings. The city deemed the new truck a necessity after several serious fires on North Street, most notably the Academy of Music fire on January 28, 1912.

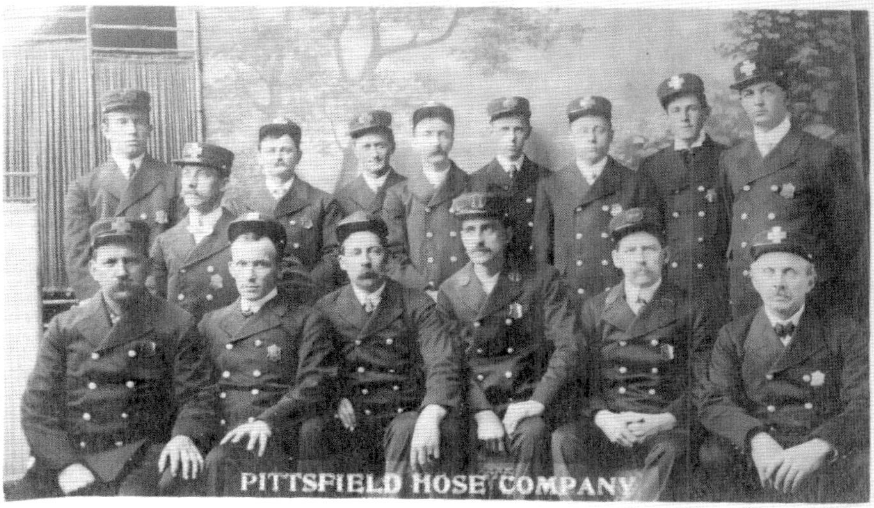

On June 3, 1844, the center, east, and west Pittsfield fire districts were formed. An engine house was built on School Street. By 1876, according to Pittsfield historian Edward Boltwood, Pittsfield's firemen were "well-organized, well-equipped, spirited, and competent." The four companies were the Housatonic Company, the George Learned Company, the S.W. Morton Company, and the Greylock Hook and Ladder. In 1891, the City of Pittsfield took control of the fire department.

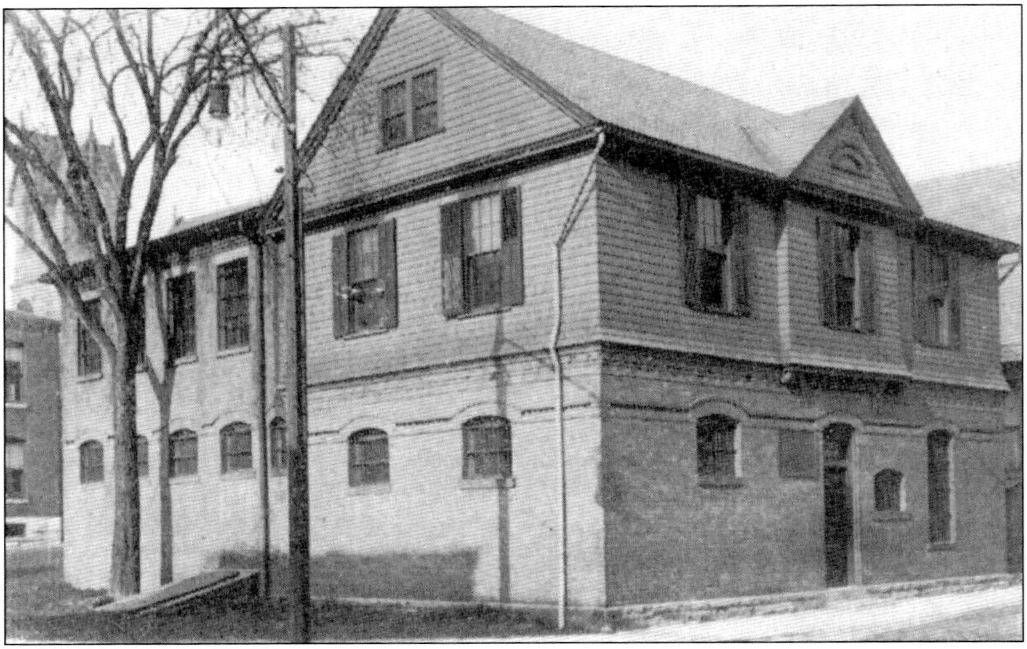

In 1877, Pittsfield ended the system of electing constables and established a regular police force under Chief John Hatch. This brick and shingle building at School and Allen Streets was used as Pittsfield's police station from 1879 to 1939, when the current station was constructed nearby. The old station house was used as the Old City Hall Annex, then demolished in 1968 to make way for a parking lot.

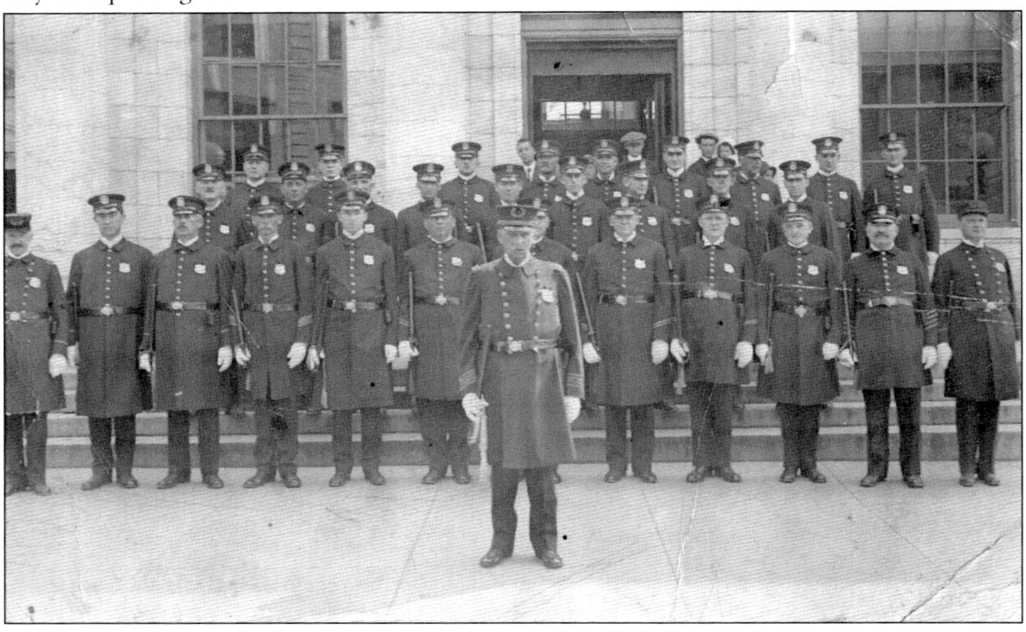

Members of the Pittsfield Police Department, sporting their dress uniforms and holding night sticks, pose for photographer W.H. Benedict on the steps of the post office at the corner of Fenn and Allen Streets. Based on the uniforms, this postcard dates to about 1915.

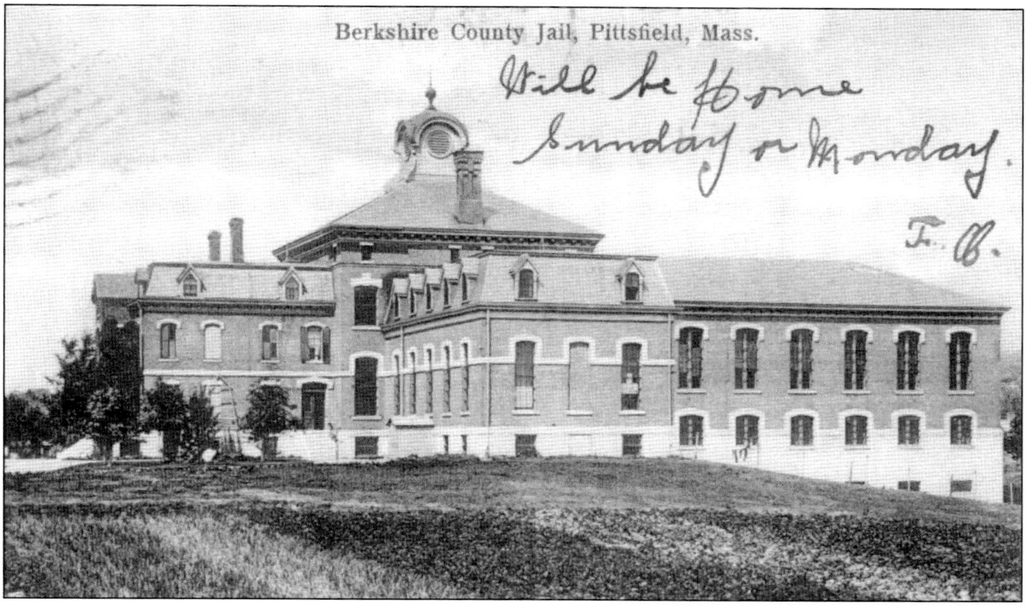

The Berkshire County House of Correction, on Second Street, was built in 1871 on land purchased from Abraham Burbank for $6,500. This intimidating building not only housed the city's convicts, it also was a place of executions. On August 16, 1878, murderer John Ten Eyck was hanged under the supervision of Sheriff Root. This building served as the jail until 2001, when it was replaced by a new facility on Cheshire Road.

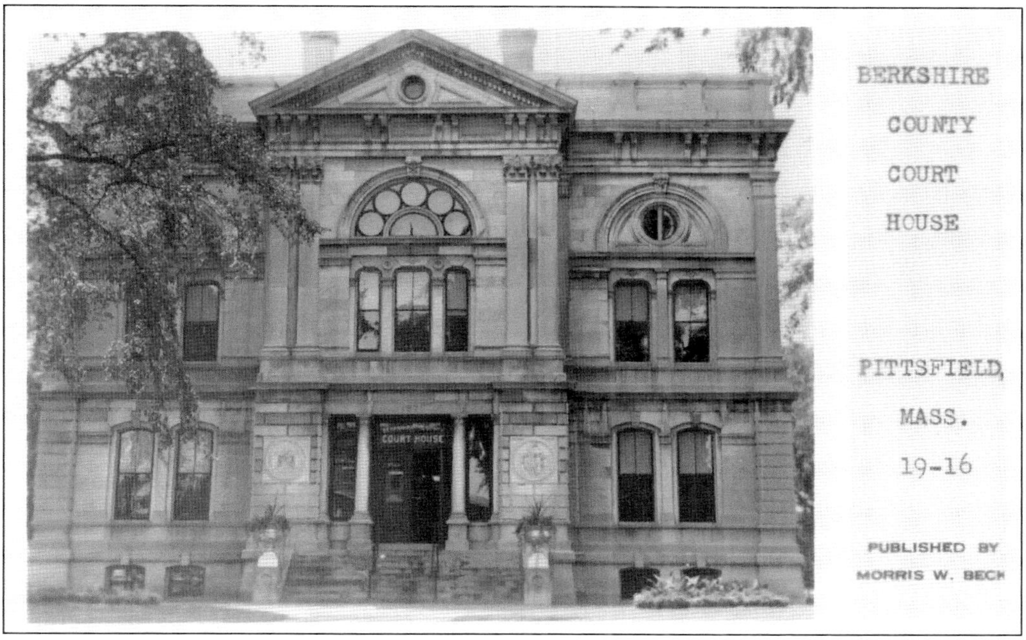

In 1868, the Massachusetts Legislature voted to move the Berkshire County seat from Lenox to Pittsfield, with the stipulation that Pittsfield donate a site for a new county courthouse. The town paid $35,000 for the Peace Party House and its lot, moving the house across the street. A white marble courthouse was completed in 1871 at a cost of $200,000. It is still in use today.

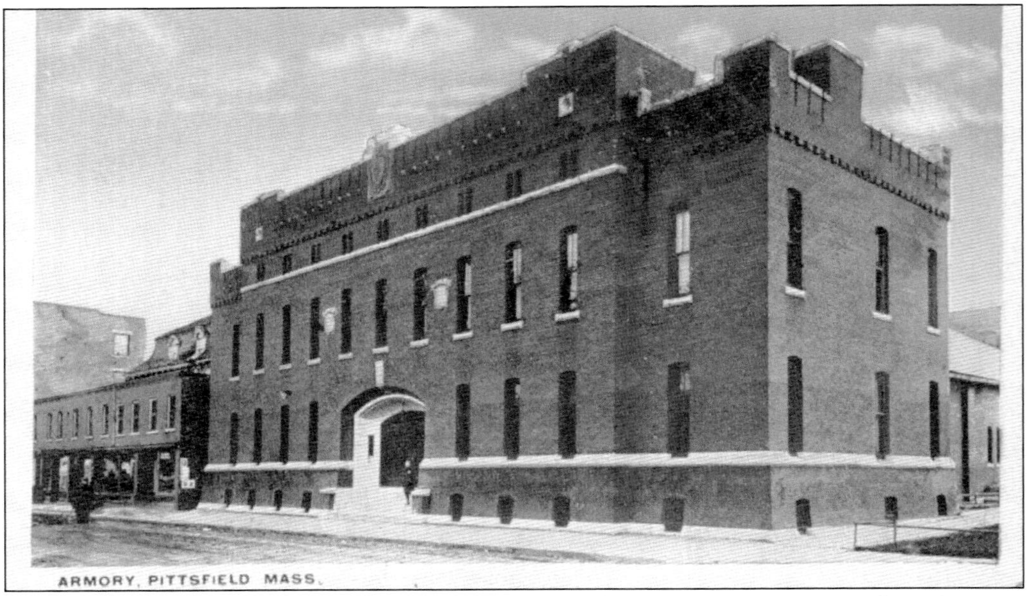

In 1901, the 2nd Massachusetts Volunteer Infantry formed Company F. Without its own headquarters, the company used the Academy of Music until 1908, when this brick building with limestone trim was constructed on Summer Street. Similar to other Massachusetts armories, it had a drill shed of 80 by 110 feet. Company F was summoned into service in June 1916 to protect the southern US border. The armory no longer stands.

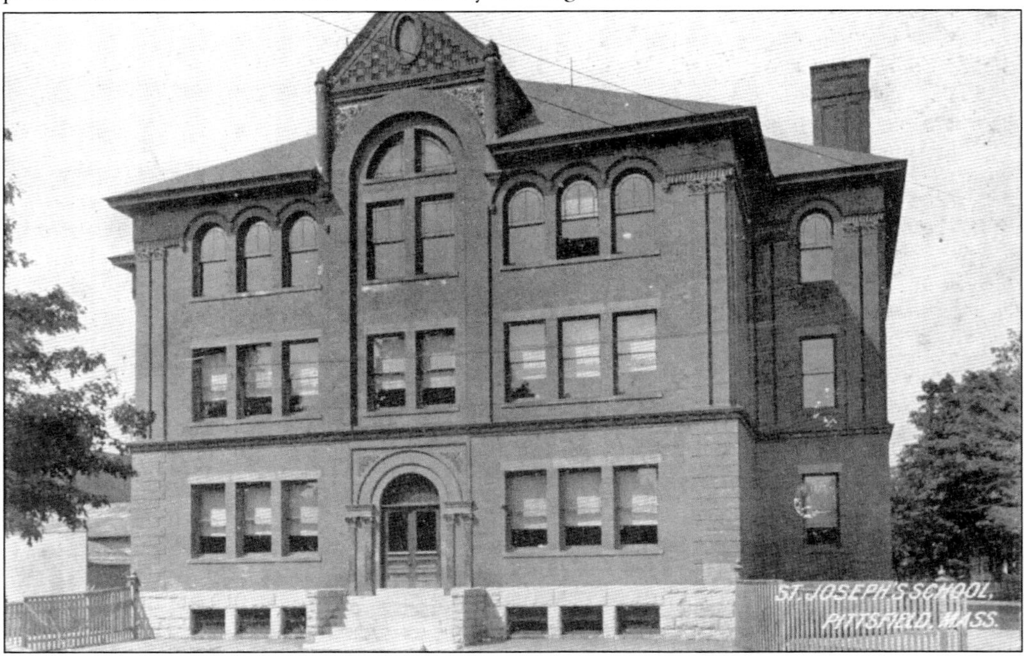

The Sisters of St. Joseph set up a free academy in their convent on North Street in 1897. In 1899, this school building was constructed on nearby North Pearl Street. With three floors, 10 classrooms, and an auditorium, it served both elementary and high school students. By 1915, there were 688 students enrolled. It was razed in 1992.

St. Joseph Central High School, originally part of the Sisters of St. Joseph Academy, moved in 1899 to a building shared with the elementary school. In 1942, in a major expansion, the comprehensive coeducational four-year high school moved to its present location at 22 Maplewood Avenue. Its student population includes both local and international scholars seeking a private Roman Catholic education. This postcard is a pastel created by Dale M. Zola in 1997.

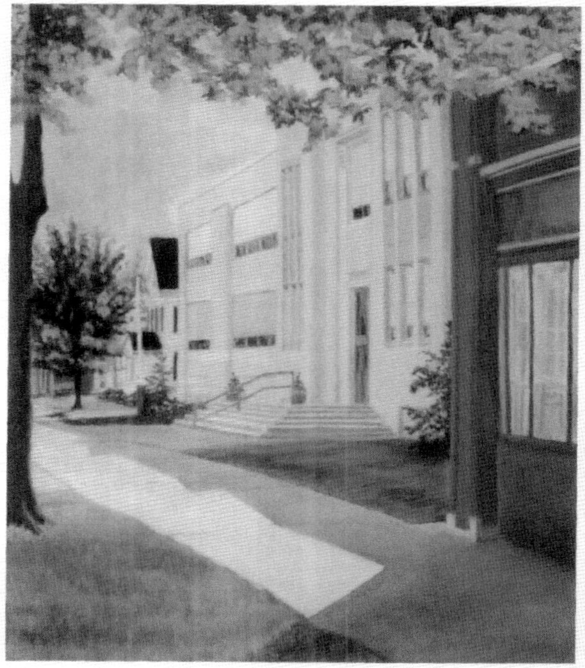

St. Mary's Parochial School was built in 1941 to serve the expanding population on Pittsfield's east side. Grades one through four were on the upper floor, while the first floor served as the church's sanctuary. By 1944, the new St. Mary the Morning Star Church was built, and the school expanded to grades one through eight. The school closed in the 1970s, and the church followed in 2008.

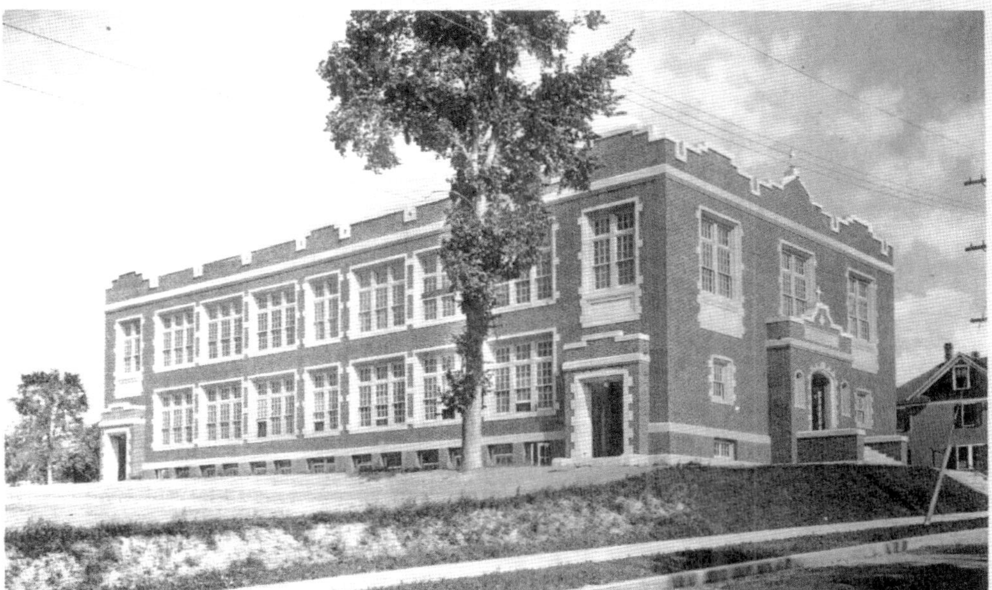

ST. MARY THE MORNING STAR. PITTSFIELD, MASS.

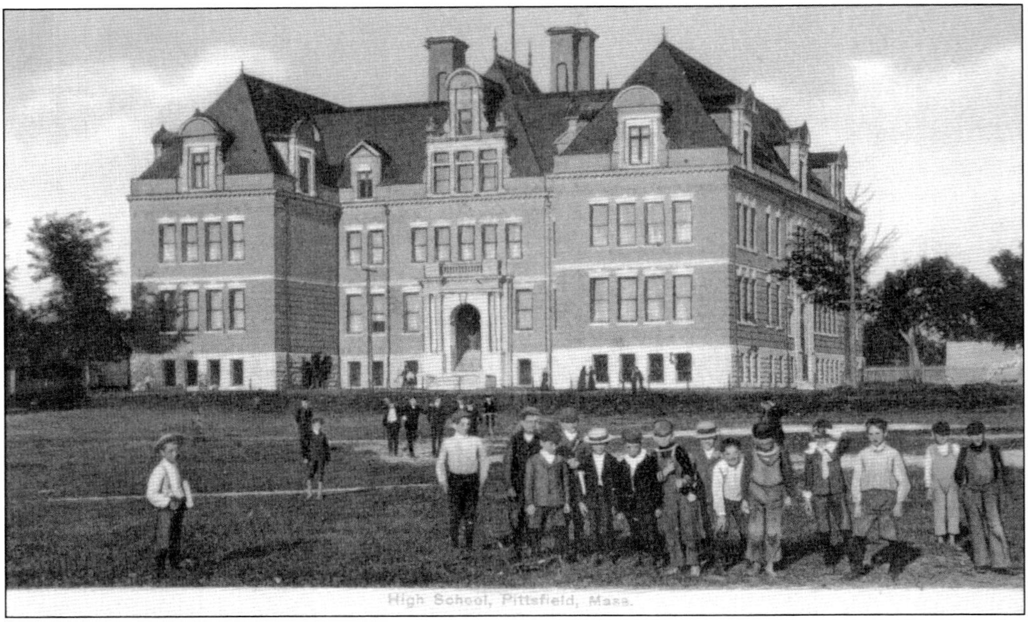

After Pittsfield's high school on South Street burned in 1895, the common was chosen for the site of this new larger school. It was finished in 1898 but by the 1920s was overcrowded enough that a new school was built on East Street. The Old Central High School building housed the Berkshire Community College before being converted to apartments.

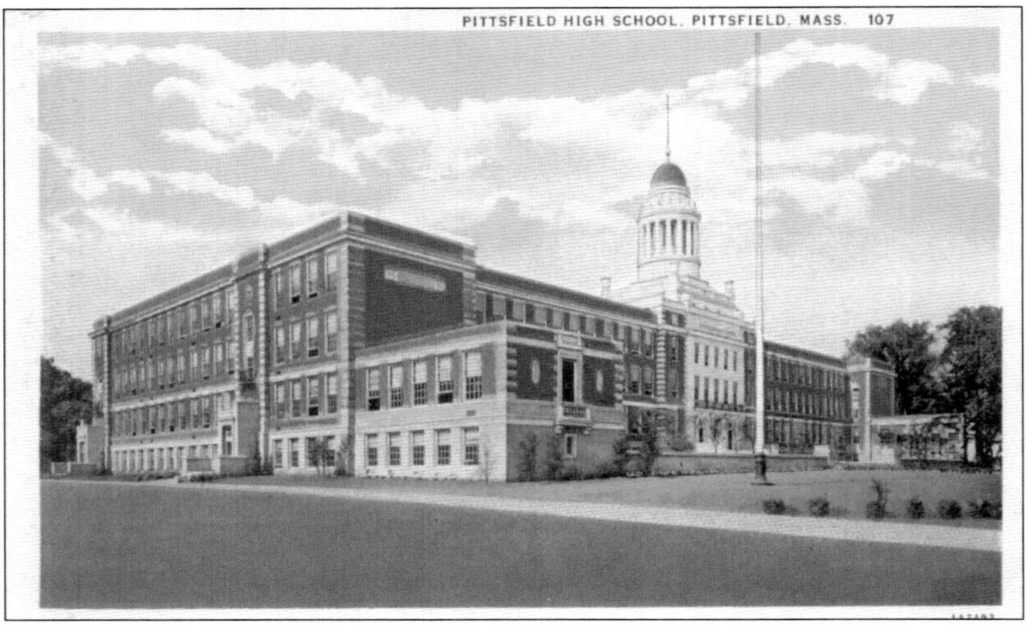

In the late 1920s, three mansions on East Street were demolished to provide space for the Pittsfield High School. On September 9, 1931, the new school, designed by local architectural firm Harding & Seaver opened to 1,450 students, and it remains in use today. However, by 1962, it was overcrowded, and in 1969, Taconic High School, on the west side of Pittsfield, opened its doors.

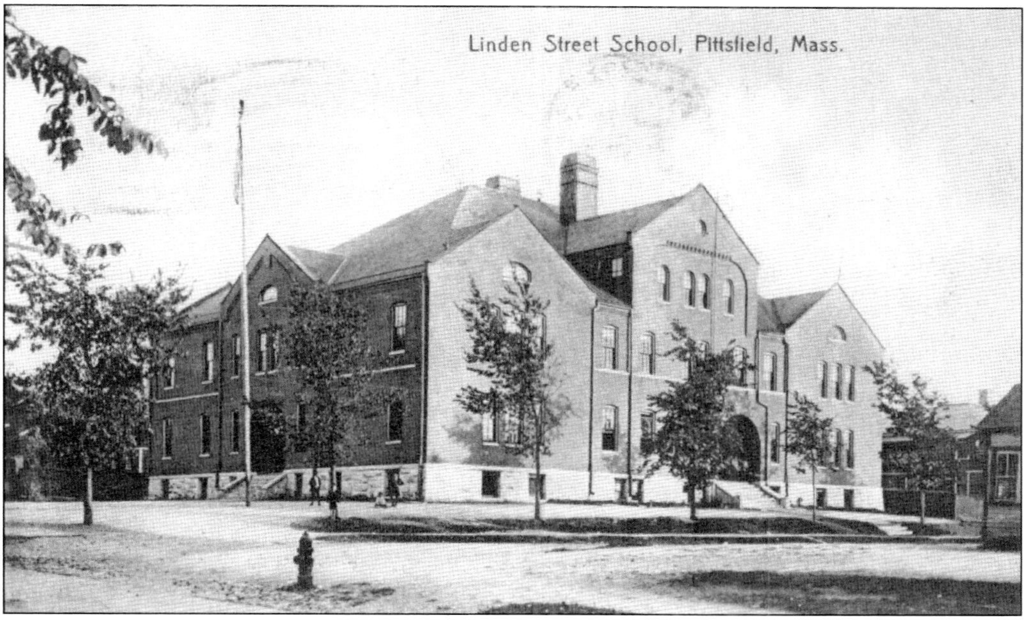

The Linden Street School was renamed to honor Joseph Tucker, a respected district court judge. Originally constructed in 1889 at a cost of $50,000, it had a capacity for 700 pupils. In 1926, it was renovated and enlarged with the addition of a third story. The school burned in 1976, and the site is now a city playground.

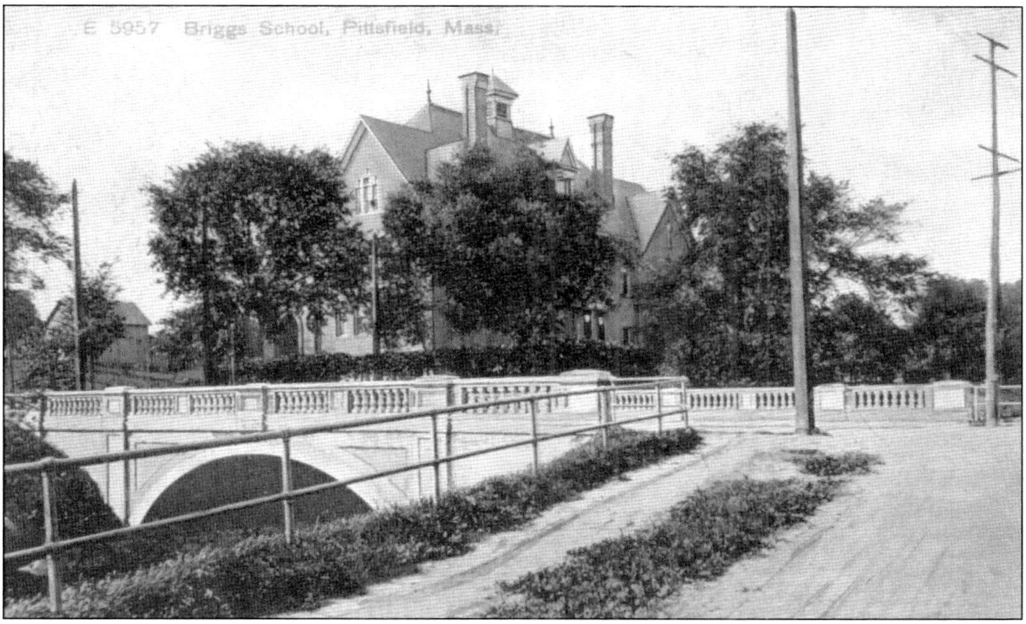

The Briggs School opened in 1897 at the corner of West and John Streets as part of the ever-expanding school system. It was named in honor of George Briggs, who served as governor of Massachusetts in the 1840s. The building, delayed by bad workmanship, had its walls condemned as insecure. They were taken down and rebuilt. The second time proved the charm, as the building still stands today.

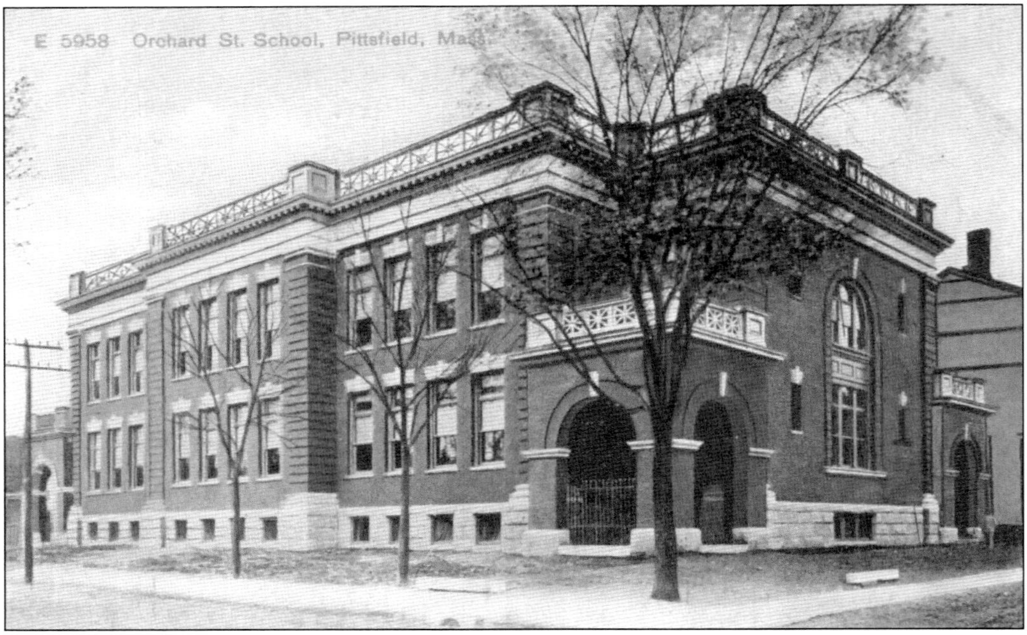

In 1905, the William M. Mercer School opened at the corner of First and Orchard Streets. It had a capacity of 500 students. Dr. Mercer served on the Pittsfield School Board for 36 years. Appropriately, the building is now the administrative headquarters for the Pittsfield Public School Department.

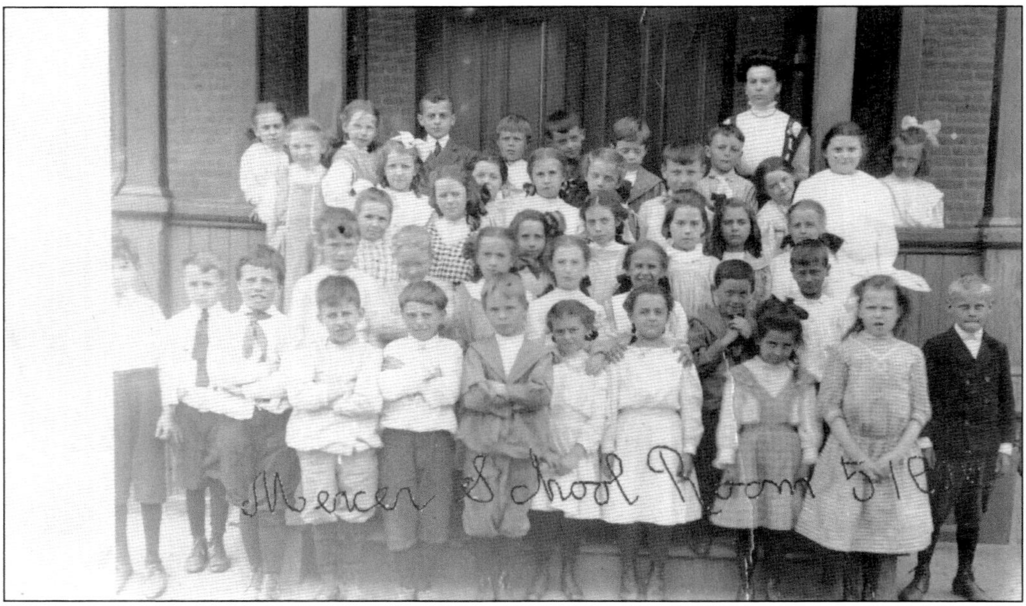

In 1909, these children pose with their teacher on the steps of the new William M. Mercer School. Dr. Mercer (1842–1908) was a popular physician who practiced medicine in Pittsfield for 40 years and championed the cause of public education. The young scholar standing directly in front of the teacher is Carl Kirchner. This photograph was given to the historical society by his wife, Lillian Kirchner.

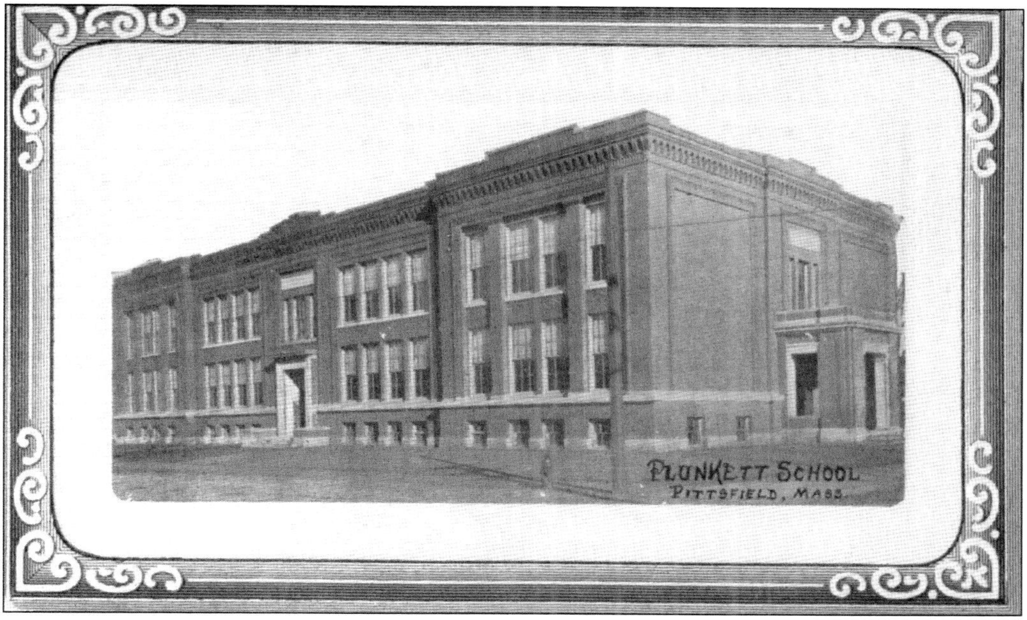

The William R. Plunkett School, built in 1909 at the corner of First and Fenn Streets, was designed by Pittsfield architectural firm Harding & Seaver. After the school closed in 1977, the building had various uses, including manufacturing and a preschool. After attempts to save the building failed, it was demolished in 2014.

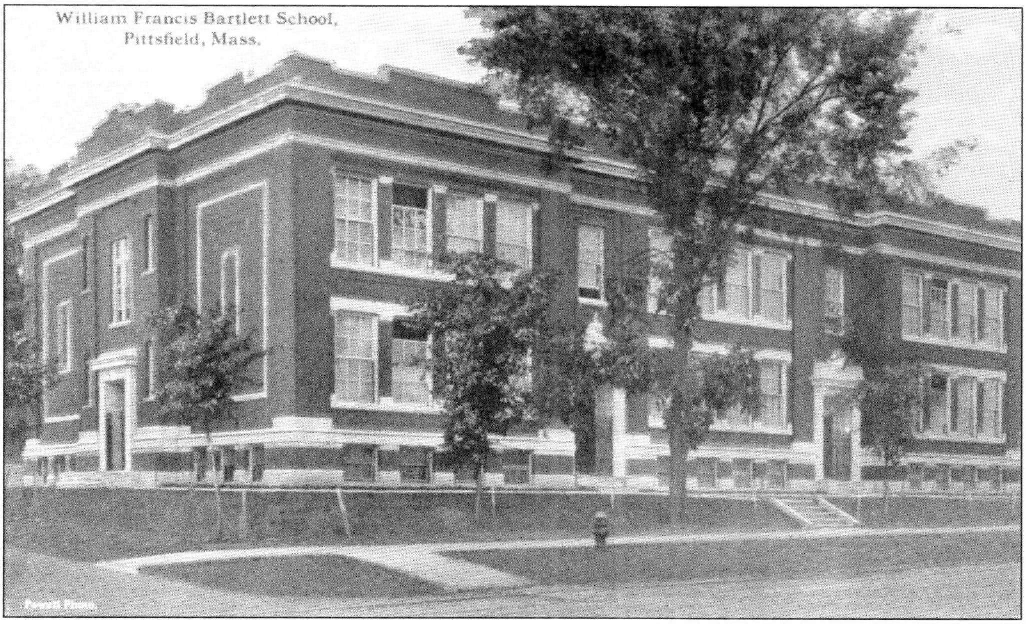

The William Francis Bartlett School, named after Pittsfield's famous Union army general, was opened between 1910 and 1912. Located on the corner of Onota Street and Woodbine Avenue, it had a capacity of 400 students and was built at a cost of $75,000. It now houses rental apartments.

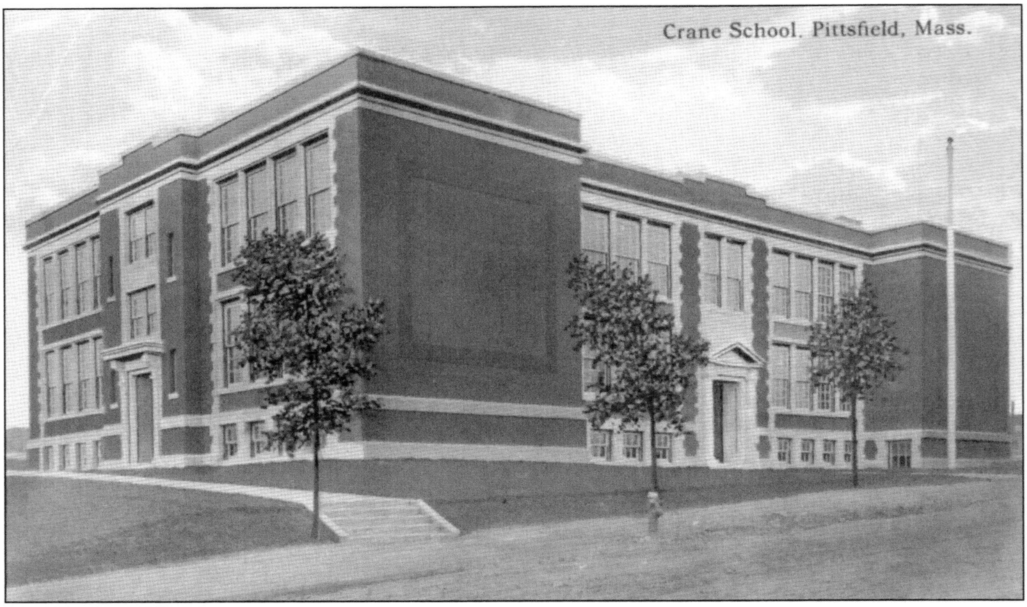

The Crane School opened on Dartmouth Street in 1913, thanks to the generosity of the Zenas Marshall Crane family. It served the Morningside neighborhood for several decades. This classic building was converted, first to rental apartments in the 1980s, and more recently to condominiums.

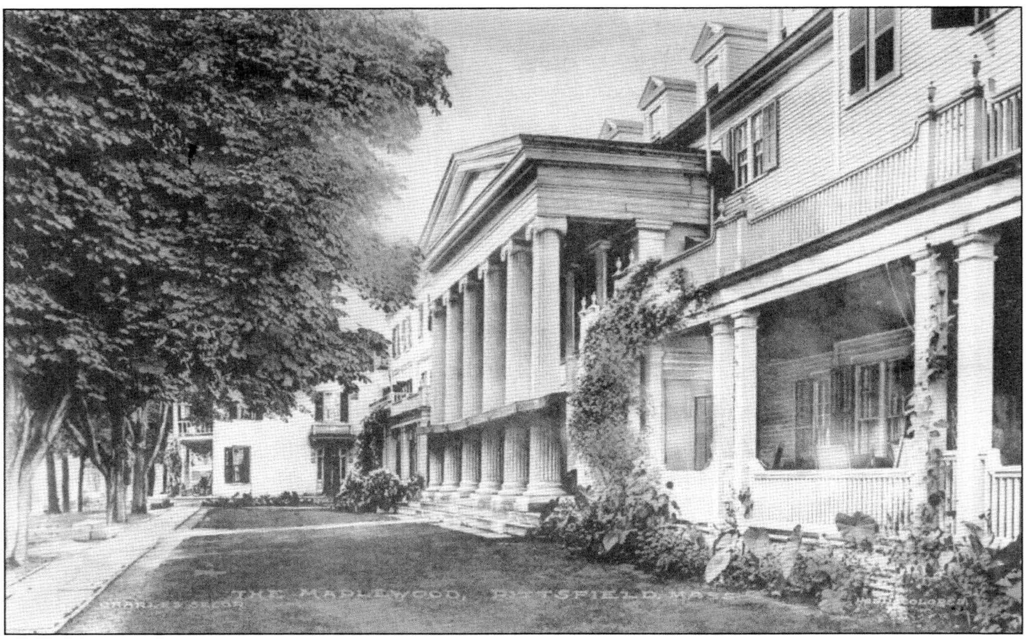

The Maplewood Young Ladies' Institute was a private girls' school from 1841 to 1884. It was located on North Street land that was once used for a prisoner-of-war camp during the War of 1812. The school was academically well regarded, enrolling up to 200 girls from around the country. By 1886, it had been converted into the Maplewood Hotel. Today, a small section survives as condominiums.

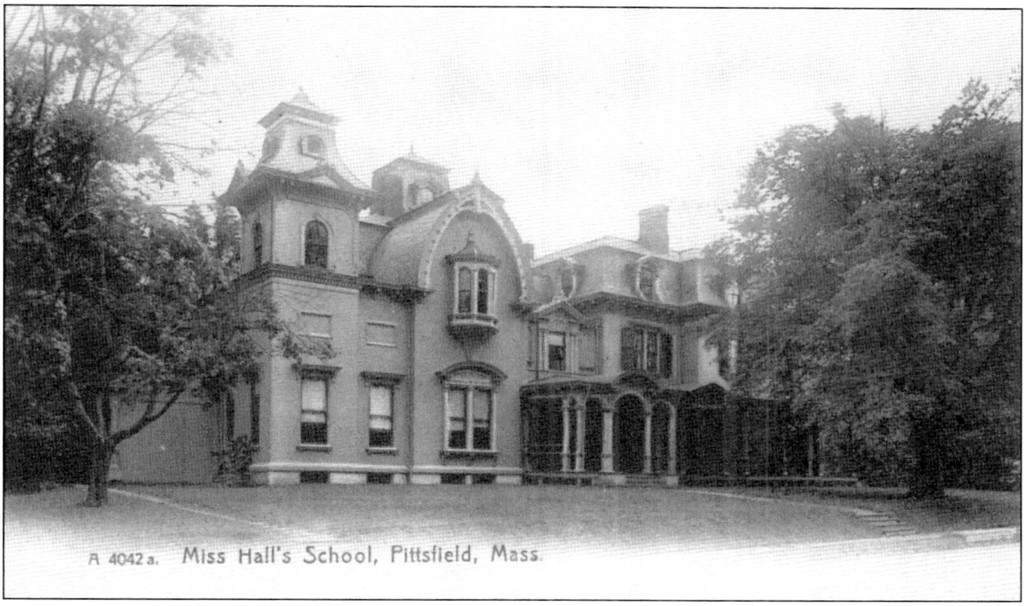

Miss Hall's School dates from the early 1800s, when Nancy Hinsdale opened Massachusetts's first boarding school for young women. Later owners included Mary Salisbury and Mira Hinsdale Hall. In 1902, Mira Hall moved the school from the corner of South and Reed Streets to Elmwood Court Mansion on Bartlett Avenue. By 1913, there were more than 100 students.

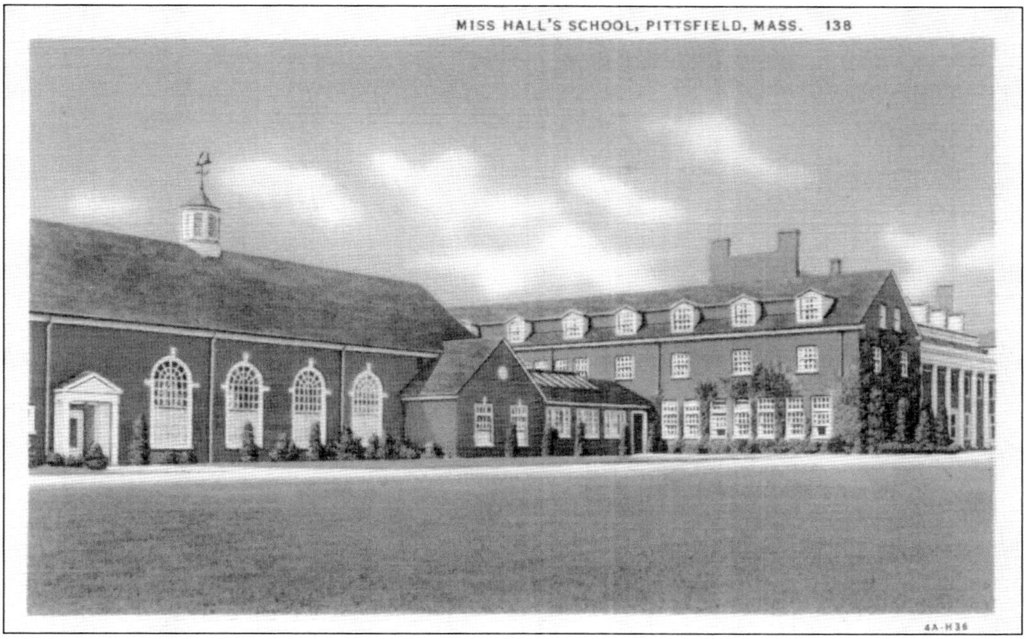

In 1908, Hall purchased Col. Walter Cutting's 75-acre Meadow Farm on Holmes Road, where she relocated her school. In 1923, the institution was destroyed by fire and replaced with a new building. In 1974, the school became coeducational, and its name changed to the Hall School. A decade later, it again became Miss Hall's School for girls and continues to educate young women from around the world.

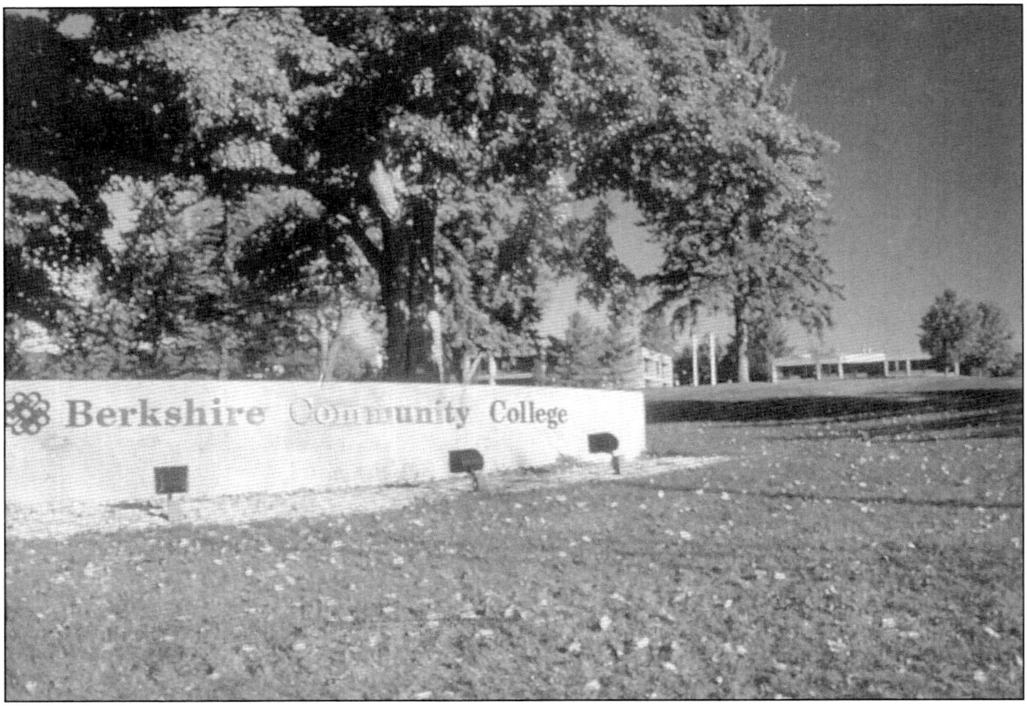

Berkshire Community College, the oldest community college in Massachusetts, is located on a rural campus on outer West Street. Founded in 1960 at the old Pittsfield High School, the two-year college now offers 35 degrees and 12 certificate programs ranging from business administration to visual and performing arts. (Courtesy of Rabbi Harold and Audrey Salzmann.)

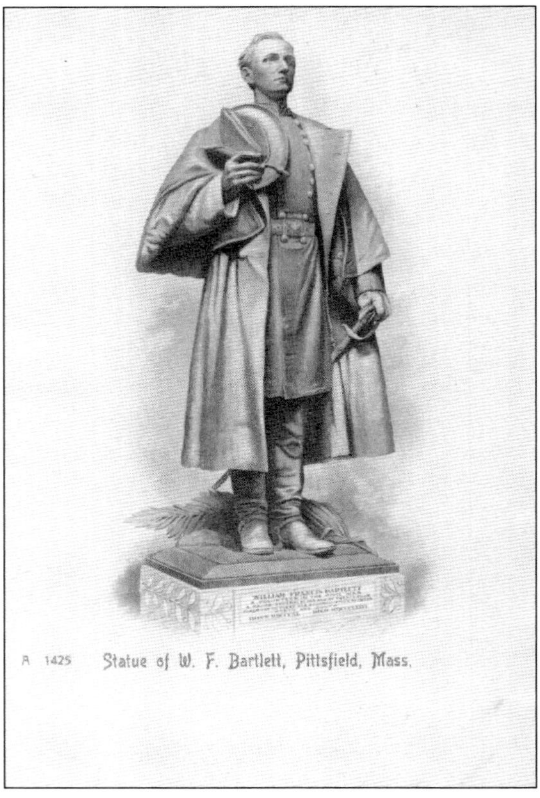

As a Harvard junior, William Francis Bartlett came to Pittsfield in 1862 to drill the 49th Massachusetts Infantry and serve, for a time, as the regiment's colonel. Bartlett served with distinction, was wounded four times, taken prisoner, and commissioned a brevet major general at the Civil War's end. This statue by Daniel Chester French is at Berkshire Community College. Herman Melville honored Bartlett with his poem "The College Colonel."

Five

Health and Wellness

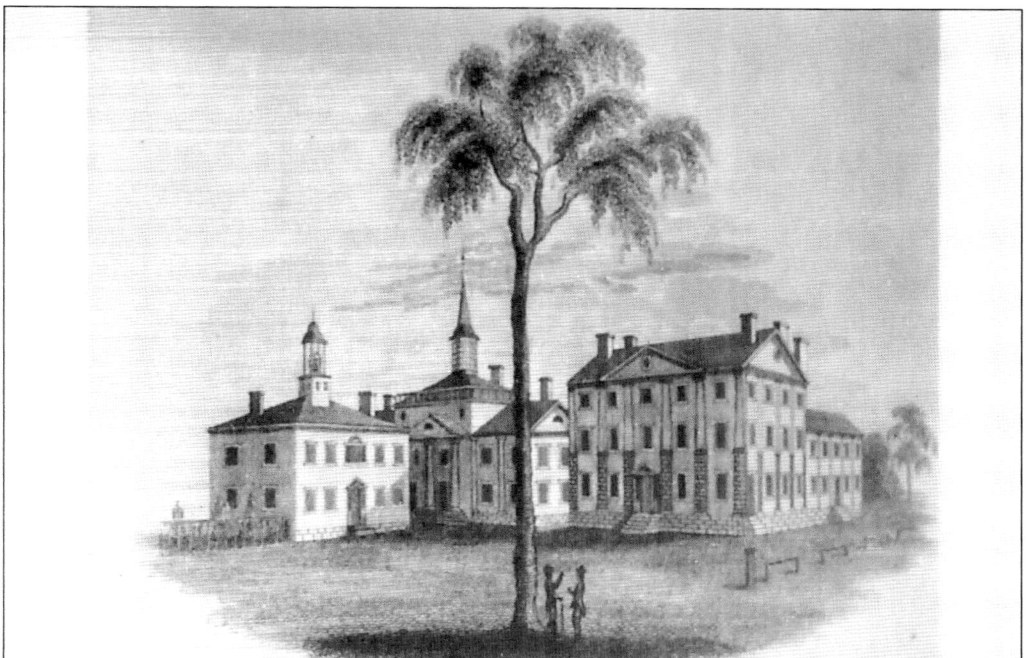

In 1823, the Berkshire Medical Institute opened at the Pittsfield Hotel, near Park Square. Classes included surgery, anatomy, obstetrics, and chemistry. Despite controversy regarding grave robbing, it brought pride to Pittsfield. An 1850 fire prompted construction of a better building on South Street. After enrollment dwindled, it closed in 1867. In 44 years, it trained 1,138 doctors, including the first African American doctor in Massachusetts in 1858.

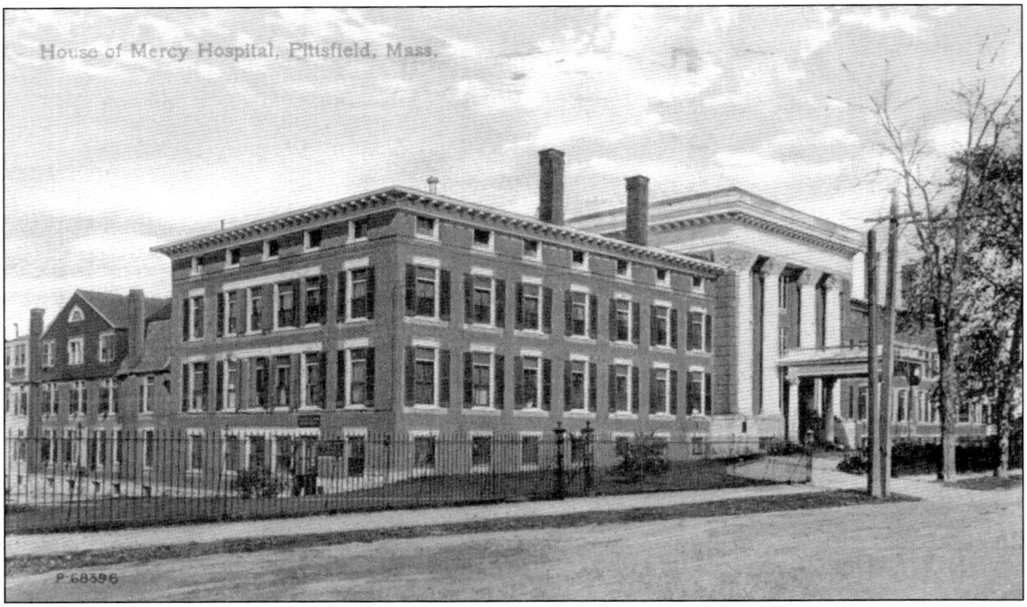

The Warriner Building, part of the House of Mercy medical complex, opened in 1911 and was constructed on land at the corner of North and Wahconah Streets. That large tract of property had been bequeathed to the city by Solomon Russell for the purpose of hospital expansion. The new building was named in honor of Maria Warriner in response to her significant financial donations.

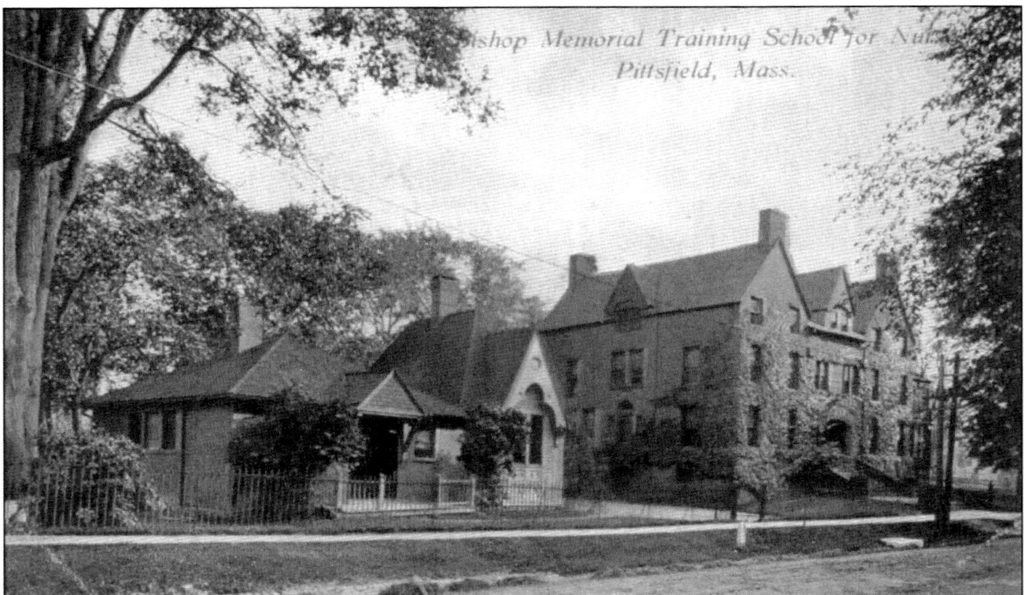

The Henry W. Bishop III Memorial Training School for Nurses (right) was established in 1889 by Henry W. Bishop II in memory of his son, "whose pain and suffering was eased by the capable ministering of systematically trained nurses." It closed in 1968 after training hundreds of nurses. That building still stands, while the smaller Milton Memorial Isolated Cottage (left) and the Rebecca Mortuary Chapel (center) are gone.

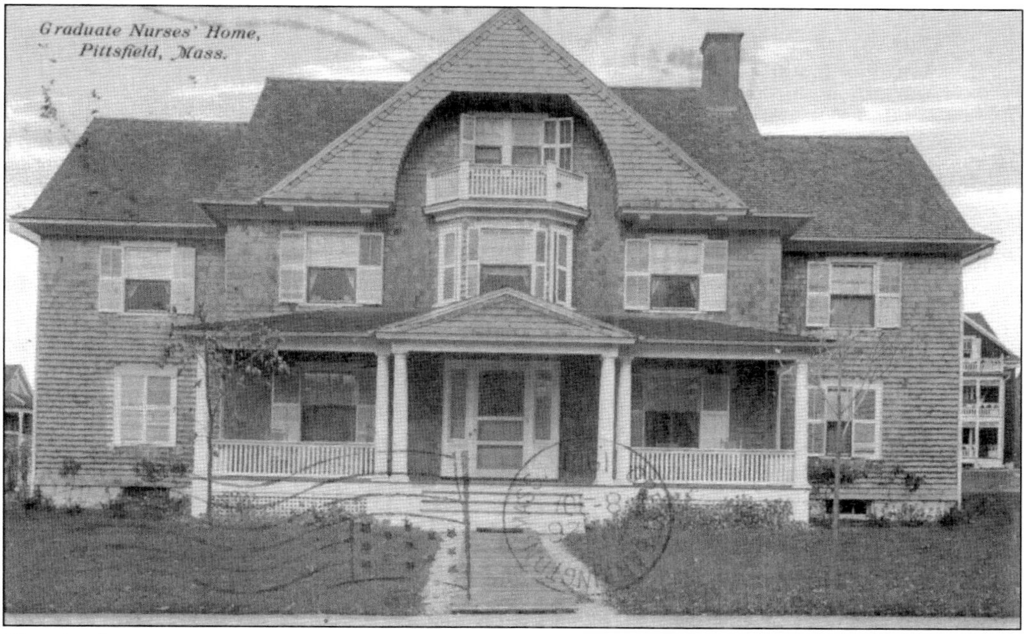

The Graduate Nurses Home was built in 1909. The association's membership was drawn from the alumnae of the Bishop Memorial School for Nurses. At the time, it was one of only a few such homes in the country. The building at 42 Russell Terrace was used for social events and meetings until the 1970s, when it was demolished to make way for the east wing of the Berkshire Medical Center.

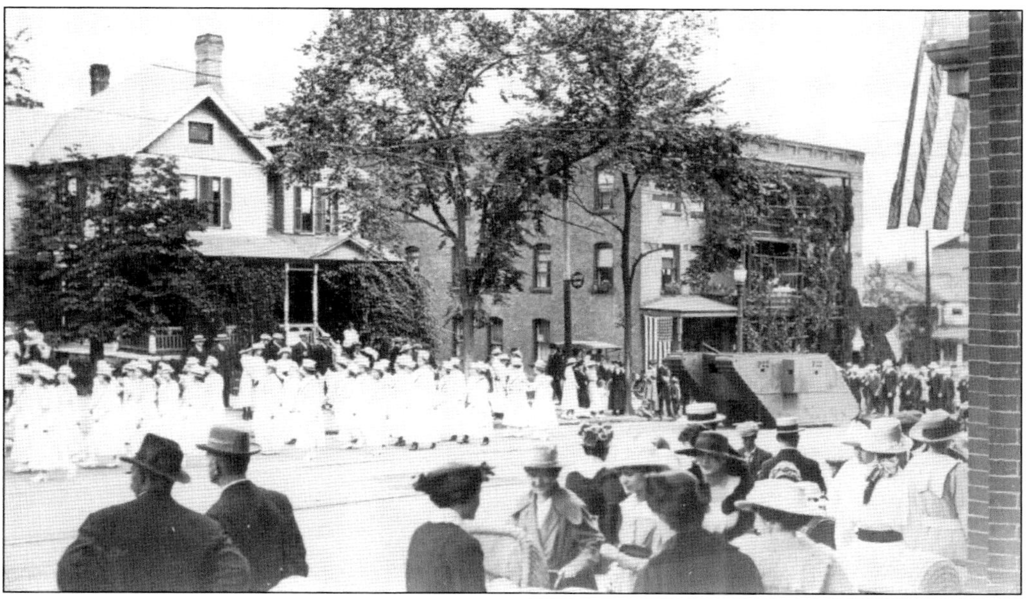

Not only were Pittsfield's nurses dedicated to helping the people of the city, but they also liked a good parade. Here, they are participating in the 1918 Fourth of July parade, demonstrating their patriotism and support of the United States of America.

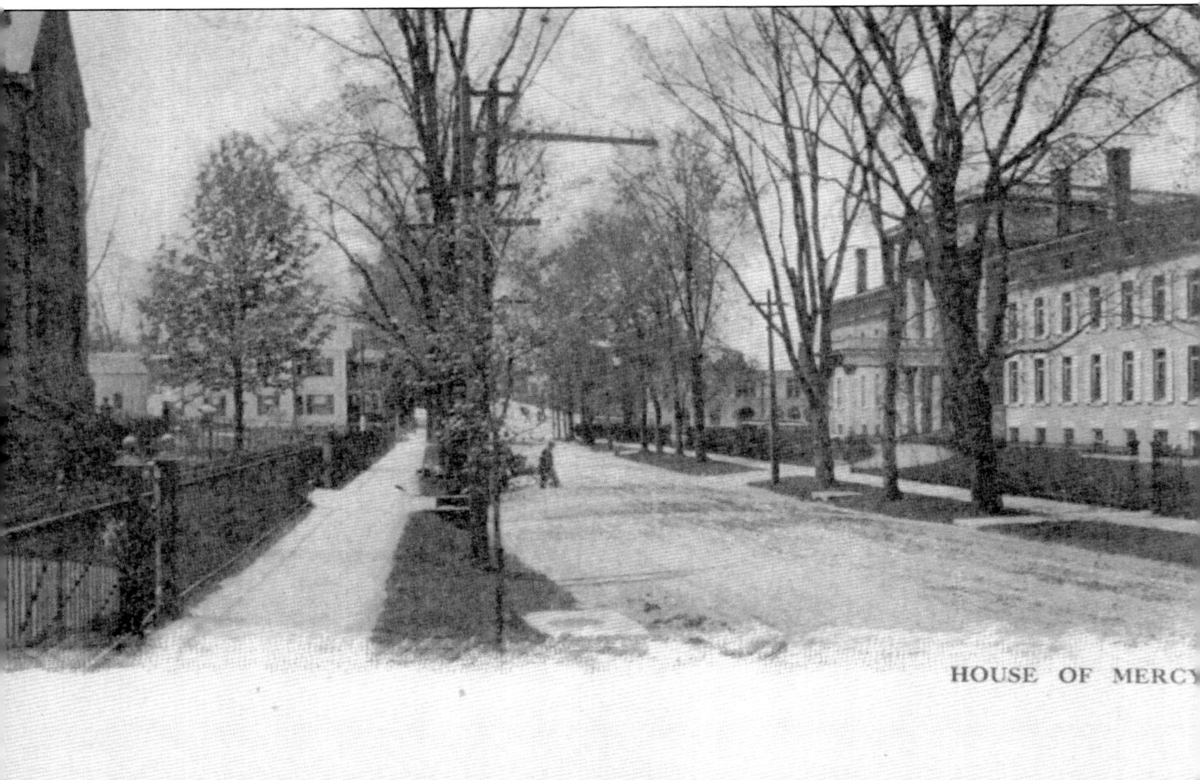

The Reverend John Todd of the First Church Congregational promoted the idea for a community hospital in his Thanksgiving 1874 sermon. Harriet Plunkett and a group of local women took up the challenge, "for the purpose of establishing and maintaining in Pittsfield a House of Mercy for the care of the sick and disabled, whether indigent or not." When the converted house on Francis Avenue opened in 1875 with eight beds, it was the first cottage hospital in the United States.

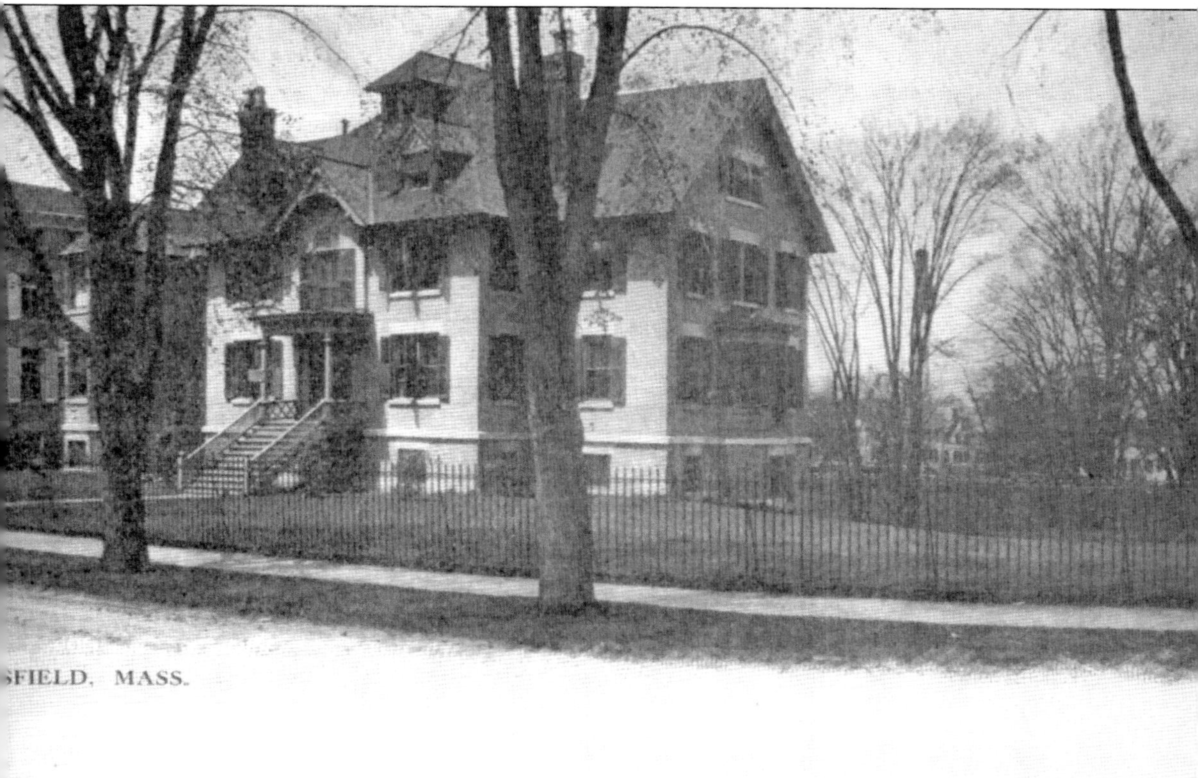

The hospital built by women gradually expanded through the decades, eventually becoming Pittsfield General Hospital and then Berkshire Medical Center. Louise Pollock, a founding board member, personally supplied ice cream to all the patients and nurses every Sunday until her death in 1928.

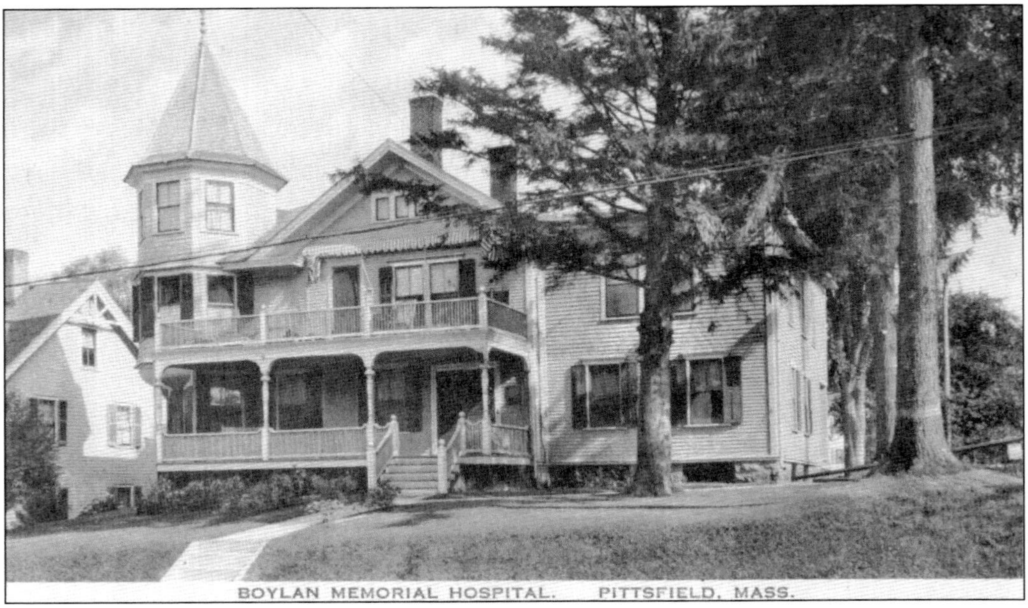

In 1916, the Bishop of Springfield dedicated the new Boylan Memorial Hospital, consisting of two houses on Springside Avenue, seen here. The 25-bed hospital was under the care of the Sisters of Providence. In 1917, the diocese purchased the Allen mansion on East Street, creating a 28-bed maternity hospital. By 1926, these inadequate buildings were replaced by a general hospital, St. Luke's. In 1968, it merged with Pittsfield General Hospital.

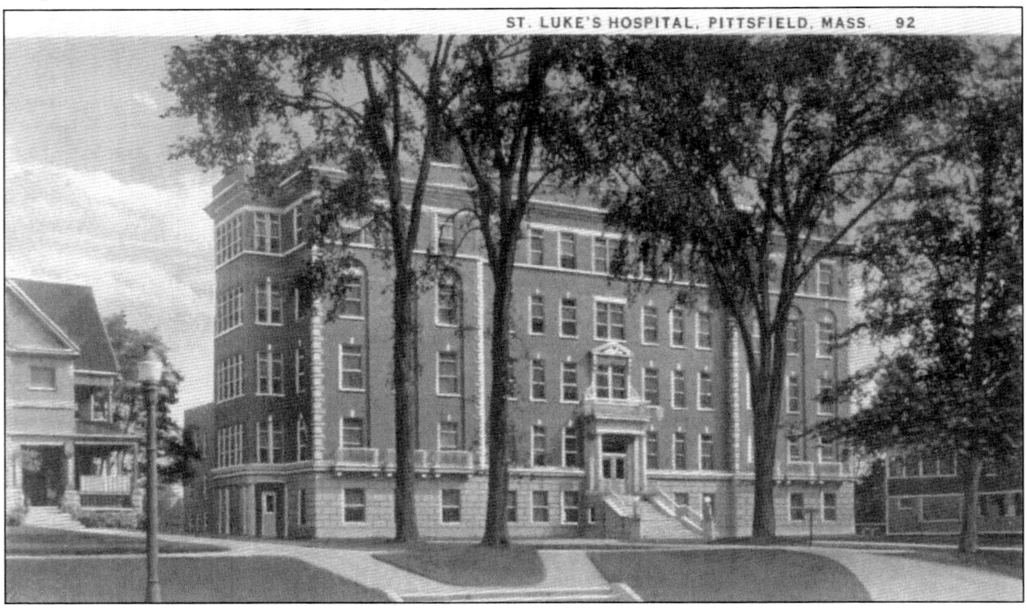

On May 1, 1926, the first patient was admitted to the five-story brick building at 379 East Street. St. Luke's Hospital, so called because St. Luke is the patron saint of physicians, had 75 rooms and 12 wards. In 1955, the hospital installed televisions in the rooms. St. Luke's was affiliated with Albany Medical School and had its own nursing school. In 1977, the building was sold for senior housing.

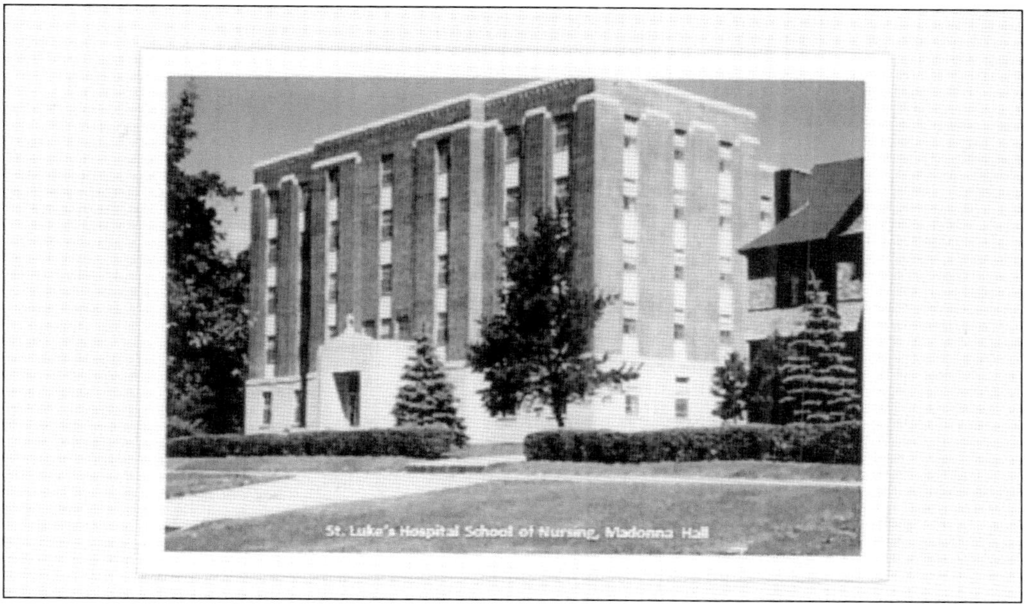

St. Luke's Hospital School of Nursing's Madonna Hall was built in 1951 at 333 East Street. It served as home and school for 130 nursing students who resided there during their three years of study under the guidance of the Sisters of Providence. Included within the hall, now a state office building, were classrooms and clinical laboratories. Close to 1,200 students had graduated before the school closed in 1974.

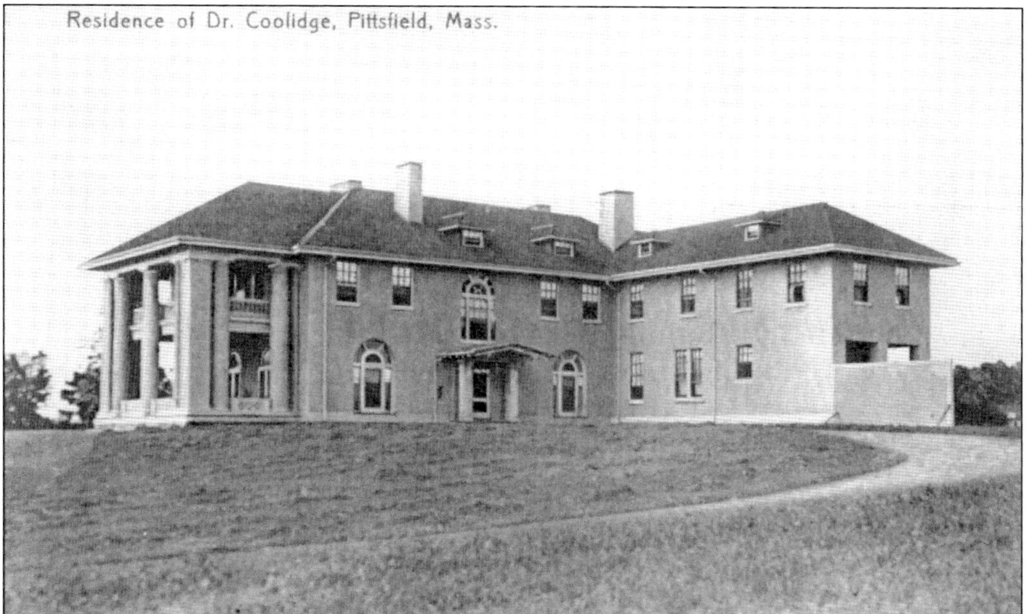

Upwey Field, seen here, was the summer cottage built for Dr. Frederick and Elizabeth Sprague Coolidge on West Street. After Coolidge died from tuberculosis in 1915, his widow donated Upwey Field to the Berkshire School for Crippled Children. With the intent of teaching boys mechanical skills, it opened in 1918 with 15 students. The mansion is again in private hands.

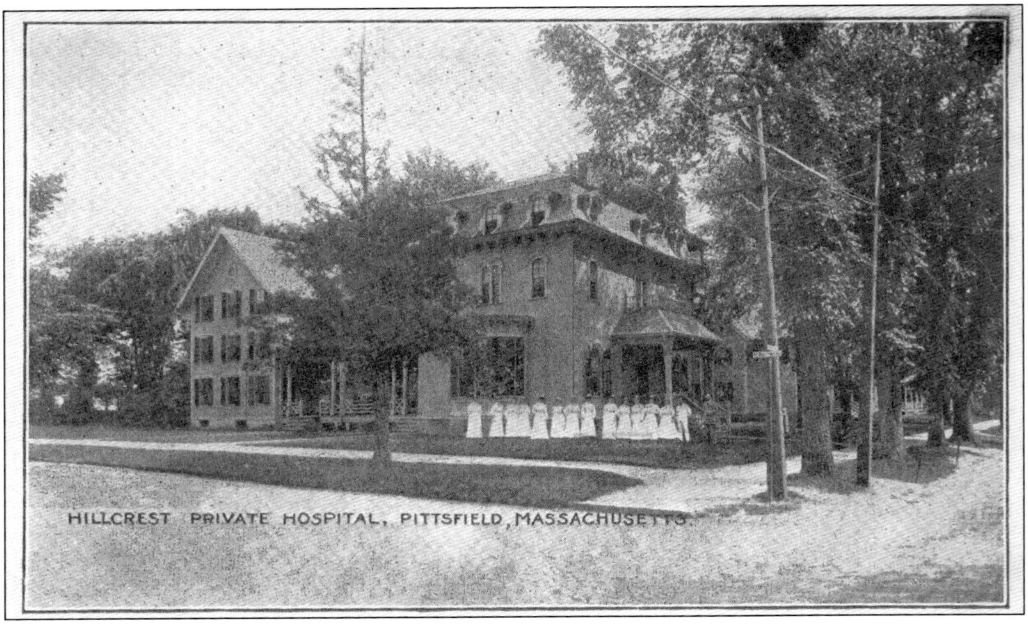

In 1908, the 24-bed Hillcrest Surgical Hospital was founded in a rented house at North Street and Springside Avenue, seen here. It was soon expanded in size and in services, becoming a general hospital in the 1920s. In 1947, the hospital treated 1,510 patients, performed 637 operations, and saw 217 babies born. That same year, the hospital kicked off a fund drive to raise $1 million for a 150-bed facility.

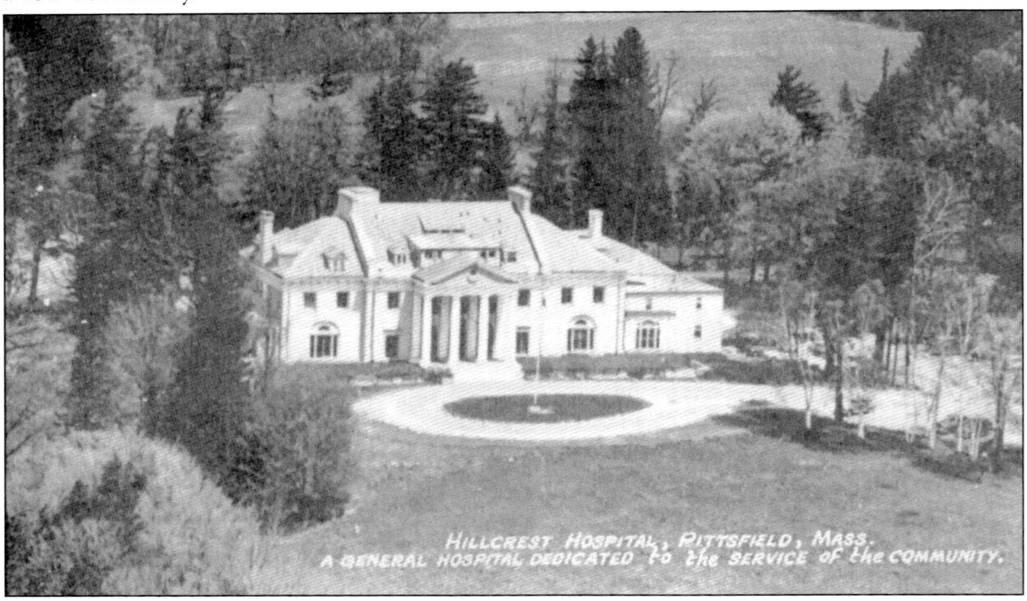

In 1948, Hillcrest Hospital purchased and renovated the historic Tor Court estate. The Gilded Age summer cottage on West Street was built for the Salisbury family in 1909. The hospital opened in 1951 with 100 beds. A large addition was completed in 1970, and the Family Health Center was added 1987. Hillcrest Hospital merged with Berkshire Medical Center (BMC) in 1998. BMC's Hillcrest Campus now includes a cancer center.

Six

Business and Industry

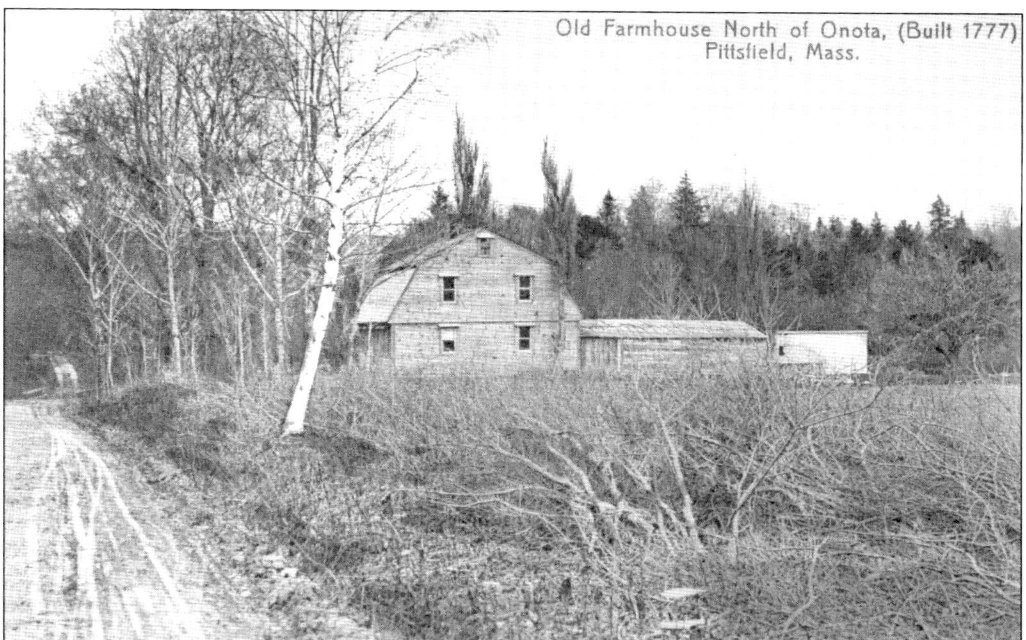

This 1777 farmhouse represents Pittsfield's earliest economic development. Settlers were eager to farm the fertile Housatonic River valley. In 1810, the Berkshire County Agricultural Society organized the first county fair in the United States. The fair grew out of Elkanah Watson's exhibition of Merino sheep in Park Square in 1807. In 1849, with its abundant waterpower, Pittsfield developed into an industrial powerhouse. The agricultural society disbanded in 1901.

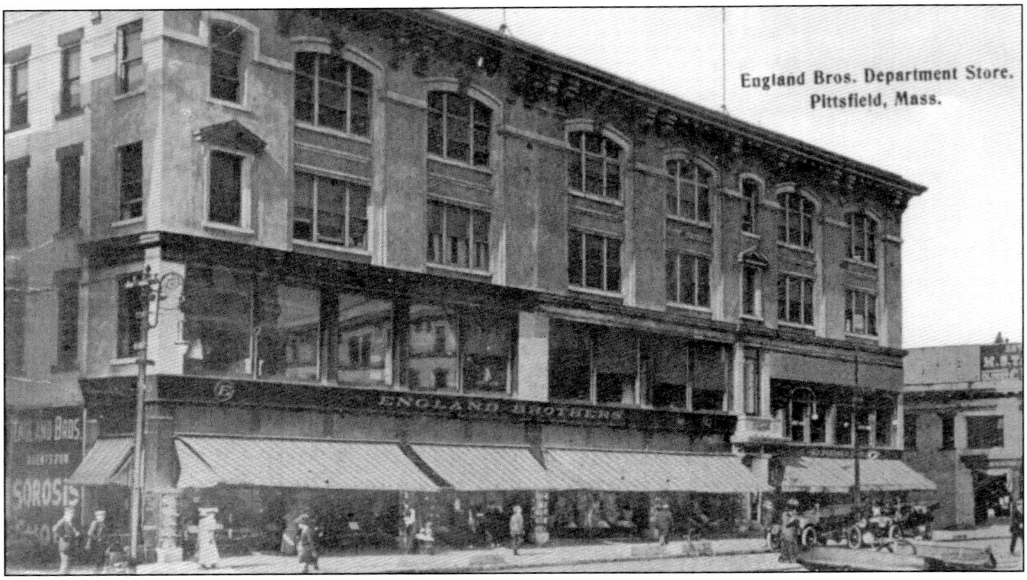

Moses England founded his dry goods store on North Street in 1857. First located on the east side of North Street, it moved across the street in 1891. Greatly expanded by Moses's three sons, England Brothers was once the largest department store in western Massachusetts. Two floors were added in 1926, complete with elevators with sliding gated doors. In 1916, over 200 employees served the crowds of shoppers.

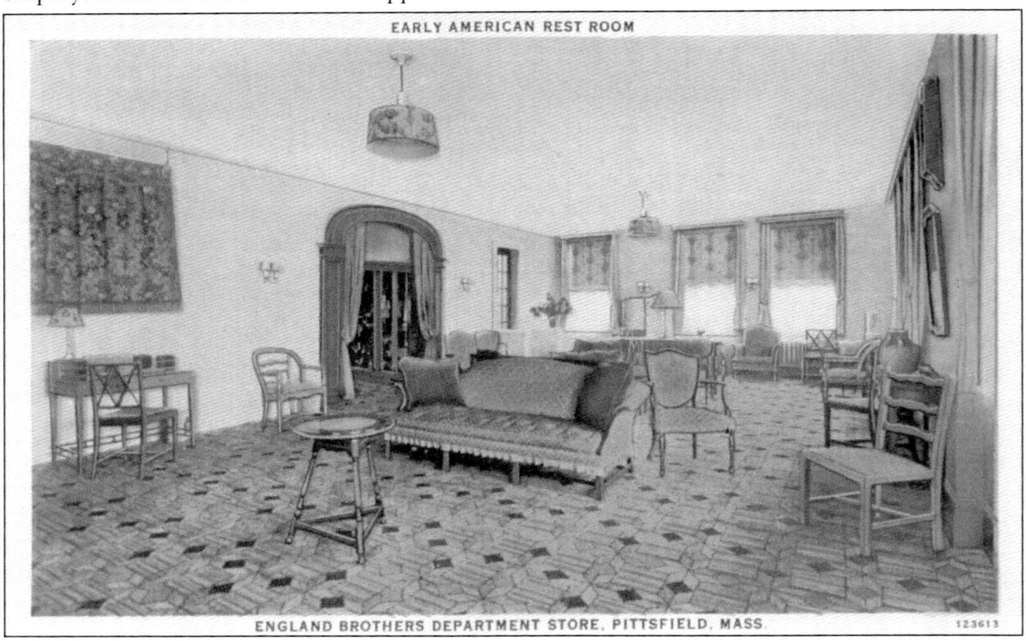

This comfortable women's lounge was on the third floor of England Brothers department store. There was a matron on duty to see to everyone's needs. The restrooms were to the left, through the archway, and contained coin slots for use of the stalls. This well-appointed room provided a quiet and comfortable respite during a hectic day of shopping. Access was easy due to the two escalators installed in 1949.

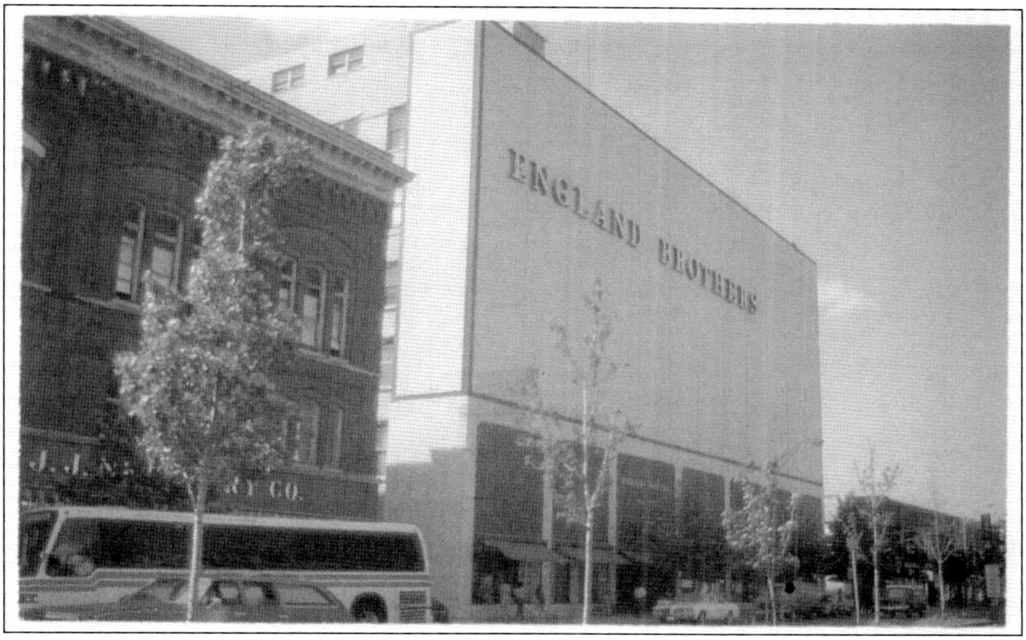

This view of England Brothers shows its 1966 modern facade. The store closed in 1988 after 131 years offering the "finest in quality, style and service at fair prices." In 1998, the building was demolished with difficulty, as it was very well built. Pittsfielders reminisce about the animated North Pole workshop in the display windows and Santa Claus helping children with Christmas wishes.

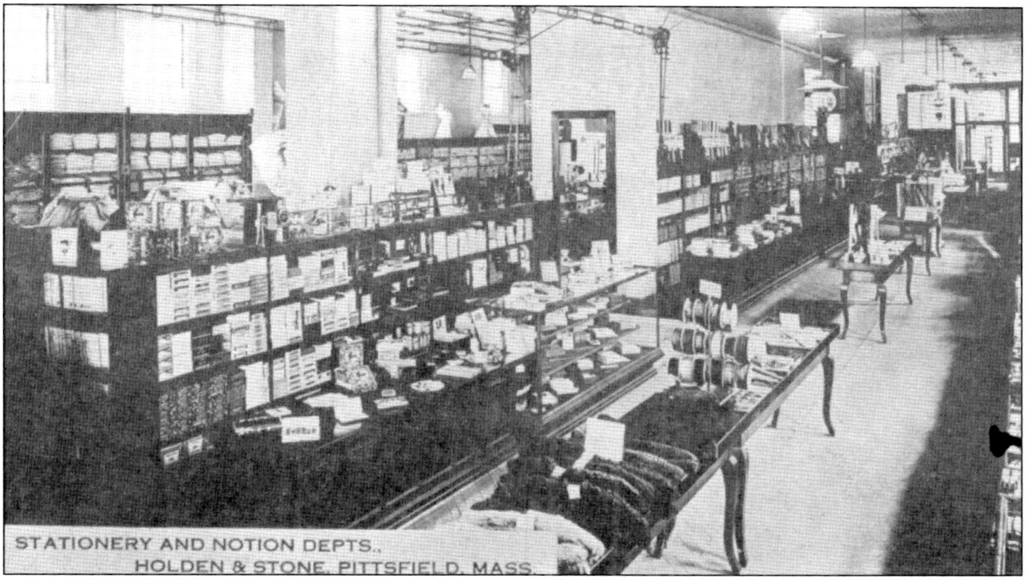

Holden & Stone, founded in 1844, was one of the longest-lasting stores in Pittsfield's history, selling everything from stationery to clothing. The popular department store's owners were ahead of their time, when in the late 19th century, they promoted shorter work weeks and longer vacations for their staff. The store, whose last location was in the Onota Building on North Street's east side, closed in 1968.

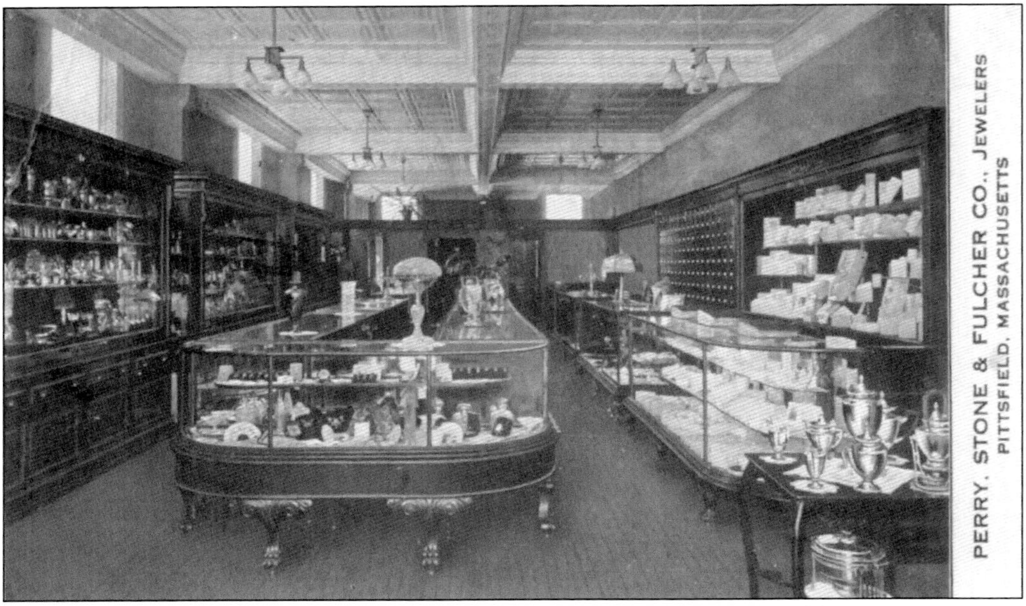

According to the 1912 Pittsfield City Directory, the Perry, Stone & Fulcher Company was located at 123 North Street. The owners were diamond merchants, jewelers, silversmiths, and stationers. Frank Fulcher was the resident proprietor, and the company had a branch store in the Hotel Aspinwall in Lenox, Massachusetts.

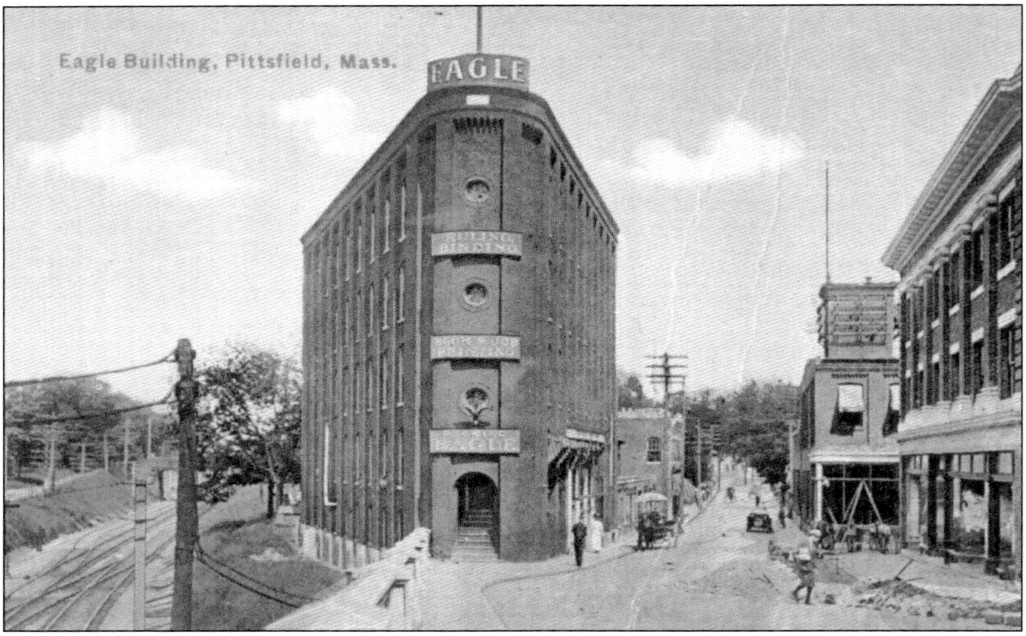

In 1904, the *Berkshire Evening Eagle* newspaper and the Eagle Printing and Binding Company moved into their new redbrick flatiron building on the north side of Eagle Street. The *Eagle*, which first published on May 9, 1892, now had facilities worthy of a newspaper with a daily circulation of over 11,000. They advertised it was the largest print plant in western Massachusetts, producing the finest commercial and library binding.

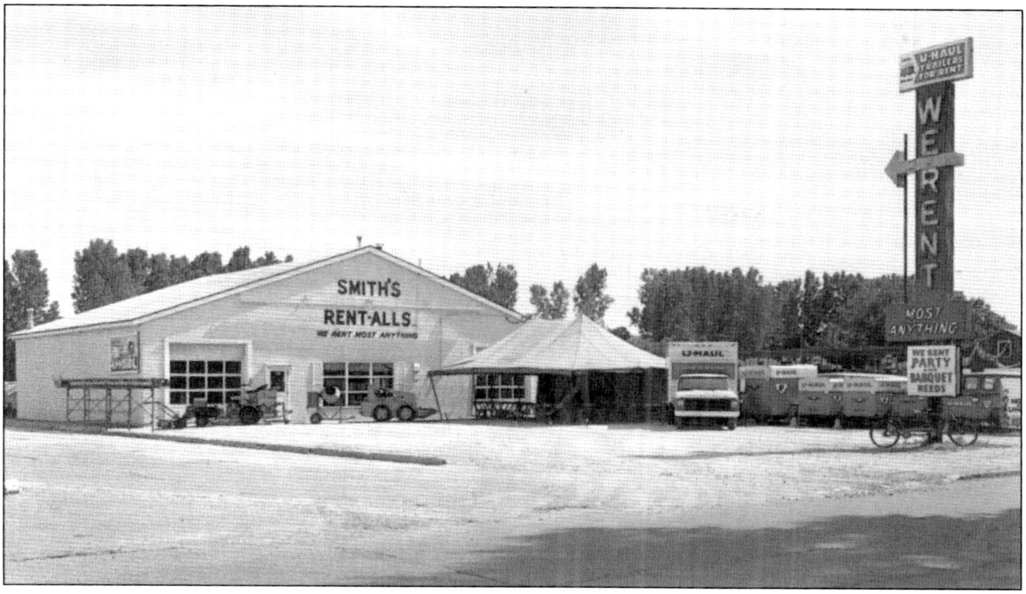

The Smith Rent-All Company was located at 720 East Street. In 1977, the company began to specialize in renting enormous tents. A news article noted, "Princess Grace, Jackie Onassis, Telly Savalas and other celebrities gathered under one of Smith's tents in Bridgewater, Connecticut to bid on Arabian horses owned by film director Mike Nichols." The building is now an automobile dealership.

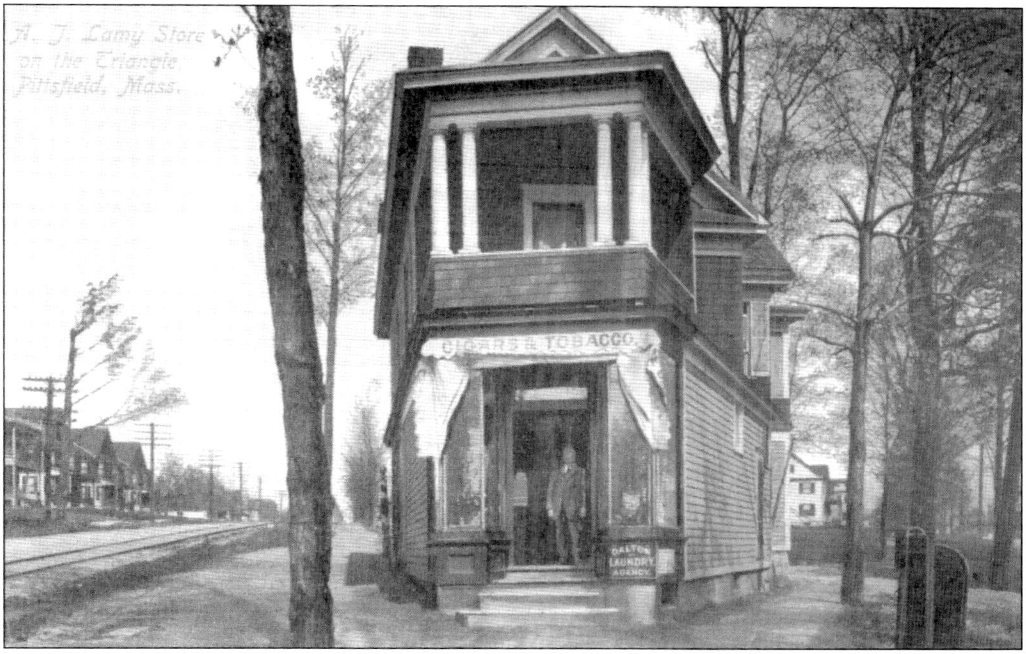

Arthur J. Lamy's building on the triangle at 2 Dalton Avenue had living quarters above the Cigar and Tobacco Shop and the Dalton Laundry Agency. Lamy's corner store, typical of many neighborhood shops in Pittsfield, offered groceries, newspapers, tobacco and ice cream—all within walking distance.

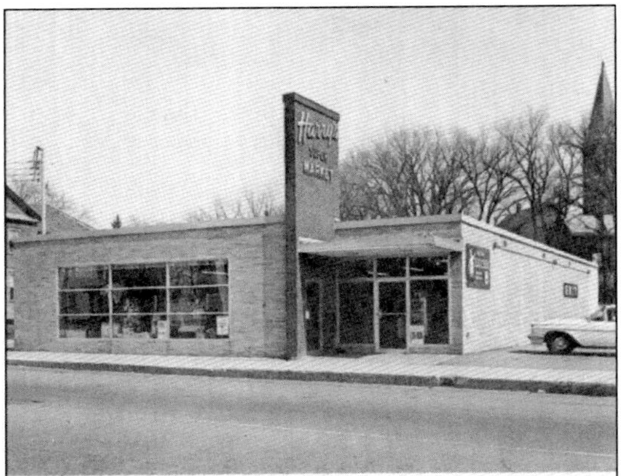

The shopping center in the north end began in 1914 with the opening of Harry's Real Variety Store at the corner of Wahconah Street and Pontoosuc Avenue. Harry Nichols Sr. and his family expanded their business empire to encompass Nichols Pharmacy and Nichols Package Store. Today, Harry's Super Market describes itself as a "locally owned, third-generation, hometown store."

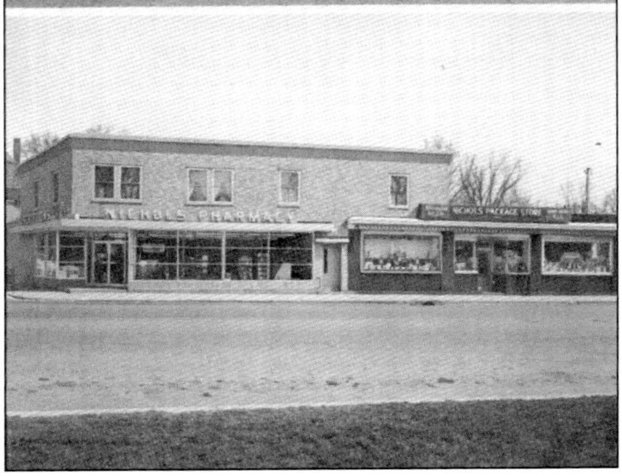

Today's Haddad Motor Group began humbly, in 1932, when George A. Haddad opened a used-car lot. In 1936, Haddad opened a Pontiac dealership in downtown Pittsfield. In 1951, Louis Haddad joined his father, and they moved their dealership to its present location (seen here) at 130 Pittsfield-Lenox Road. In 1981, George L. Haddad joined the business, which now includes Toyota, Subaru, Hyundai, and Nissan franchises.

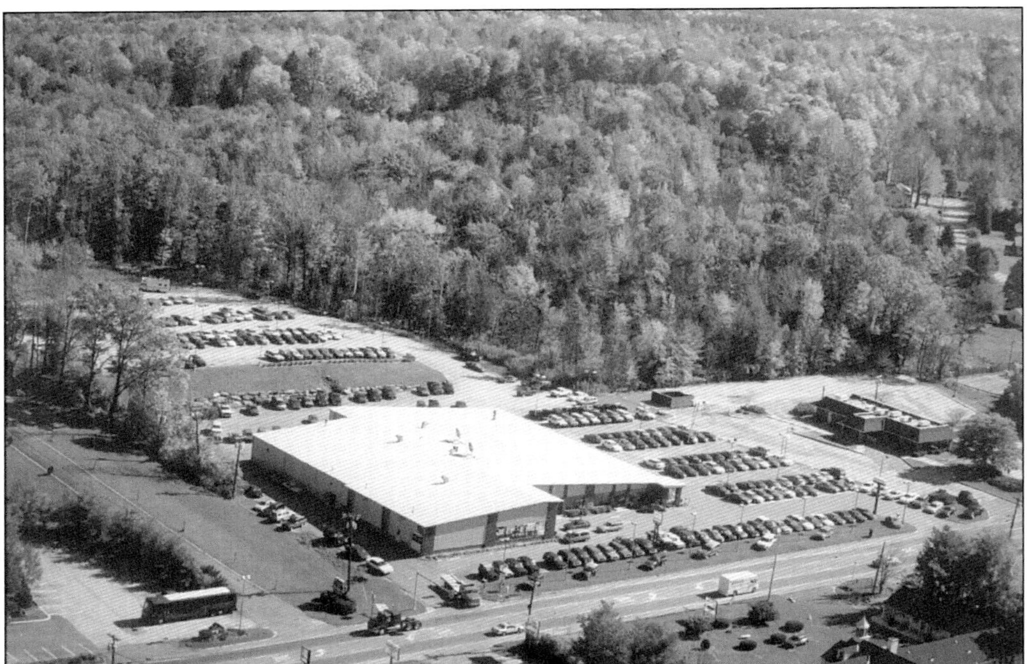

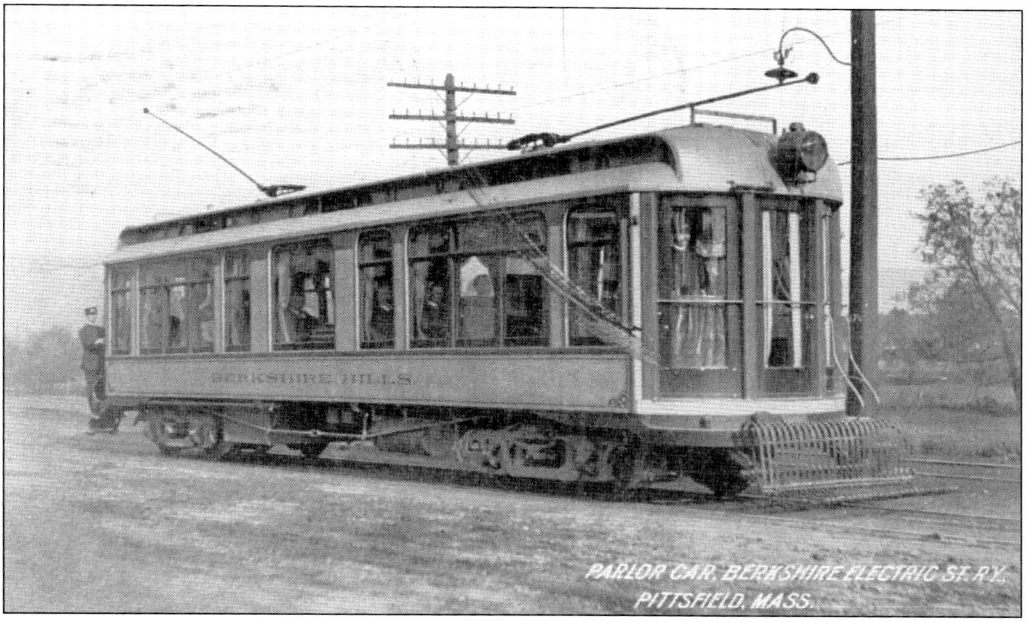

Pittsfield Electric Street Railway was formed in 1890 as an outgrowth of the horse-drawn Pittsfield Street Railway, which had been in existence since 1886. The first electric trolley car run, from Park Square to Pontoosuc Lake, occurred on July 9, 1891. Electric trolleys continued as a popular mode of transportation until the 1930s. The parlor car, seen here, awaits restoration at a trolley museum in Maine.

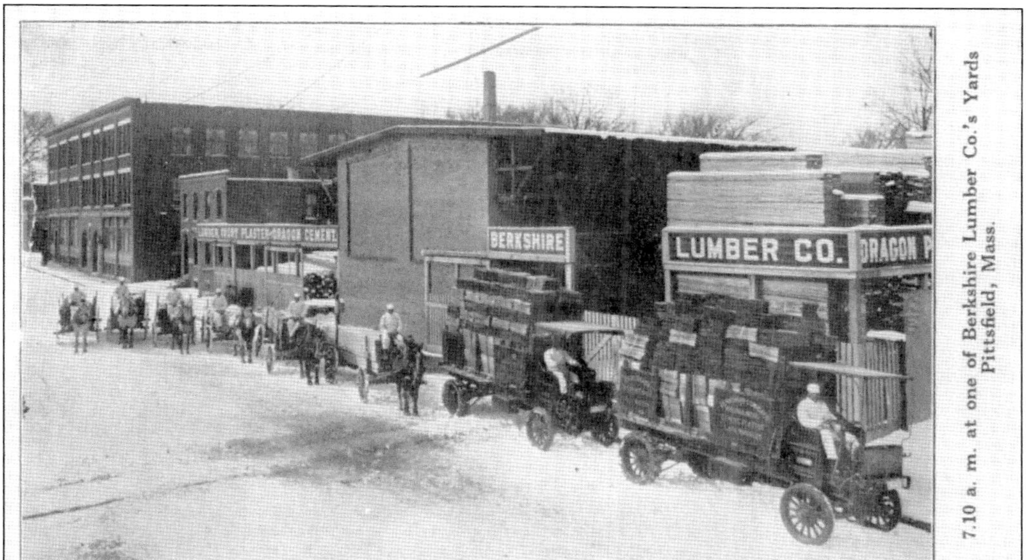

New motor trucks and horse-drawn wagons lined up early in the morning, May 1, 1910, at Berkshire Lumber Company on Columbus Avenue. Owner Charles Butler had one of the largest lumber companies in New England, controlling thousands of acres of woodlots in Massachusetts and Nova Scotia. Butler expanded in 1914, buying more lots on Columbus Avenue and Summer Street in order to gain access to train tracks.

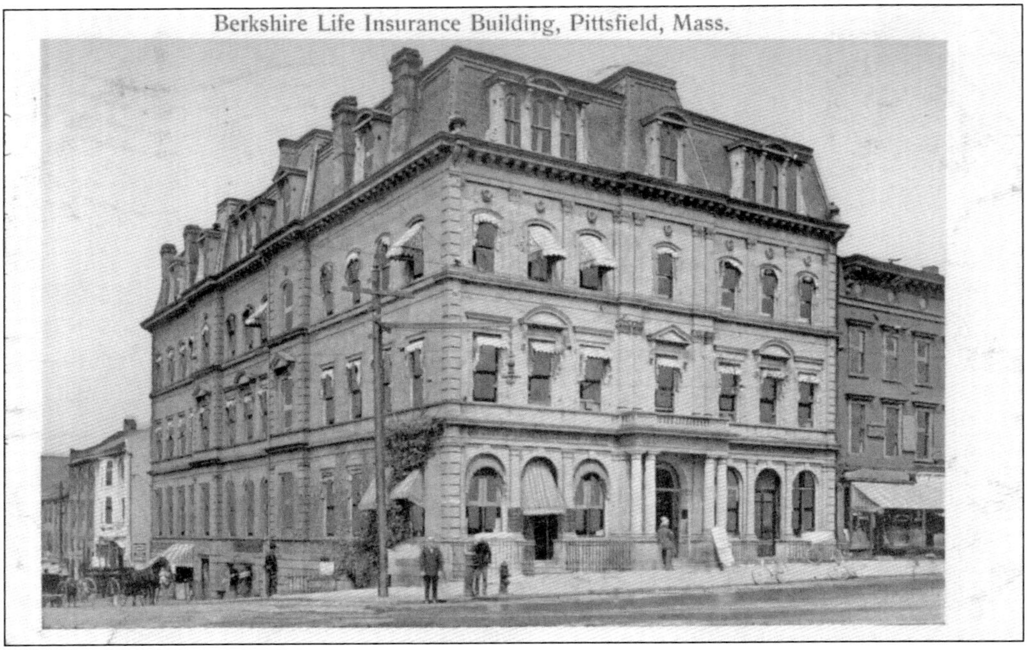

The Berkshire Life Insurance Company was founded in 1851 by former Massachusetts governor George Nixon Briggs. The company's headquarters, pictured here around 1870, was built in 1868 at the corner of North and West Streets. In 1911, the mansard roof was replaced with two additional stories. The building housed many businesses, even after Berkshire Life moved to South Street in 1959. The grand old building still stands.

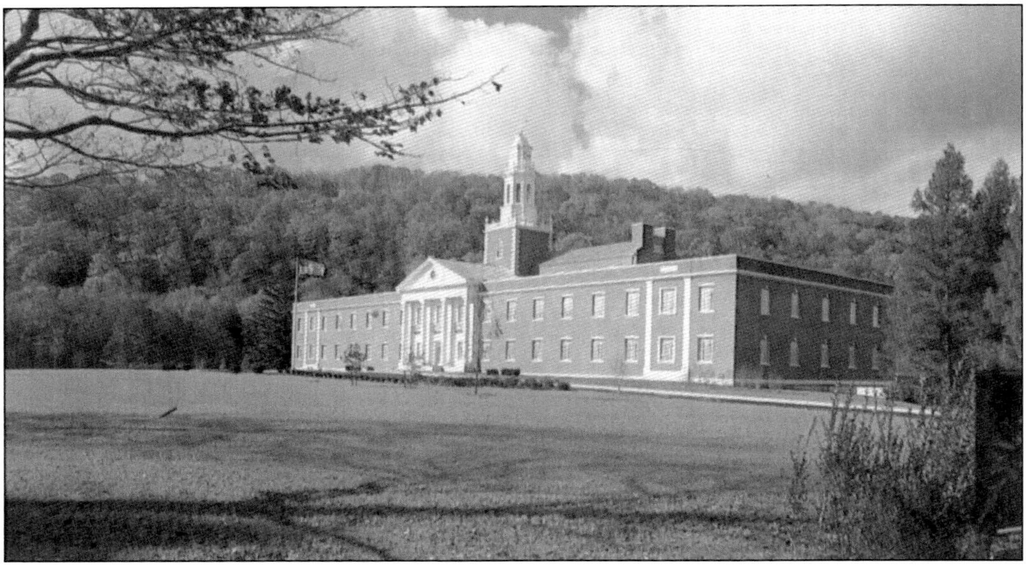

After 100 years in business, the Berkshire Life Insurance Company had outgrown its downtown headquarters. In 1952, it purchased 23 acres at 700 South Street (Route 7) across from the Pittsfield Country Club and moved into the new building in 1959. In 2001, Berkshire Life became a subsidiary of the Guardian Life Insurance Company of America with headquarters in Pittsfield and field offices nationwide.

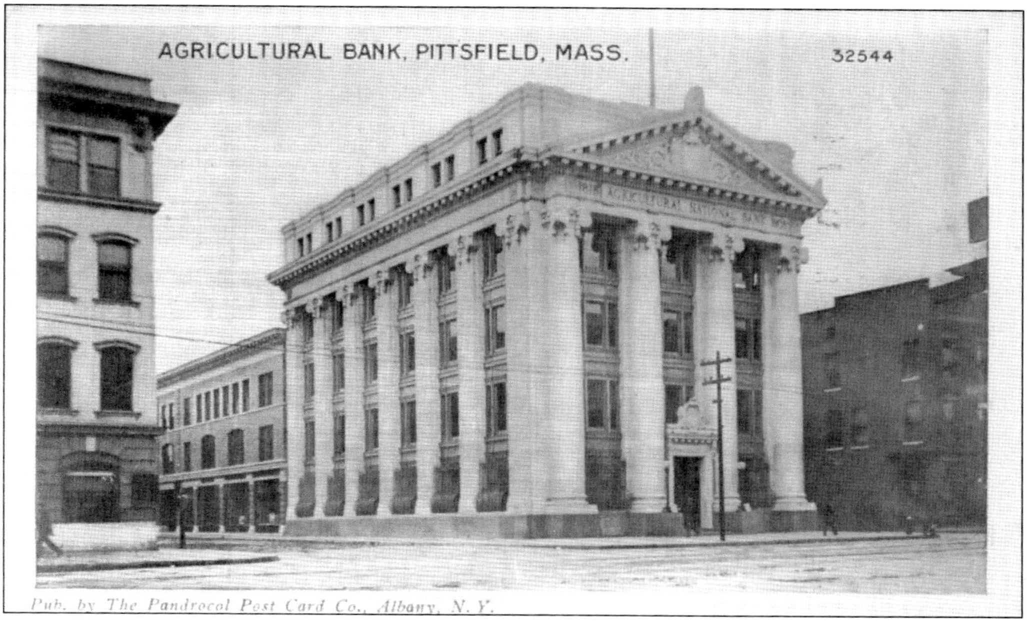

Nathan Appleton, a wealthy Bostonian who predicted that Pittsfield would grow from a small farm town to a textile manufacturing center, founded the Agricultural National Bank in 1818. In 1908, the bank's third and final location was chosen, and construction began on the $250,000 white marble Greek Revival structure that stands today on North Street between Fenn Street and Dunham Mall.

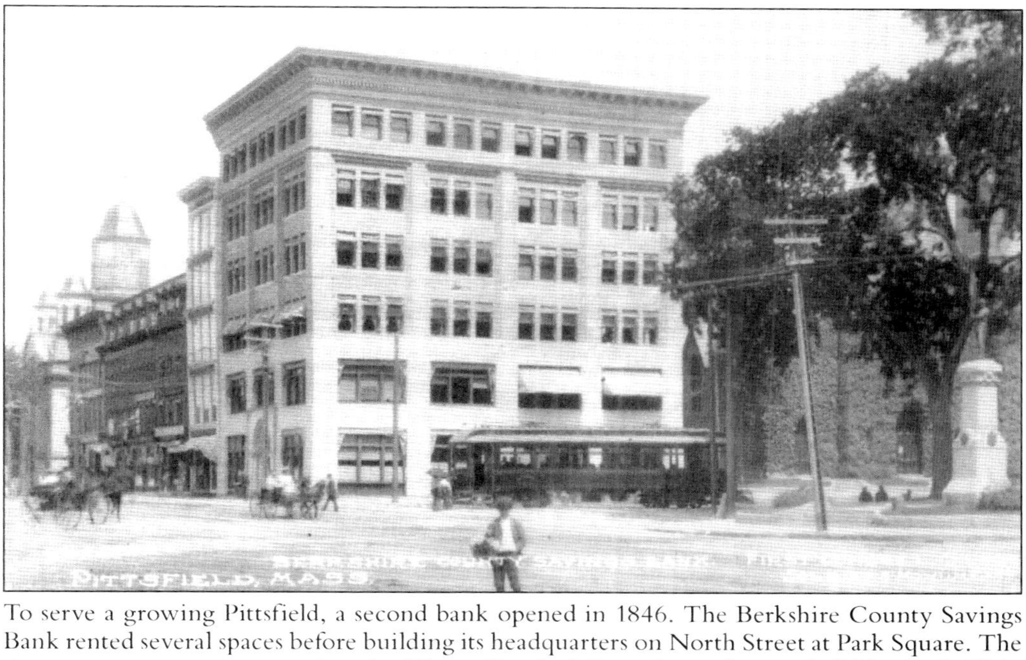

To serve a growing Pittsfield, a second bank opened in 1846. The Berkshire County Savings Bank rented several spaces before building its headquarters on North Street at Park Square. The six-story structure was touted as the "first office building of a modern scale." The Park Club, a businessmen's organization, rented the third floor for a time, and the building was expanded in 1926.

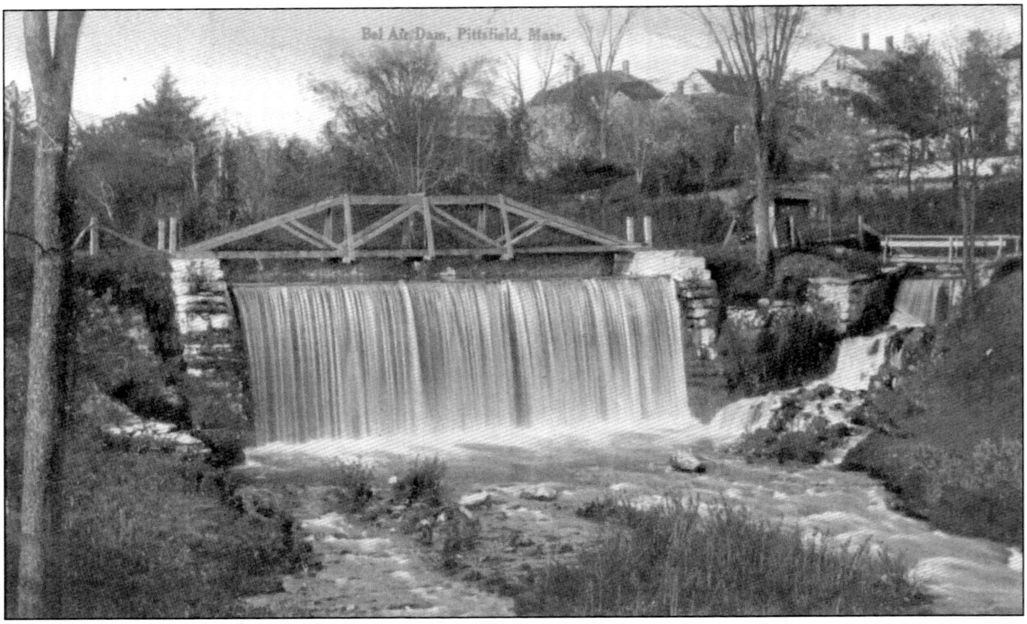

In 1832, E.M. Bissell built a four-story brick factory along the west branch of the Housatonic River near Wahconah Street. It failed due to inadequate waterpower. Pittsfield Woolen Company took over the plant, made extensive improvements, and constructed the stone dam seen here. In 1873, another woolen mill, the Bel-Air Manufacturing Company, assumed ownership of the same location. Though that company also failed, its name stuck to the dam.

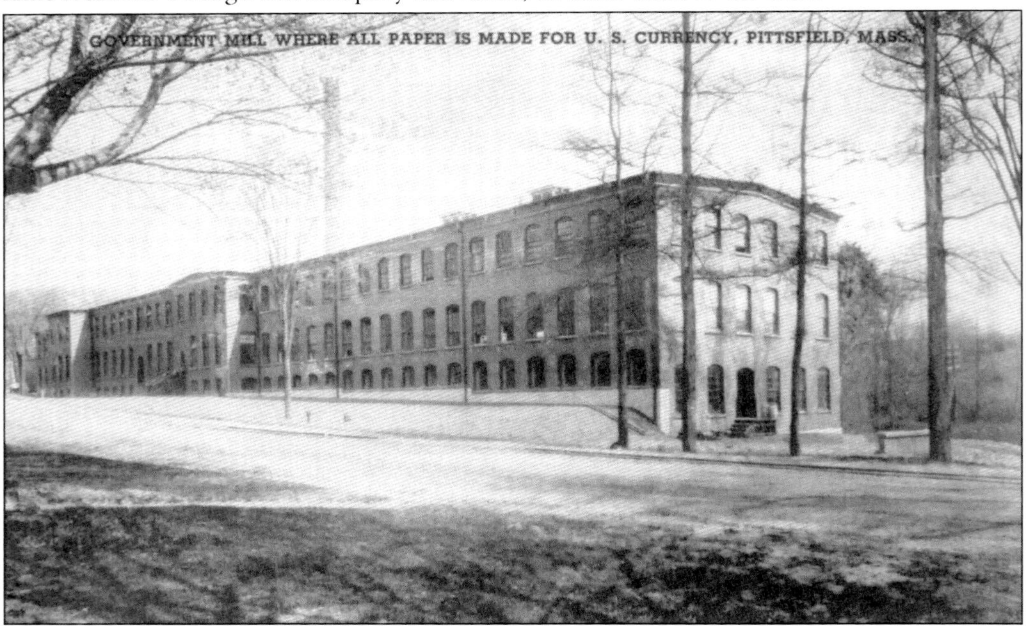

In 1863, Thomas Colt built a paper-making factory on the east branch of the Housatonic River. Crane & Company of Dalton purchased it in 1879 to make fine paper for treasury notes and currency. Following a fire in 1892, the plant was rebuilt as the US Government Mill, seen here. Crane has been the sole supplier of paper for US currency since 1879.

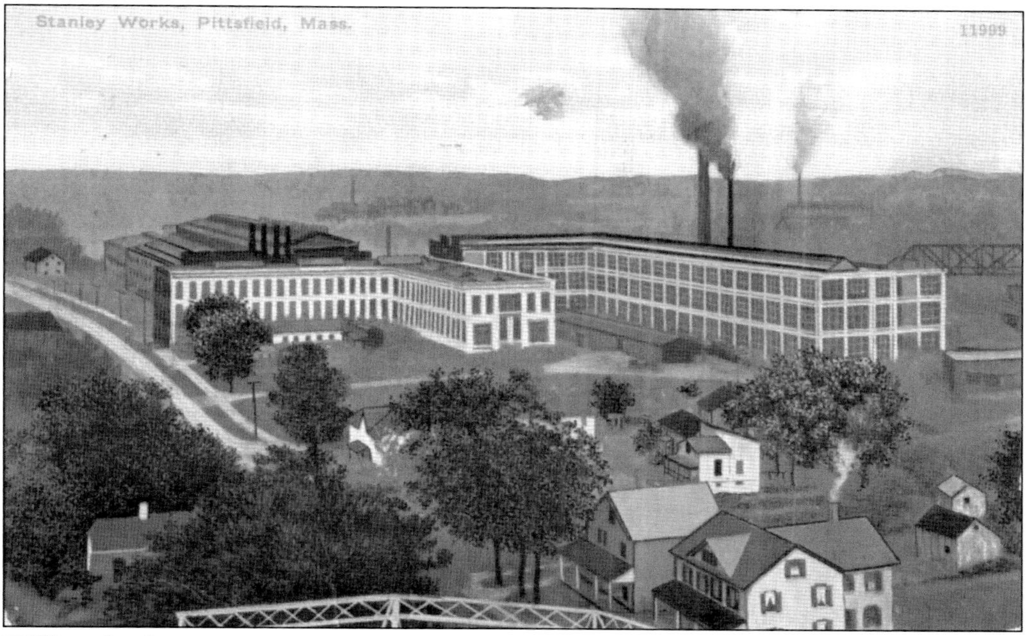

William Stanley Jr. was an American physicist who held 129 patents for electrical devices. He was the first to develop an electrical transformer, in 1886, leading to the electrification of Main Street in Great Barrington, Massachusetts. In 1890, Stanley moved to Pittsfield and founded the Stanley Manufacturing Company. The company was sold to Ferdinand Roebling in 1899, then to General Electric in 1903.

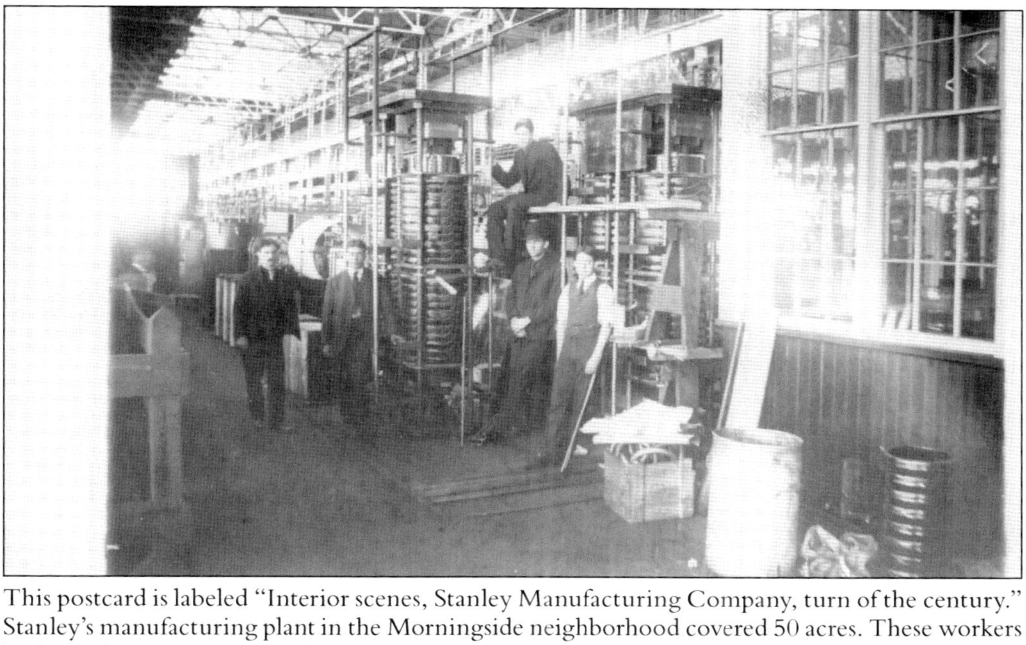

This postcard is labeled "Interior scenes, Stanley Manufacturing Company, turn of the century." Stanley's manufacturing plant in the Morningside neighborhood covered 50 acres. These workers built the first 100 light transformers in the country and later the first transformers of 10,000 volts and higher. William Stanley stated, "I believe we turned out the first commercial condensers for the alternating current in Pittsfield."

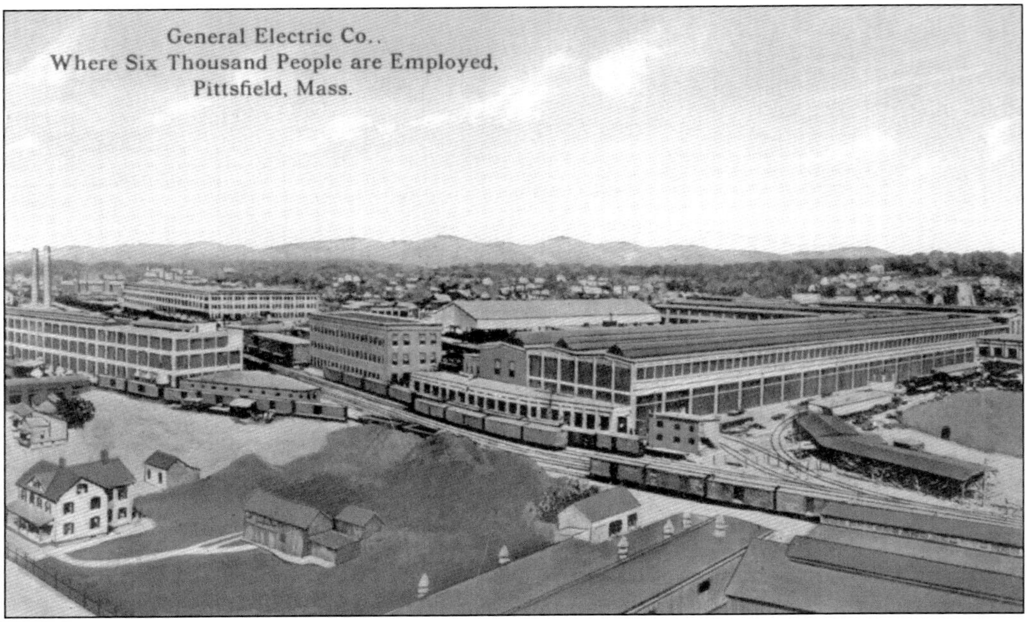

After General Electric purchased the Stanley Manufacturing plant in 1903, it dominated Pittsfield's economy for much of the next 80 years. By 1950, over 10,000 were employed in the transformer department, making Pittsfield the power transformer capital of the world. It was a devastating blow to Pittsfield when GE ended its transformer manufacturing in 1987.

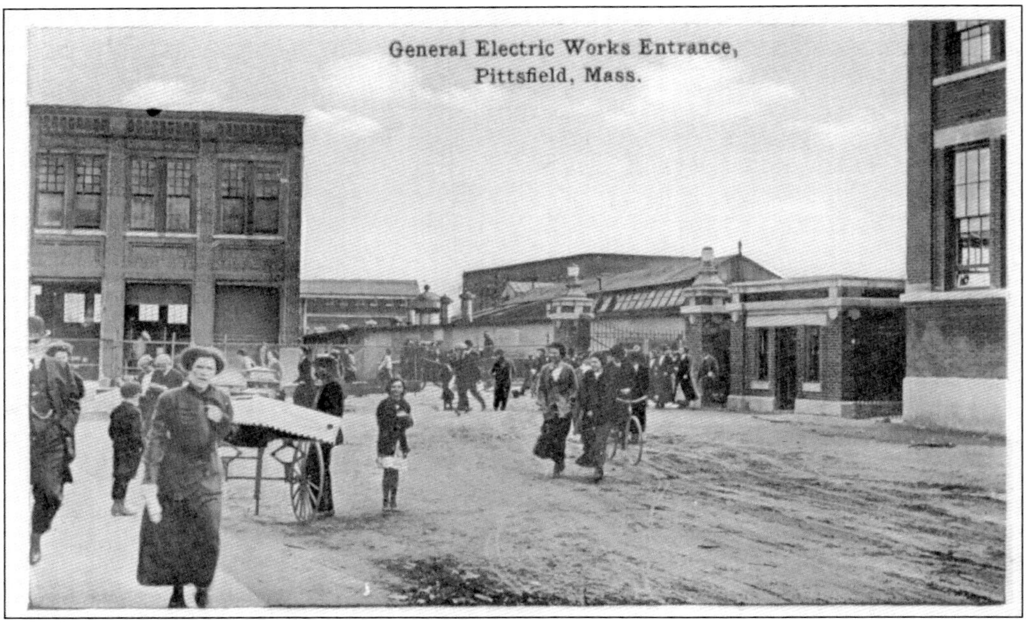

Thousands of workers streamed through General Electric's gates each day. GE's impact on Pittsfield through the 20th century was dramatic and far-reaching. Workers could shop at the company store, take continuing education courses, bank at the credit union, read the GE newspaper, use the Stanley Club, and partake of innumerable parties, celebrations, and parades. In addition to transformers and defense materials, GE plastics and Lexan were manufactured in Pittsfield.

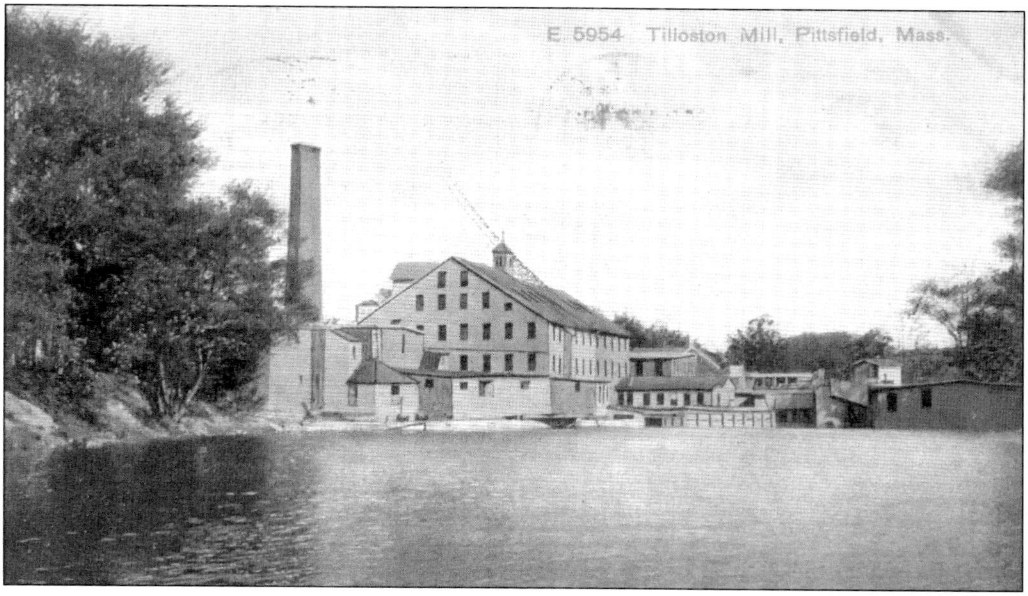

Otis L. Tilloston purchased the Osceola Woolen and Flouring Mill in West Pittsfield in 1864. Over the next 20 years, with several partners and additions, the Tilloston Mill encompassed 150 acres and 16 tenement houses. Machinery was continually added to increase production of "union cassimeres" (fine cloth of cotton and wool). The plant boasted 4,580 spindles, a dye house, and a finishing house.

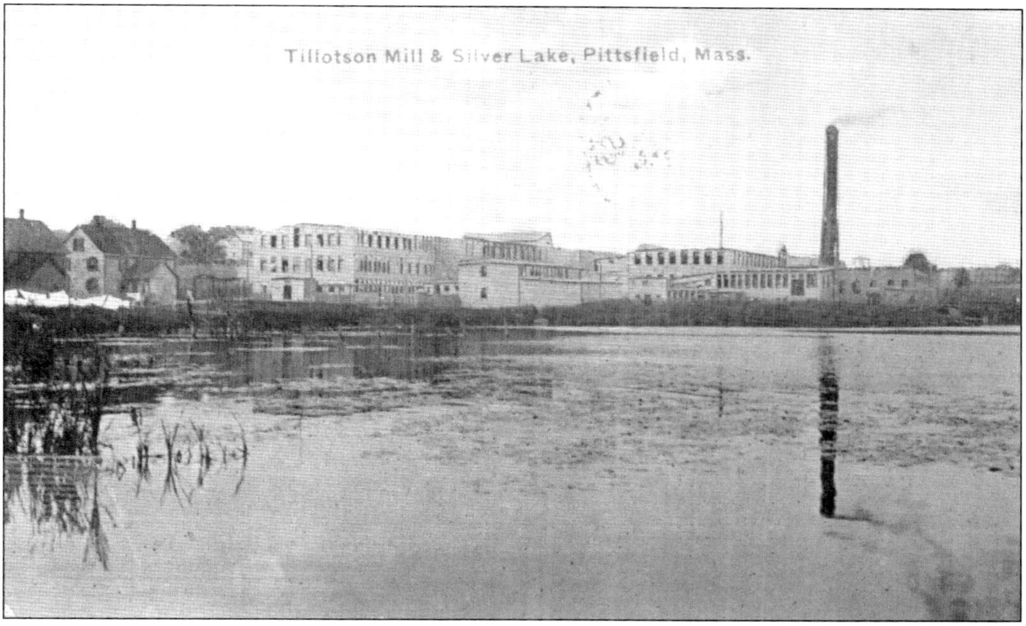

In 1901, several companies merged under the name W.E. Tilloston Manufacturing Company, expanding to include this mill on Silver Lake, on the eastern side of the city. The Silver Lake mill specialized in high-quality woolen underwear. This large mill, encompassing weaving, spinning, and knitting, employed over 600 workers. Silver Lake, minus the factories, has been restored to its natural beauty.

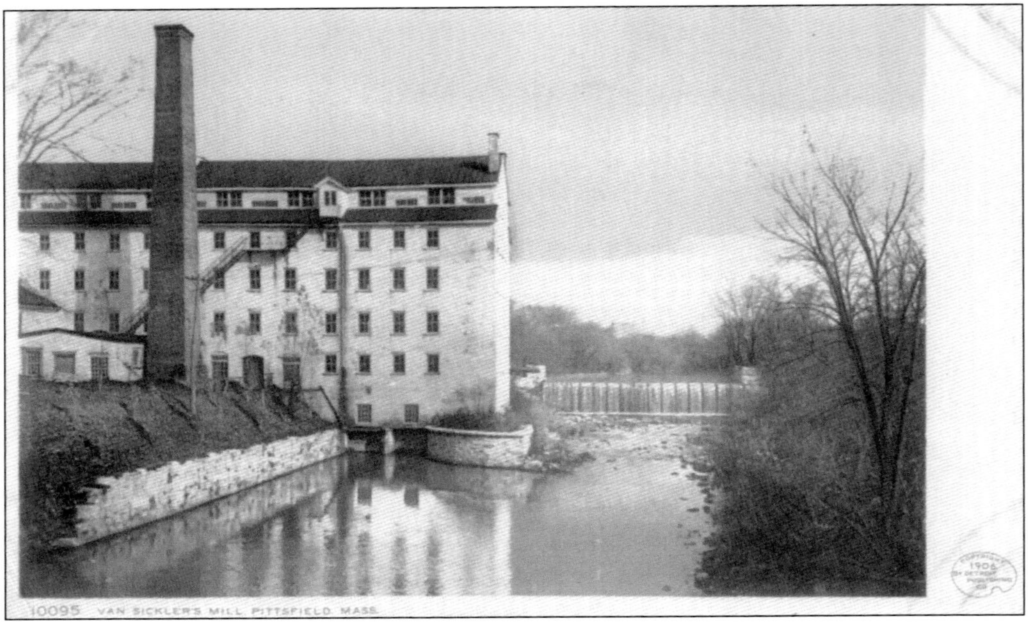

In 1876, Martin Van Sickler purchased this 1832 cotton mill on the Housatonic River, located just south of the Elm Street bridge. The factory was powered by the 1778 mill dam, the first such dam to be built in the city. The multistoried brick factory was large enough for 100 workers to produce 1.5 million yards of cotton sheeting a year.

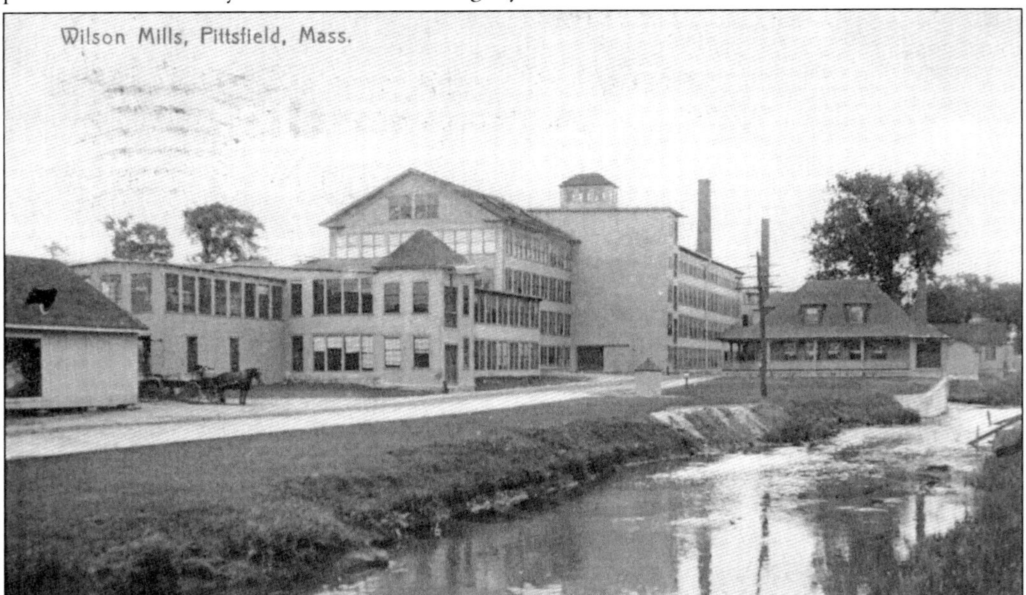

By 1900, the former Taconic Mill had become the Wilson Mill, under the direction of James and E.H. Wilson, and produced thousands of yards of woolen cloth a year. The plant was enlarged in 1904 when the Wilson brothers purchased the nearby Bel Air factory. Between 1914 and 1915, the Wilson Mills produced 125,000 blankets and 750,000 yards of cloth to outfit European armies. The factory complex closed in 1927.

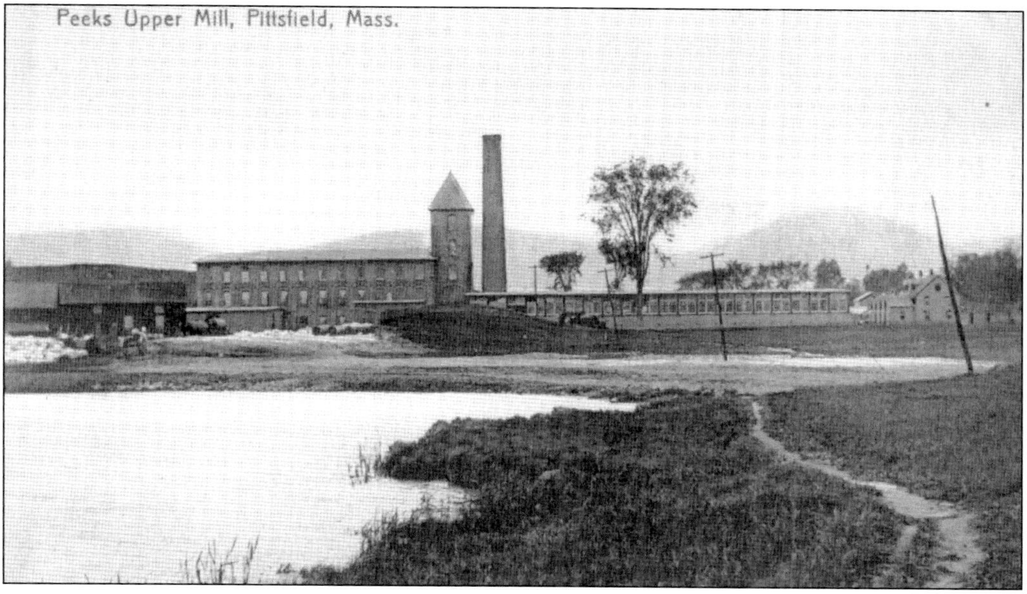

Onota Brook, now a peaceful stream flowing through West Pittsfield, once powered several mills and factories, including two mills owned by the Peck family. Together, the Upper Mill and Lower Mill produced cotton thread until 1910, when the company was sold to Berkshire Woolen and Worsted, which used the Upper Mill. Due to competition from synthetics, that company closed in 1960.

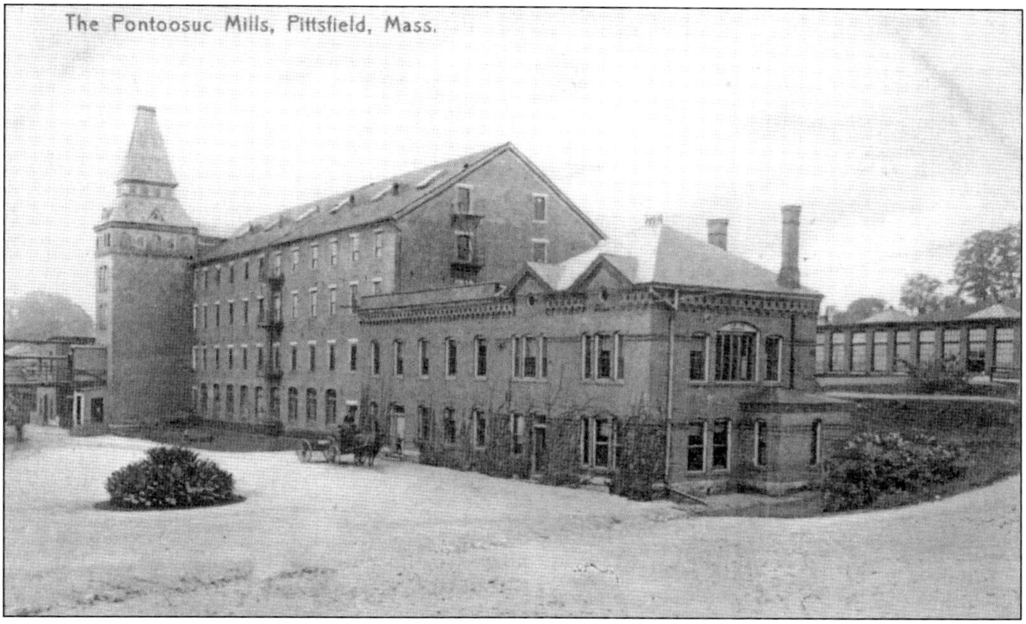

The Pontoosuc Mill was the oldest textile mill in Pittsfield, dating back to 1827. This enormous complex was located on upper North Street, south of Pontoosuc Lake. The company survived by wisely changing its product line to meet changing demands. Over the decades, fine woolens for garments and heavy cloth for blankets were made by as many as 450 employees. The company survived until 1963 under the name Wyandott Worsted.

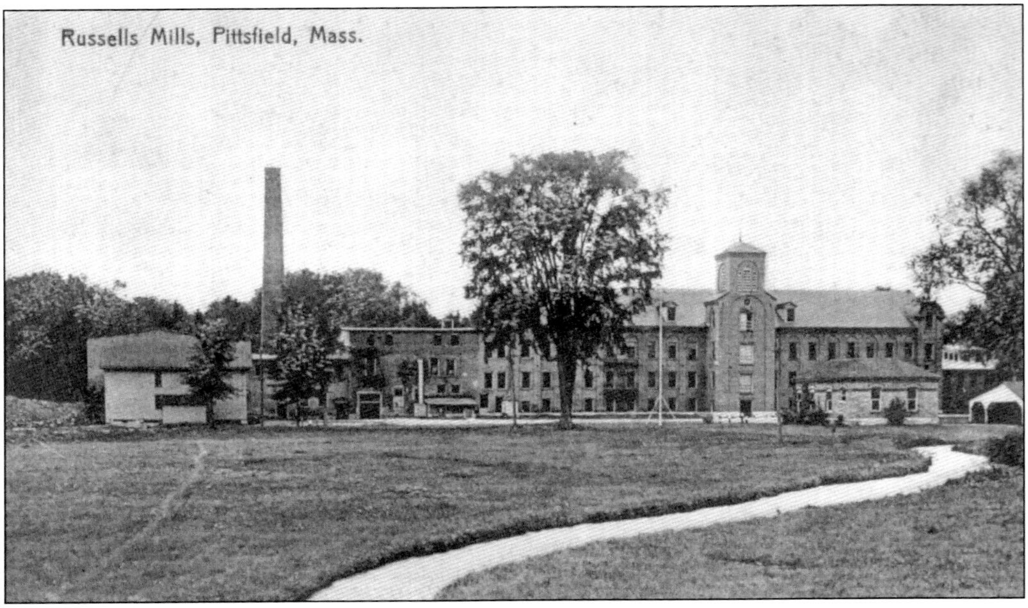

In 1863, brothers Solomon and Charles Russell built this mill on Onota Brook to produce woolen cloth, which was in high demand during the Civil War. Over the years, and with numerous additions, the plant became known as the Elmvale Worsted Company, which survived until 1960. The handsome building on Peck's Road has been adapted for warehouse and retail businesses.

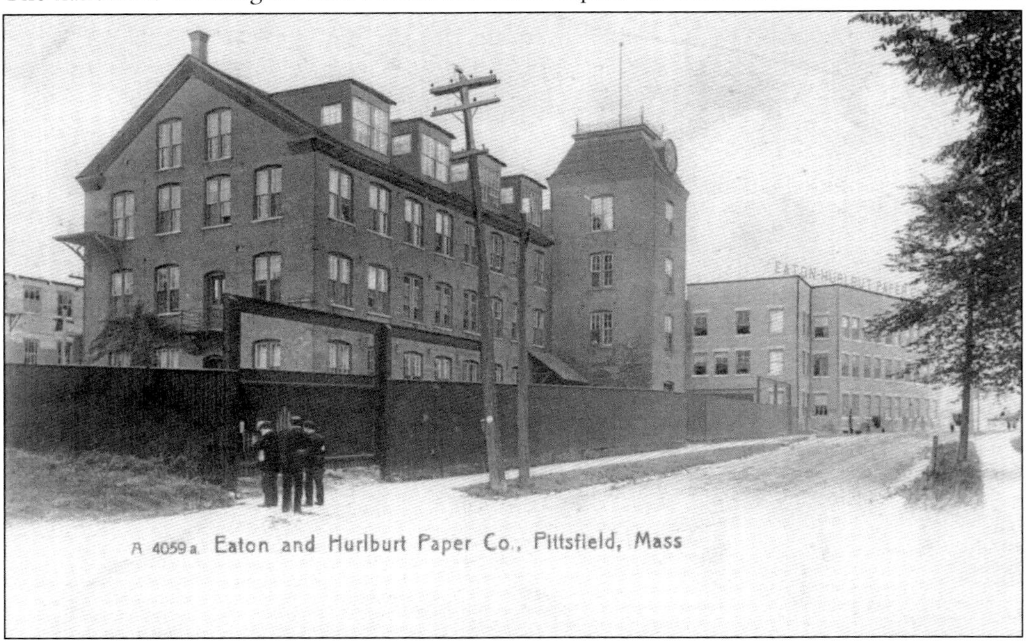

The Terry Clock Factory, built in 1883 on South Church Street, was purchased by Arthur Eaton in 1888. Over the next 100 years, under different names, this factory, seen in this 1907 view, produced vast amounts of stationery and envelopes. These products, including the famous Eaton typewriting paper, were distributed around the world. It closed in the late 1980s. Today, the buildings house the *Berkshire Eagle* and Clock Tower condominiums.

Seven

Recreation

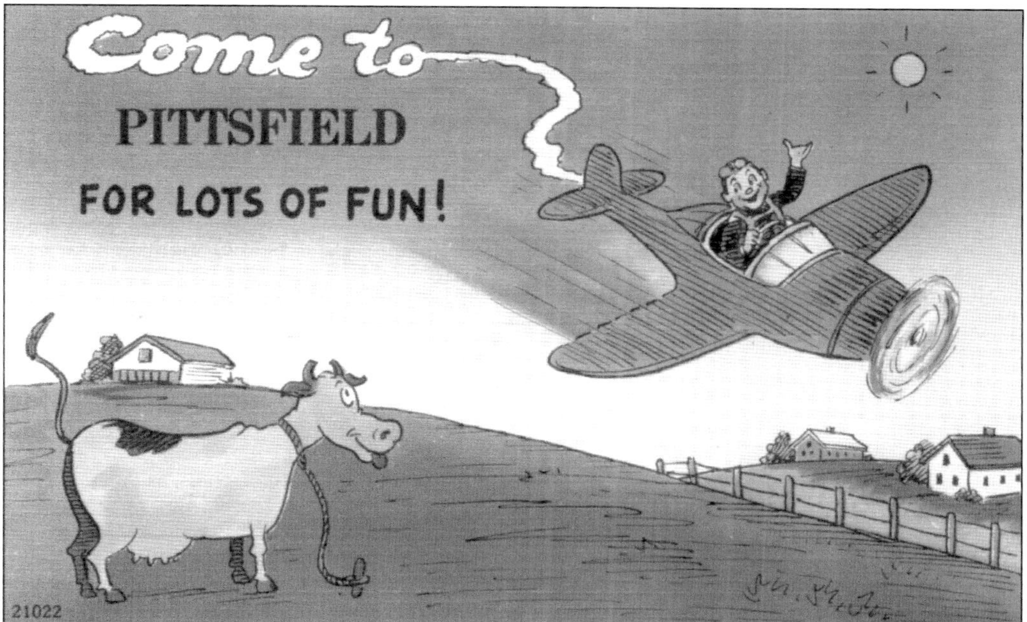

Pittsfield has mountains for hiking and skiing, lakes for swimming and fishing, and parks for playing and picnicking. Friends, families, and visitors may enjoy the clubs, both public and private, as well as extensive community activities. Come to Pittsfield—a city for all seasons.

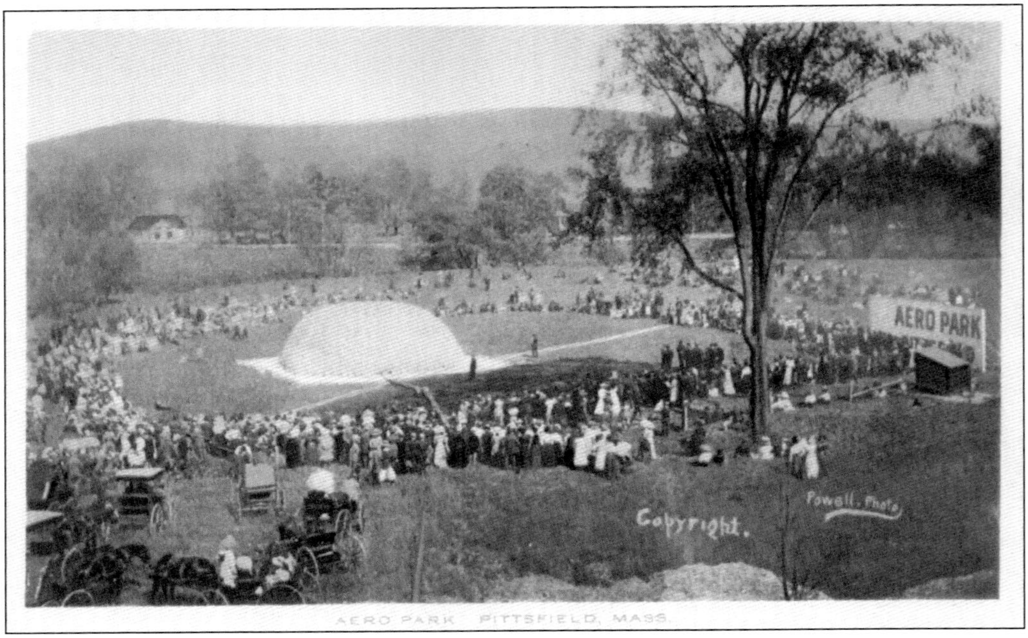

Aero Park was located at the corner of East and Newell Streets. In 1906, the park was selected by the Aero Club of America as the site for the first international balloon race in America. The Pittsfield Gas Works, adjacent to Aero Park, provided the gas for the hot-air balloons. Today, the site is Mark Belanger Memorial Park.

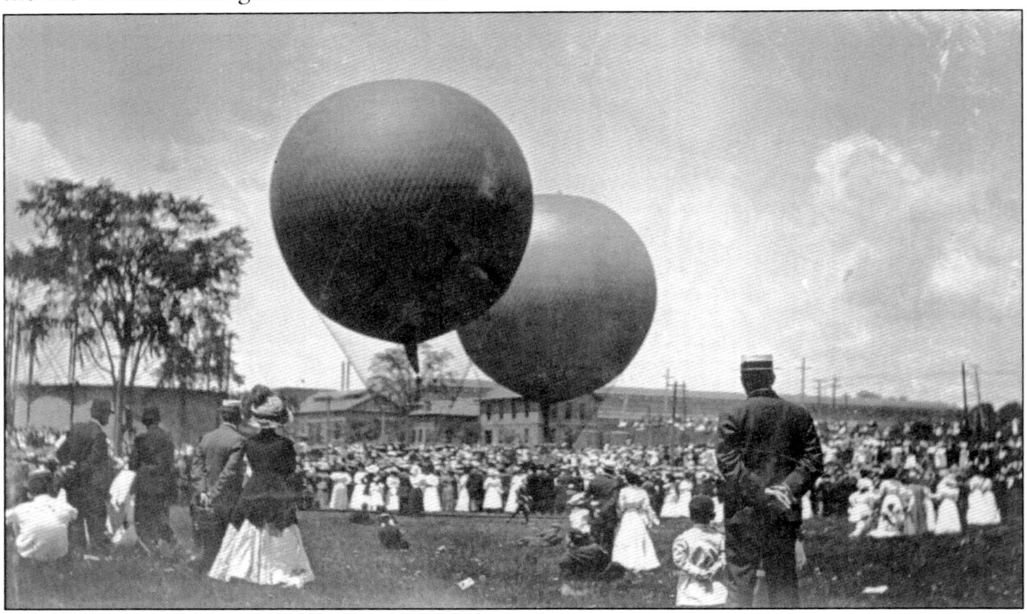

On June 20, 1909, Aero Park was the scene of excitement, as newlyweds Mr. and Mrs. Roger Burnham took off at midnight on a honeymoon flight. Pilot van Sleet landed 12 miles from Boston Common, in the lead to win the *Boston Herald*'s trophy for closest landing to the common. The scene pictured here may be from October 1906, when the *Centaur* and the *L'Orient* competed in a distance race.

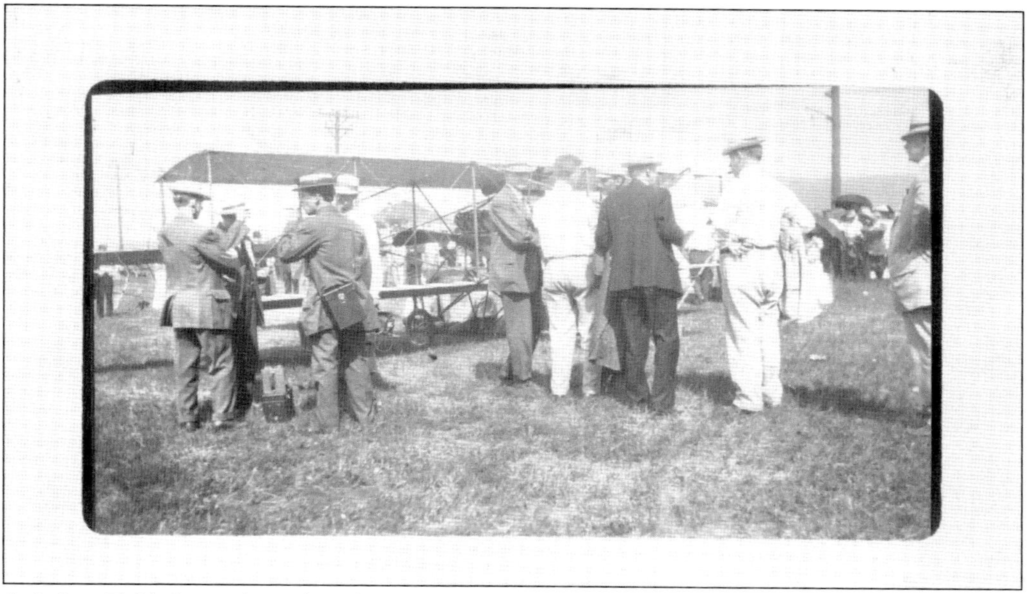

Aviation Field, located on the Allen Farm between Dalton Avenue and the Boston & Albany Railroad tracks, was the site of Pittsfield's 150th anniversary celebration on July 4, 1911. Some 32,000 spectators gathered to watch Berkshire County's first biplane demonstration. Unfortunately, the pilot, Charles C. Witmer, lost control of the Curtiss aircraft, but he did recover from his injuries at the House of Mercy hospital.

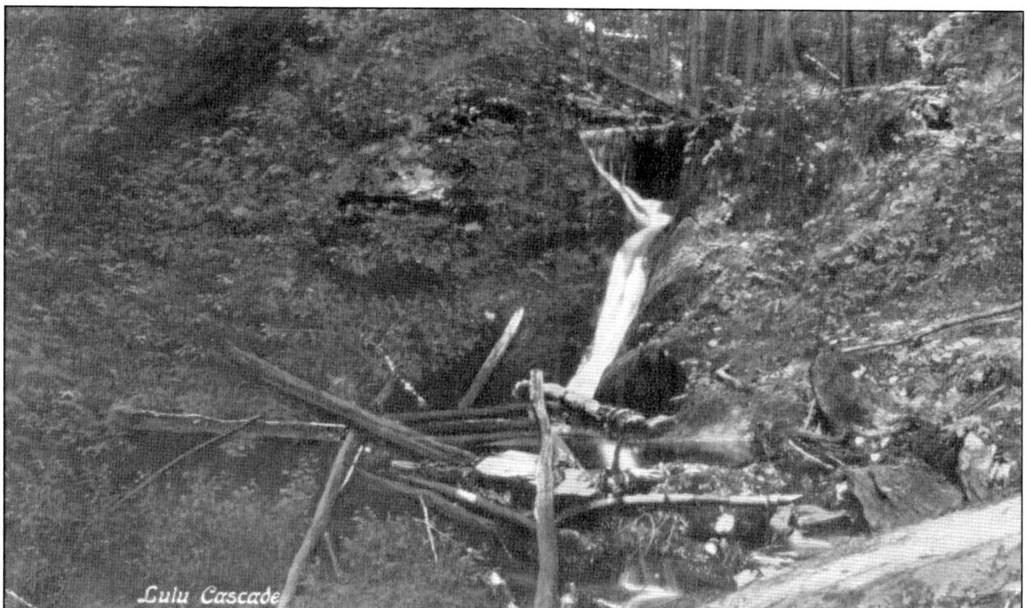

The Pittsfield State Forest, approximately 11,000 acres, is located on the ridgeline of the Taconic Mountain range bordering Pittsfield to the west. The forest, owned by the Commonwealth of Massachusetts, boasts the lovely Berry Pond, 65 acres of wild azaleas, 30 miles of walking trails, and 32 campsites. One highlight is the picturesque Lulu Cascade, a series of waterfalls in the Lulu Brook.

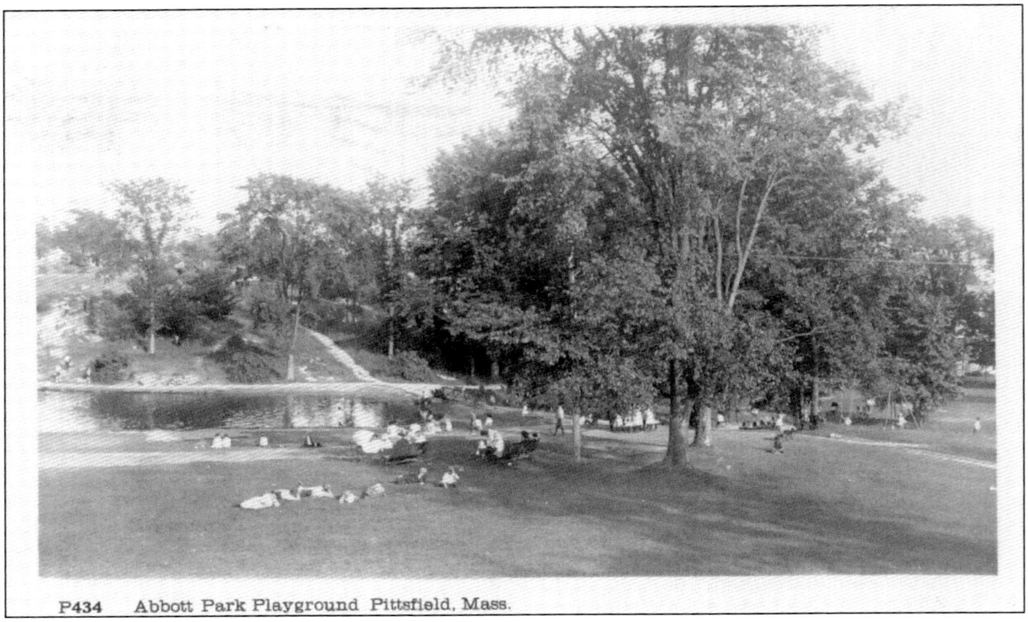

Kelton B. Miller, publisher of the *Berkshire Eagle*, donated 10 acres of land to Pittsfield in 1910. Miller set the condition that Pittsfield maintain the park forever, improving it for the good of the entire community. It was originally called Abbott Park, in honor of the Reverend Charles Abbott, who owned a nearby boys' school. Abbott Park was later renamed Springside Park.

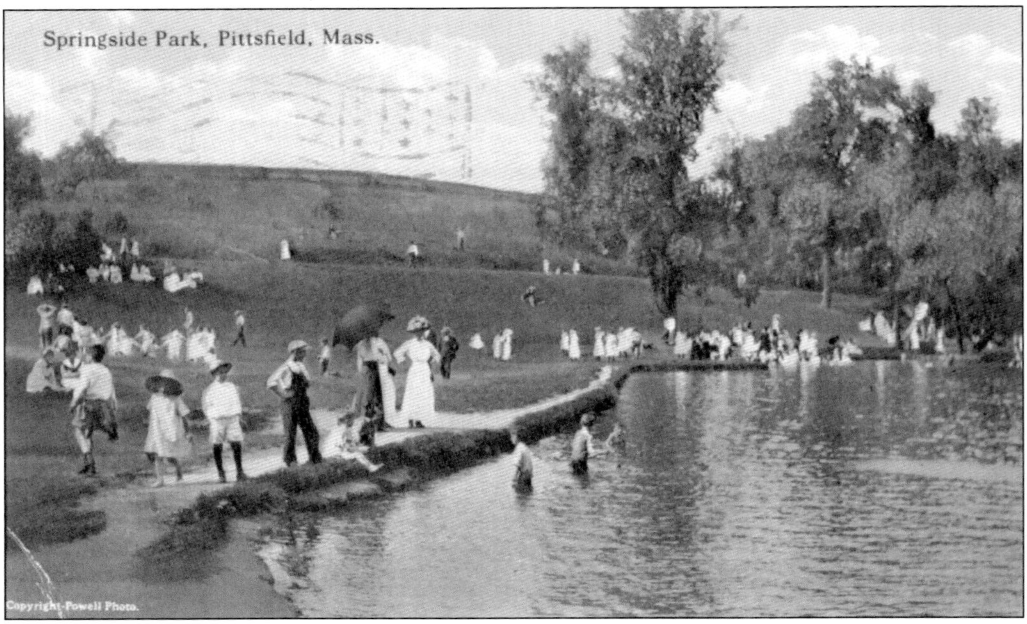

In 1912, Pittsfield's new Park and Playground Association purchased 15 more acres to expand Springside Park. In 1939, the Kelton Miller family donated an additional 75 acres. Today, Springfield Park covers 275 acres and contains greenhouses, ball fields, hiking trails, and Elmhurst (Springside House), which is undergoing restoration. In 1949, North Junior High School, now Reid Middle School, was built in the park area.

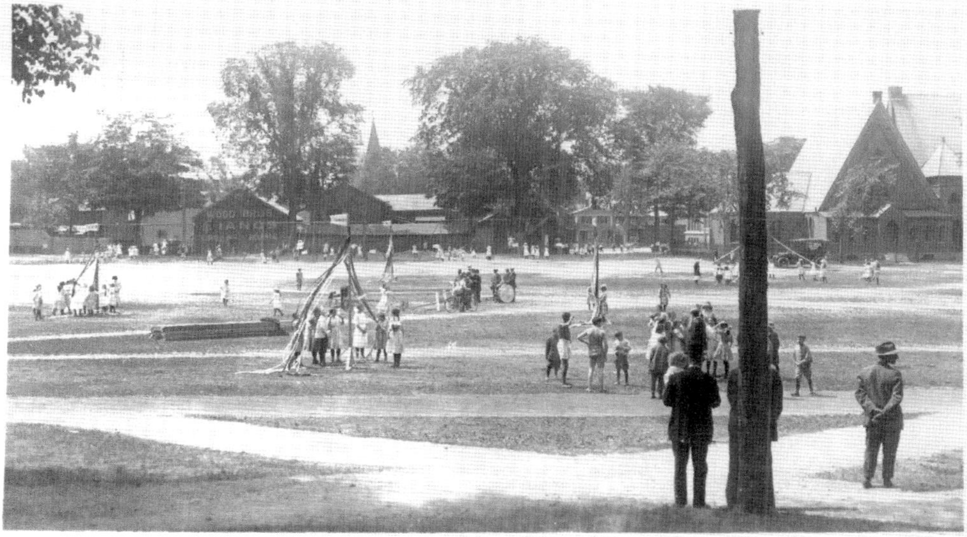

P453 The Common Playground, Pittsfield, Mass.

This area on First Street, between the train tracks and Fenn Street, was used until 1850 as the Old Burying Ground. In 1883, Pittsfield appropriated $1,500 to remove the graves and make this desolate plot of land into a town park, the First Street Common. Between 2012 and 2015, this park has undergone another dramatic revival and renovation. In this view from about 1900, the Lutheran church is to the right.

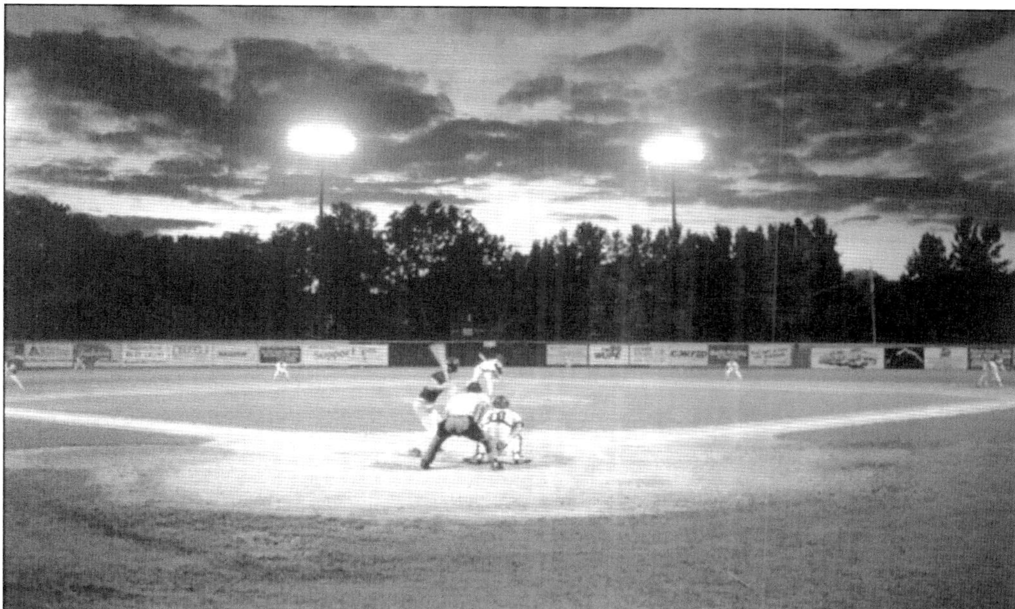

Documentation of Pittsfield's history with baseball dates to the town's passage of a 1791 ordinance banning the playing of baseball in Park Square. In 1859, the city hosted the first intercollegiate game between Amherst and Williams Colleges. Wahconah Park was built in 1892. The 4,500-seat grandstand was added in 1927. Since the batters face west, causing occasional delays as the sun set, the Pittsfield Suns team is appropriately named.

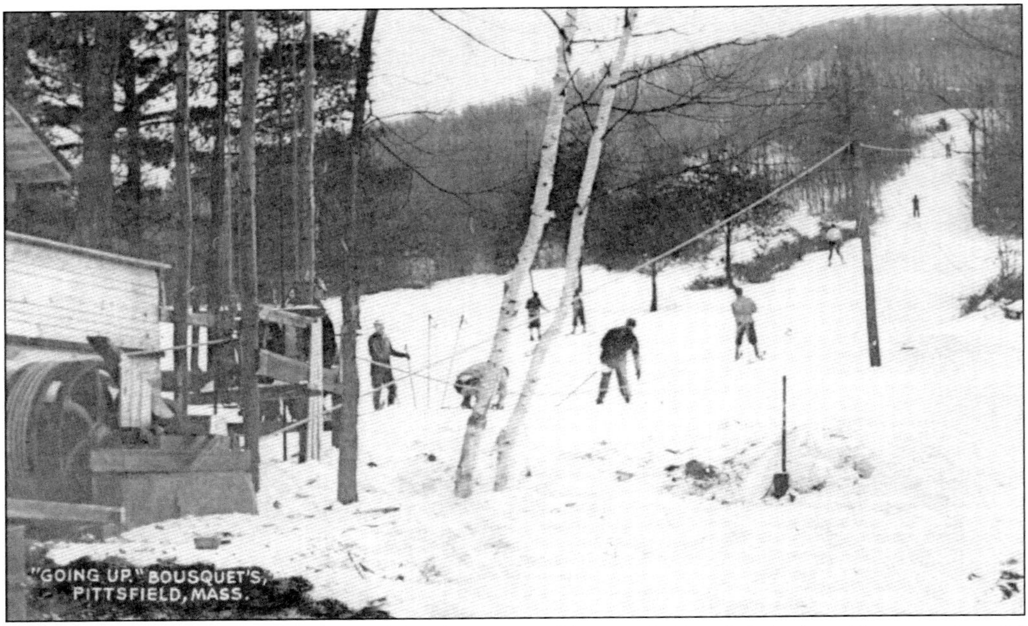

In 1932, Clarence Bousquet opened his ski area on Tamarack Road. It is the oldest existing ski area in the Berkshires and the first in the world to have night skiing, under mercury vapor lights. The first ski tow was installed in 1935, and in 1939, Bousquet invented and patented a rope tow gripper to protect the hands and arms of skiers as they were pulled up the slope.

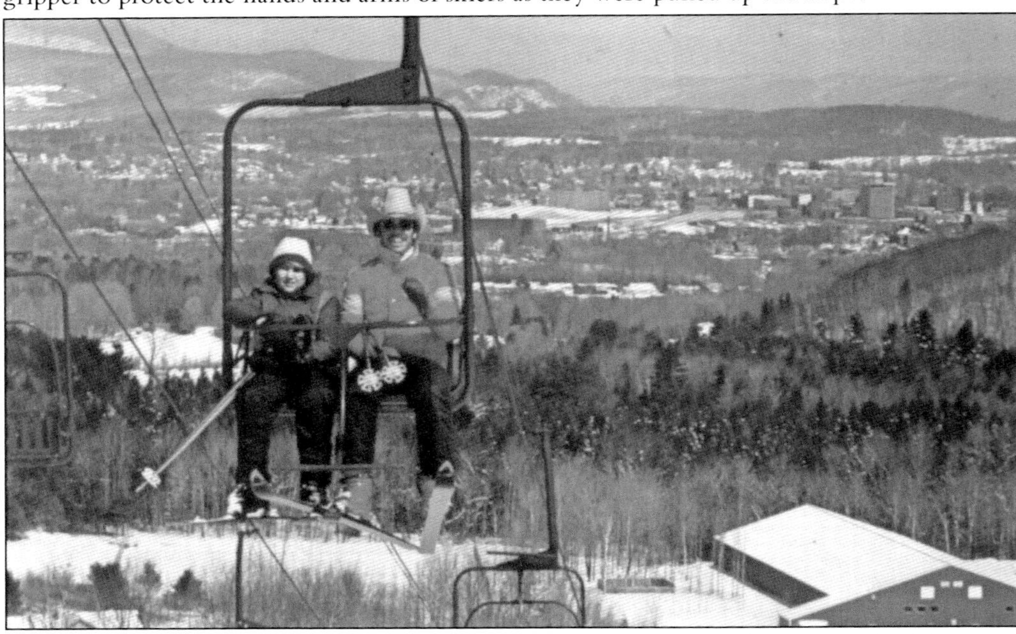

Today, Bousquet offers 24 trails, a vertical drop of 750 feet, three double lifts, and a full-service ski school. The chair lift, seen here, was installed in 1962–1963. Bousquet can boast of many famous visitors, including John F. Kennedy, and Olympians, including Heidi Voelker and Kim and Krista Schmidinger. Over the past 15 years, it has become a year-round destination, with a zip line, disc golf, and ropes course.

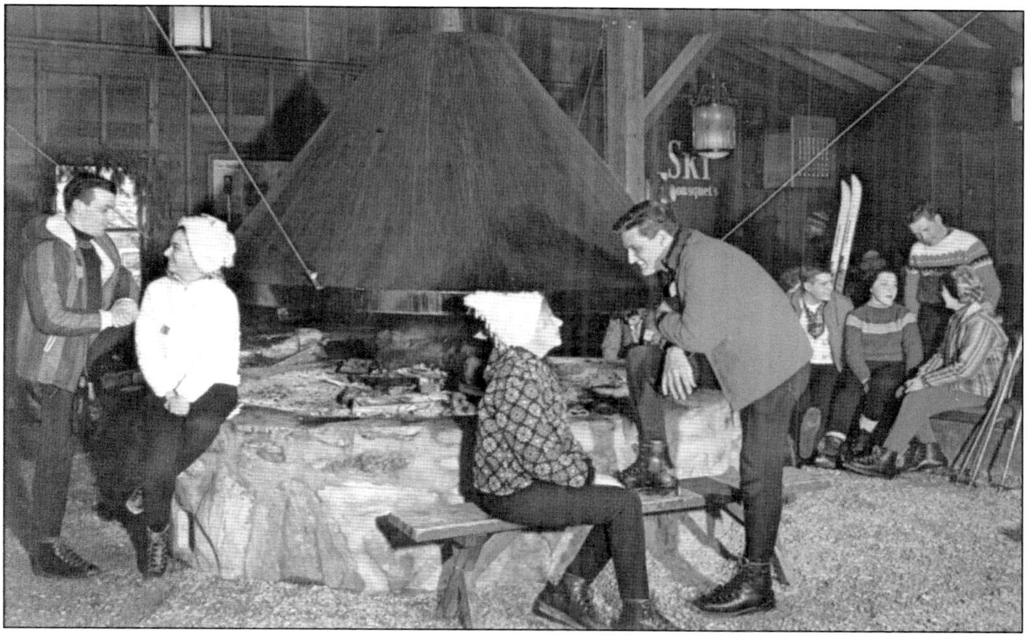

In 1956, the Bousquet Ski Area was sold to Don Soviero, who added a spacious canteen with four fireplaces—just the place for an après-ski refreshment. New York skiers who arrived in Pittsfield on the New Haven Railroad's snow trains in the 1930s and 1940s would not recognize the modern ski resort.

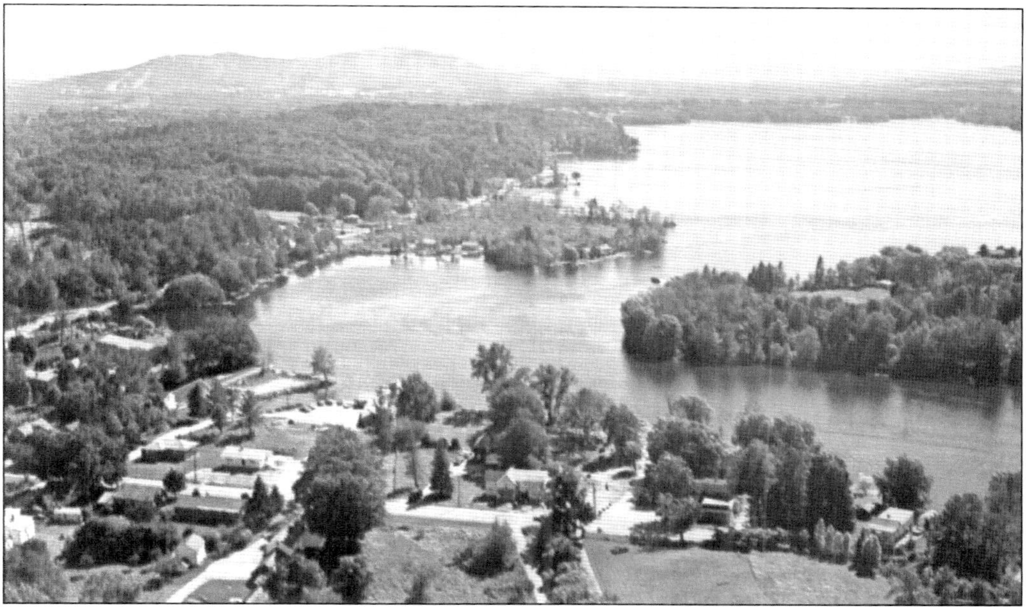

Onota Lake, a 617-acre body of water entirely within Pittsfield, is seen here from its northern shore, with Peck's Road in the foreground. In 1883, John Burbank donated a large tract of land on the eastern shore for a city park. By the year 2000, extensive improvements included a universally accessible fishing pier and a pavilion. The Lake Onota Preservation Association monitors the water quality. Thomas Island is pictured in right foreground.

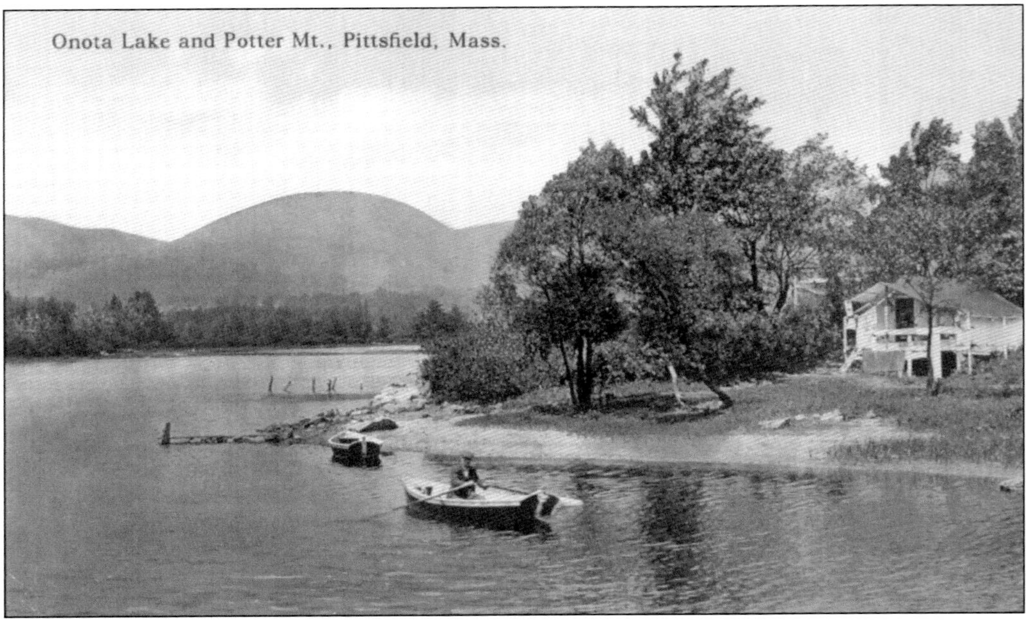

Thomas Island, in the northeast corner of Onota Lake, is the most densely populated area around the lake. Residents enjoy boating and fishing to this day. In the 1950s, newspaper articles described how hundreds of skaters enjoyed the smooth ice in Thomas Island Cove. Most of the seasonal cottages have been converted to year-round homes.

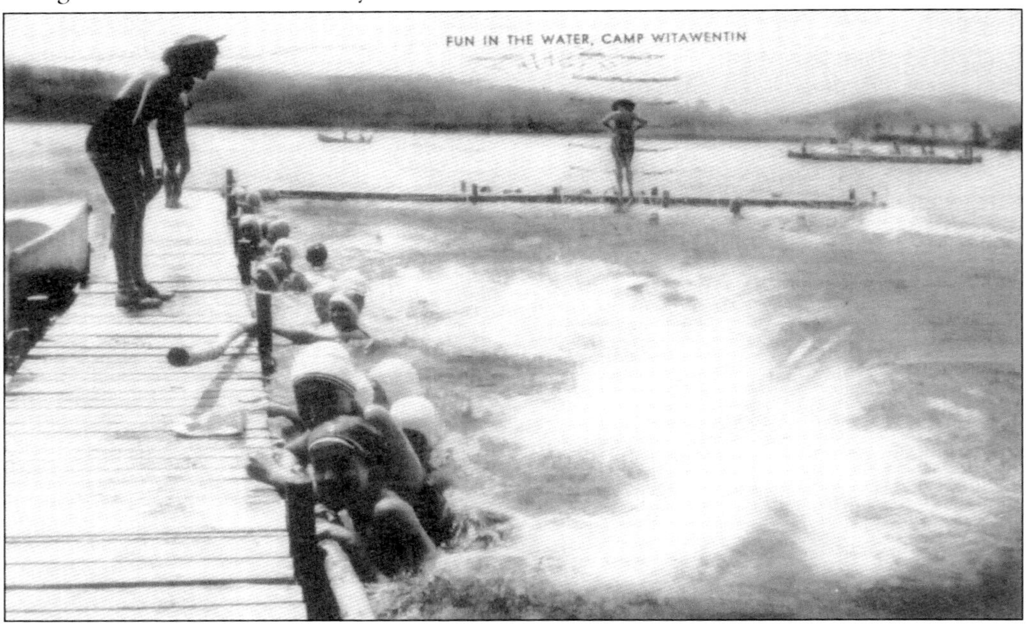

The local chapter of the Camp Fire Girls opened their first Camp Witawentin on Richmond Pond. Soon thereafter, in 1929, they moved the camp to a larger site on the western shore of Onota Lake. Swimming was an important activity, as seen on this card from the 1930s. Ironically, the camp closed from 1945 to 1950 due to a water shortage. Today, Camp Stevenson-Witawentin serves both boys and girls.

Onota Lake offers a picturesque setting for numerous sports and activities, both active and tranquil, but when the sun goes down, the fishing is extra special. With a depth in some places of 66 feet, Onota offers many places to fish—from piers, along the shore, or out on the water. Of the 21 varieties of fish, 17 are native, and four are stocked.

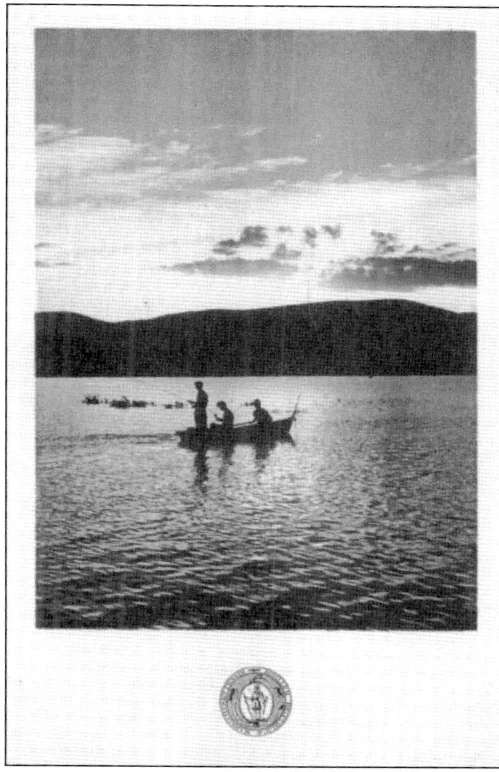

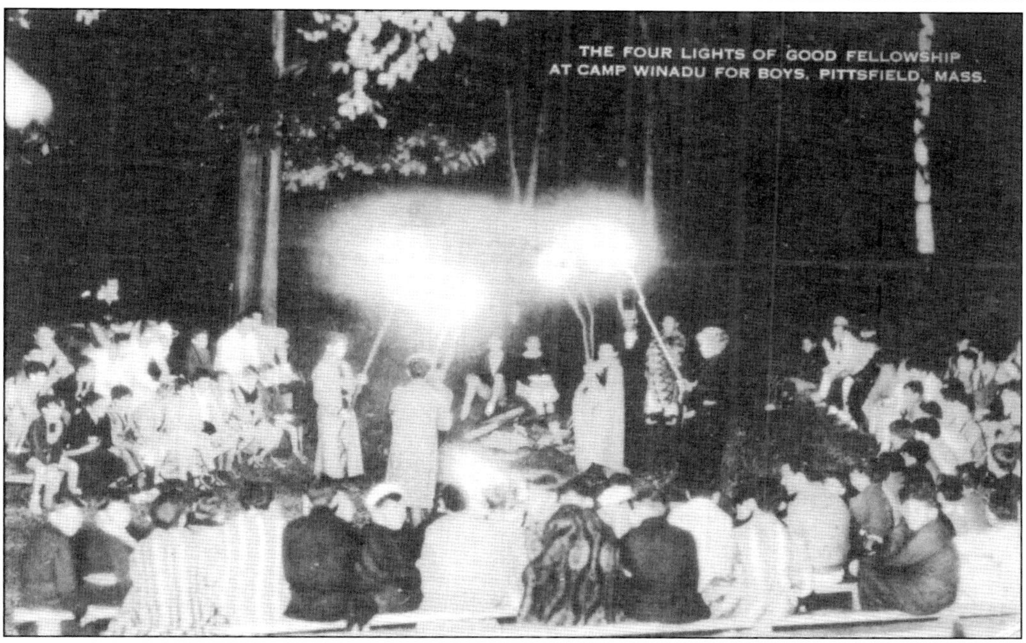

Camp Winadu, an exclusive camp for boys, was founded in 1927 on the western shore of Onota Lake. This postcard illustrates the "Four Lights of Good Fellowship." That philosophy is carried on by today's campers, whose motto is "Building Character through Sports."

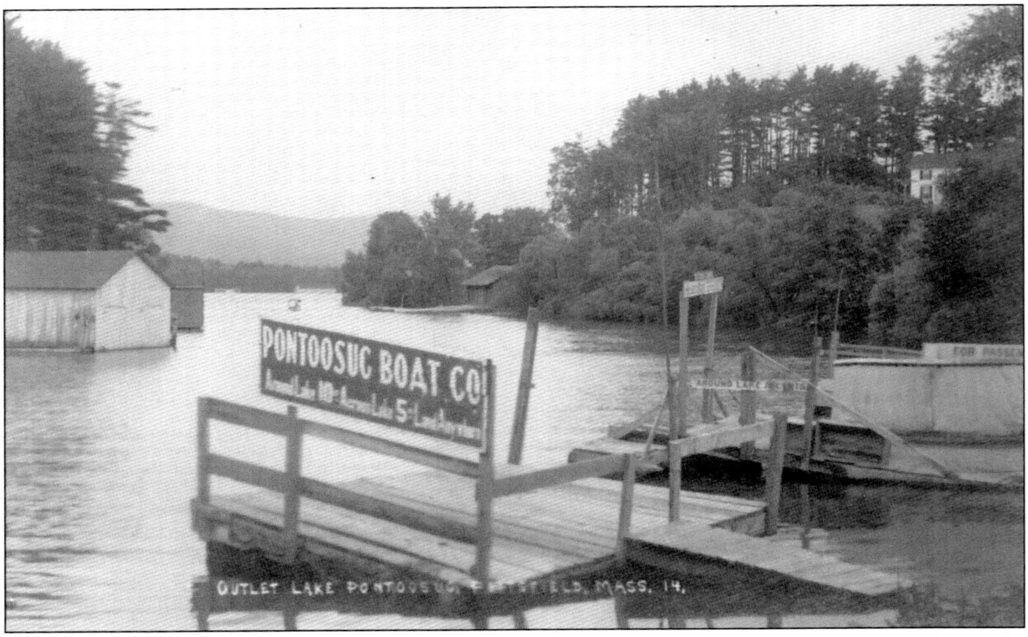

The Pontoosuc Boat Company, located near the lake's outlet, promised a cruise around the lake for 10¢, a trip across the lake for 5¢, and landing anywhere by request. Over the years, other boating companies also provided sightseeing tours. Beginning in the late 1890s to 1911, Peter Hodecker's *Lafayette*, a 300-passenger two-deck steamboat, toured the lake.

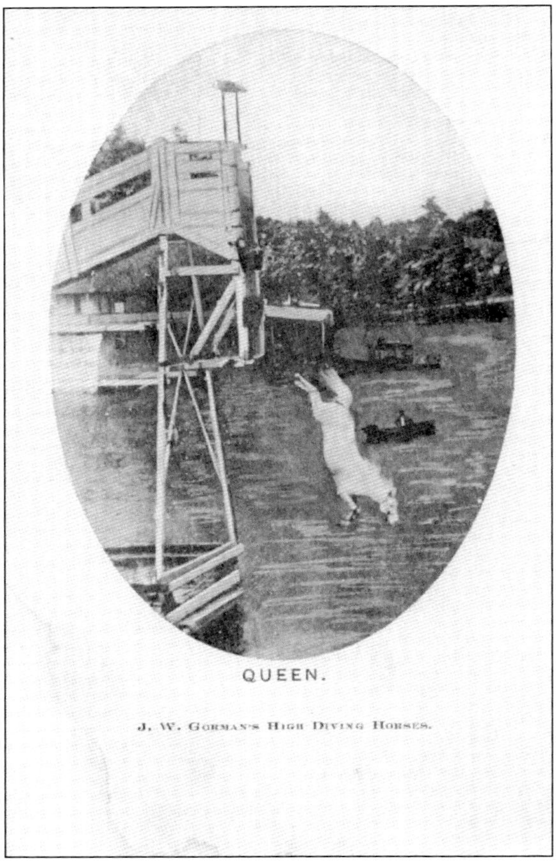

In 1909, J.W. Gorman entertained hundreds with his diving-horse show, starring King and Queen. In this view, Queen has walked up the ramp to dive gracefully into Pontoosuc Lake. Due to criticism from animal-rights groups, such exhibitions declined in popularity in the 1950s.

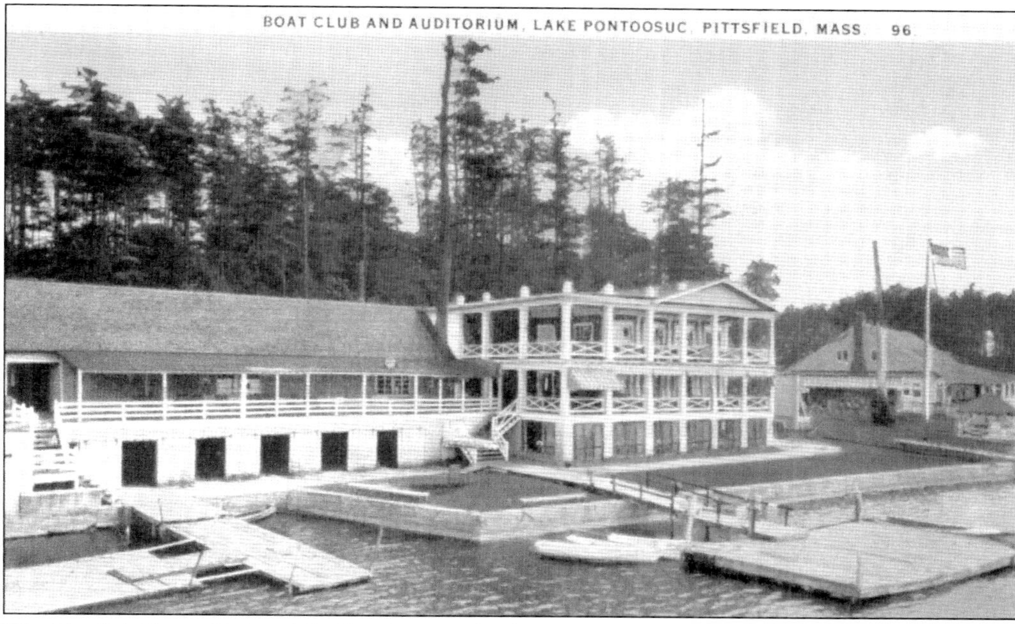

The Pittsfield Boat Club and Auditorium was built in 1909. Members could engage in water sports, have dinner, and go dancing. By 1929, it was known as the Blue Anchor Swimming and Social Club, billed as the "livest" place in town. In the 1930s, it was the Crystal Ballroom and skating rink, where young people danced to the music of Glenn Miller and other popular bands.

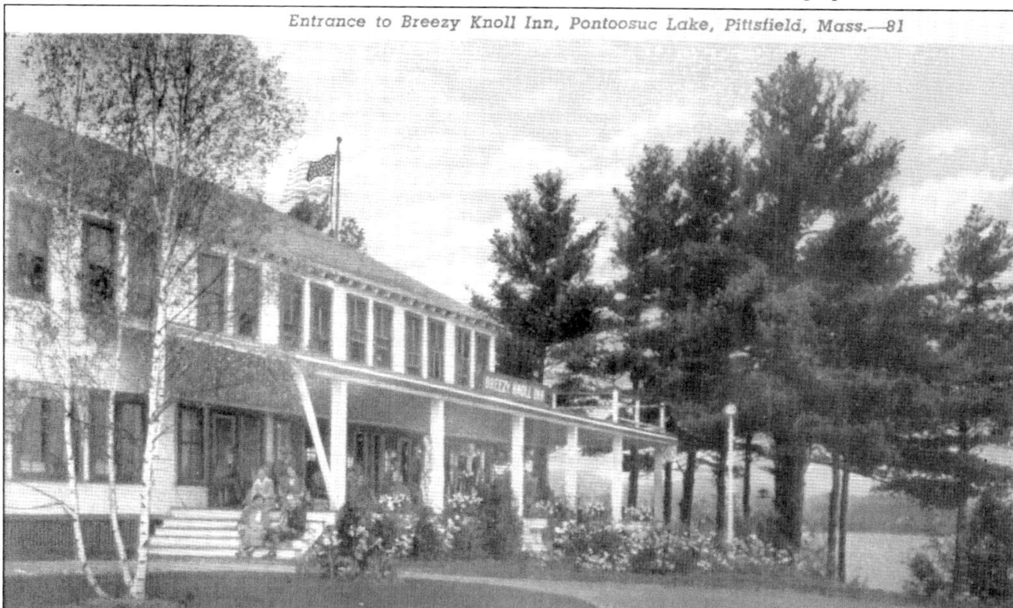

The Breezy Knoll Inn, on the south shore of Pontoosuc Lake, was established by Lenora M. Rockwell in 1914. The restaurant and 75 guestrooms were a popular summer resort, offering swimming, boating, fishing, waterskiing, and outstanding cuisine. It was a fashionable place for weddings and get-togethers of all kinds. It was sold to the Italian American Club in 1968 for $48,000.

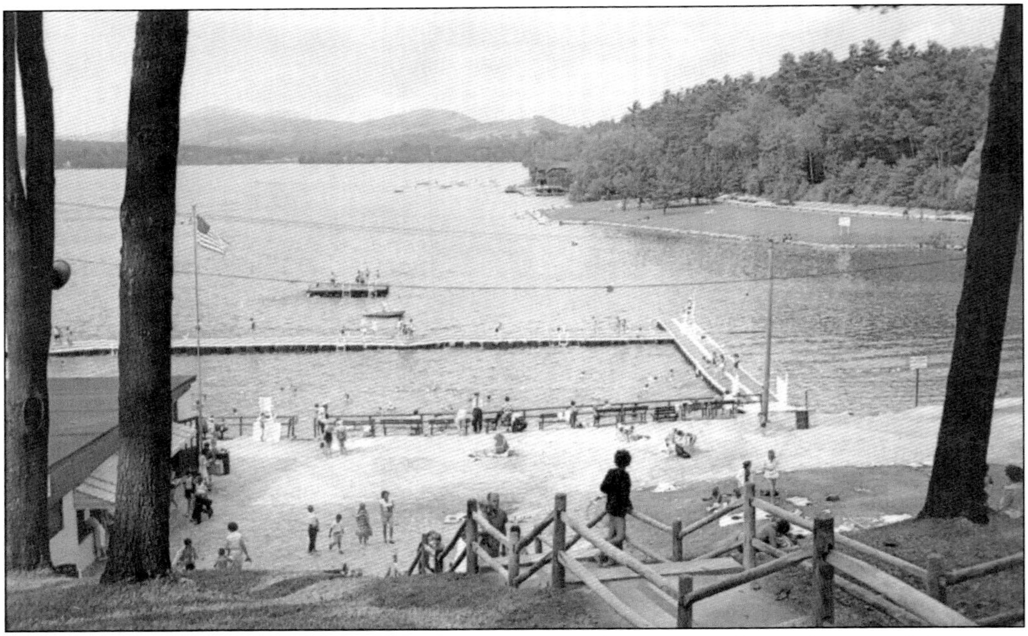

In 1913, the Pittsfield Park Commission acquired 10 wooded acres on the south shore of Pontoosuc Lake for a beach area. With a view of Mount Greylock in the distance, it soon proved popular. It was expanded in the 1940s, when the fire-damaged Blue Anchor Club was purchased by Lawrence Miller as a gift to Pittsfield. It was torn down in 1946, resulting in the 1950s view seen here.

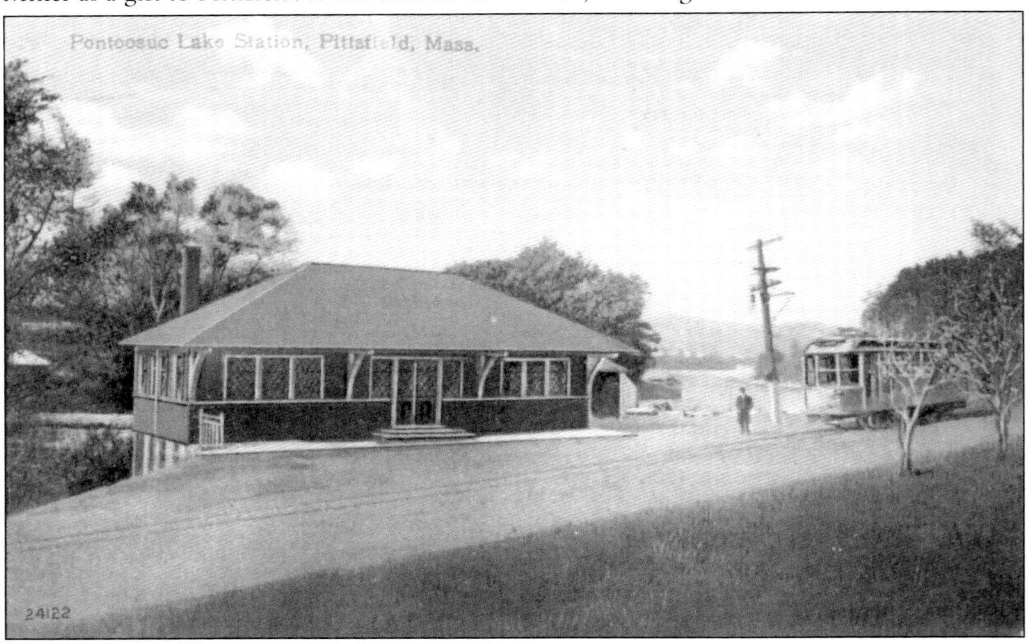

The Pittsfield Electric Street Railway Company began service between Park Square and the Pontoosuc Lake station on July 9, 1891. The route was popular from the opening day, when 3,700 passengers enjoyed the lake and surrounding scenery. By 1902, the trolley line operated a line north and south through Berkshire County, spurring development around Pontoosuc Lake.

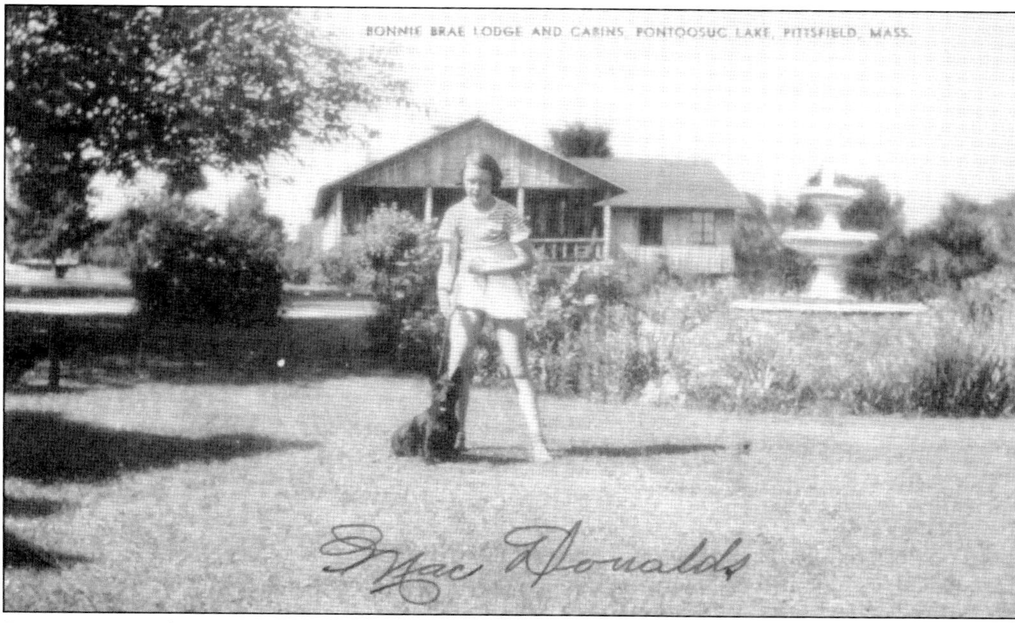

Bonnie Brae Cabins and Campsites has provided visitors with an inexpensive recreational location for decades. It is perched high above the eastern shore of Pontoosuc Lake. There are six cabins and 42 campsites, along with free hot showers, a swimming pool, and a small playground.

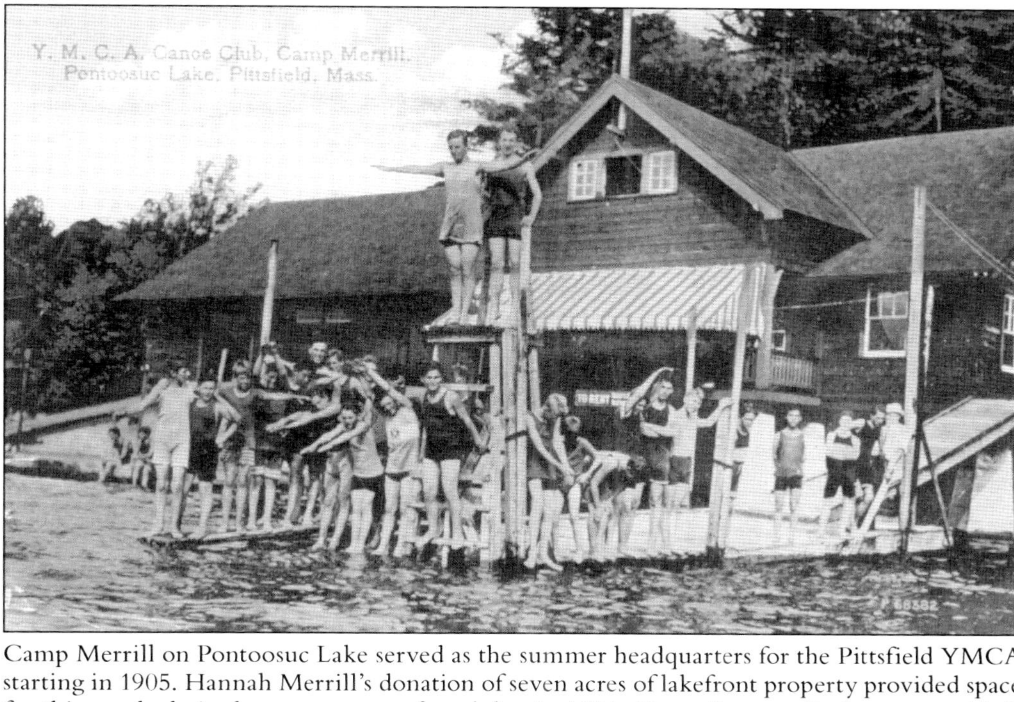

Camp Merrill on Pontoosuc Lake served as the summer headquarters for the Pittsfield YMCA starting in 1905. Hannah Merrill's donation of seven acres of lakefront property provided space for this much-desired summer camp for adults. In 1924, Camp Sumner for boys was added. The Ponterril Boat House, built as the YMCA Canoe Club, was renovated by private owners in 2012 and is now the Rusty Anchor.

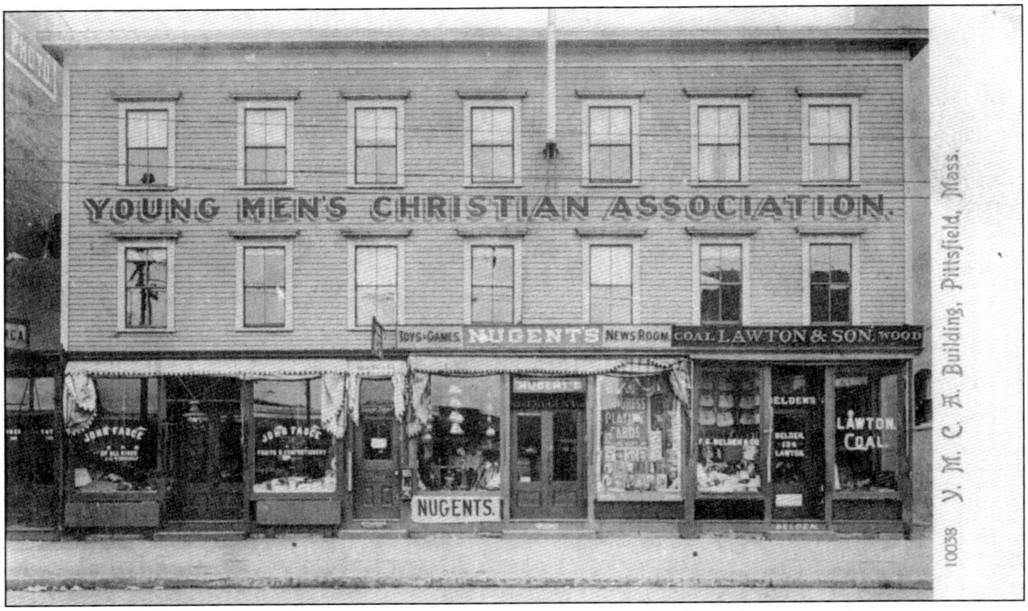

The Pittsfield YMCA was created in 1885 to provide space for "religious meetings, educational classes, a bureau of employment and a boarding house register." By 1894, the YMCA was established at 140 North Street, well equipped to meet those requirements. It had a gymnasium and showers. As seen in this view from around 1900, the first floor housed retailers such as Nugent's News Room and John Fasce's Fruit and Confectionery Shop.

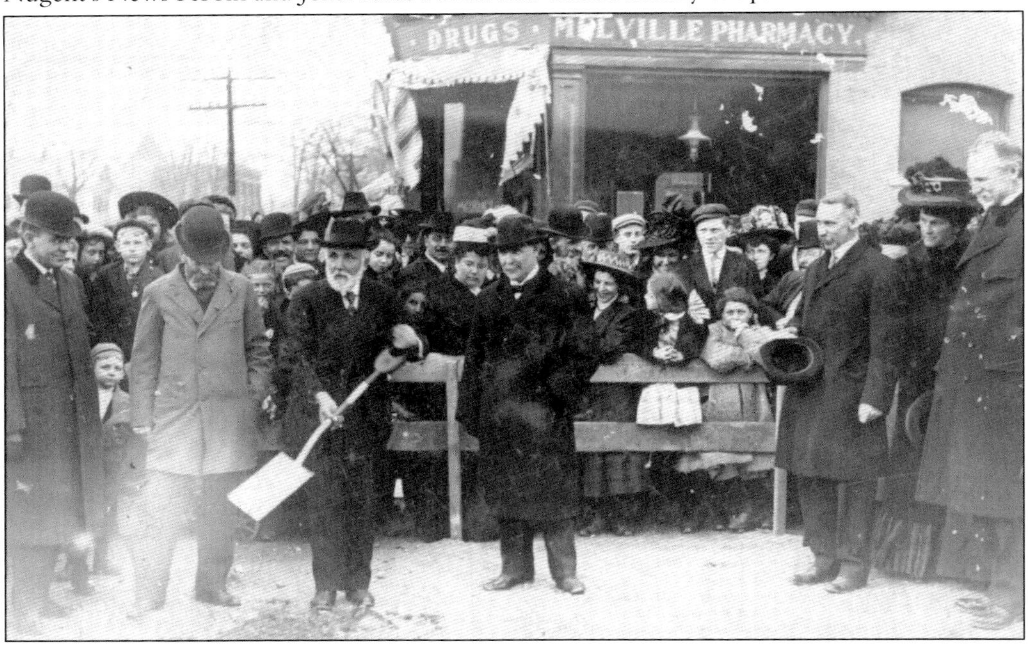

The present-day YMCA site, on the corner of North and Melville Streets, was purchased in 1906 for $50,000. Breaking ground in 1910 are, from left to right, community leaders E.D. Jones, Doc Davis, Chas Raymond, and the building's architect, Henry W. Seaver. Behind the crowd is the Melville Pharmacy, later known as the Sugar Bowl and now the home of Liberty Pizza.

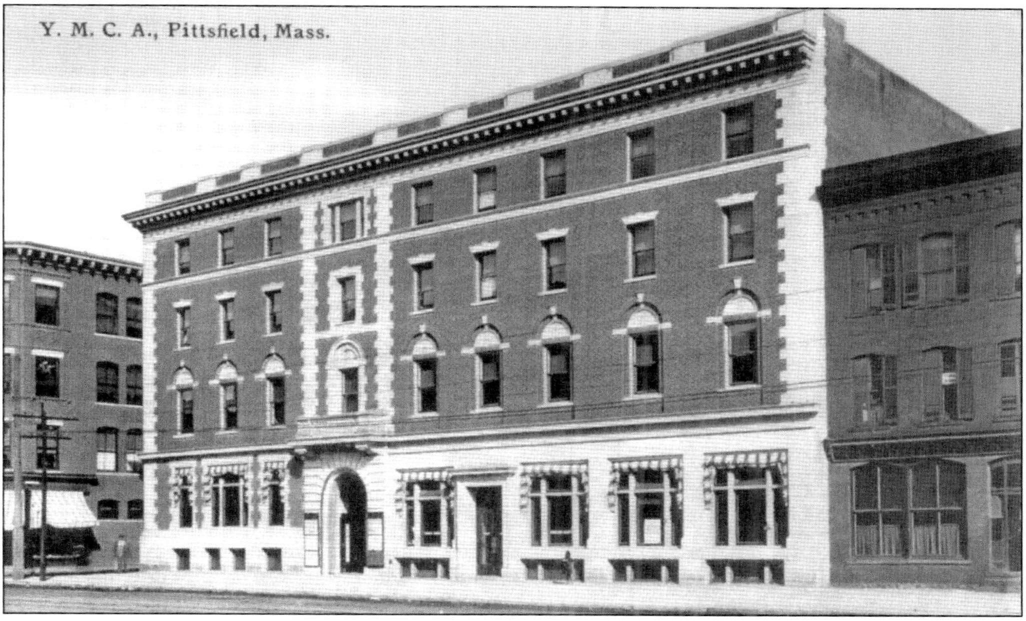

The new four-story building at 292 North Street was possibly the first YMCA in the country to devote two top floors for dormitory rooms to offset operating costs. In addition to the 74 dorm rooms, there was an auditorium, classrooms, a bowling alley, a gymnasium, and a swimming pool in the basement. The YMCA is still fulfilling its mission, offering a variety of programs for children and adults.

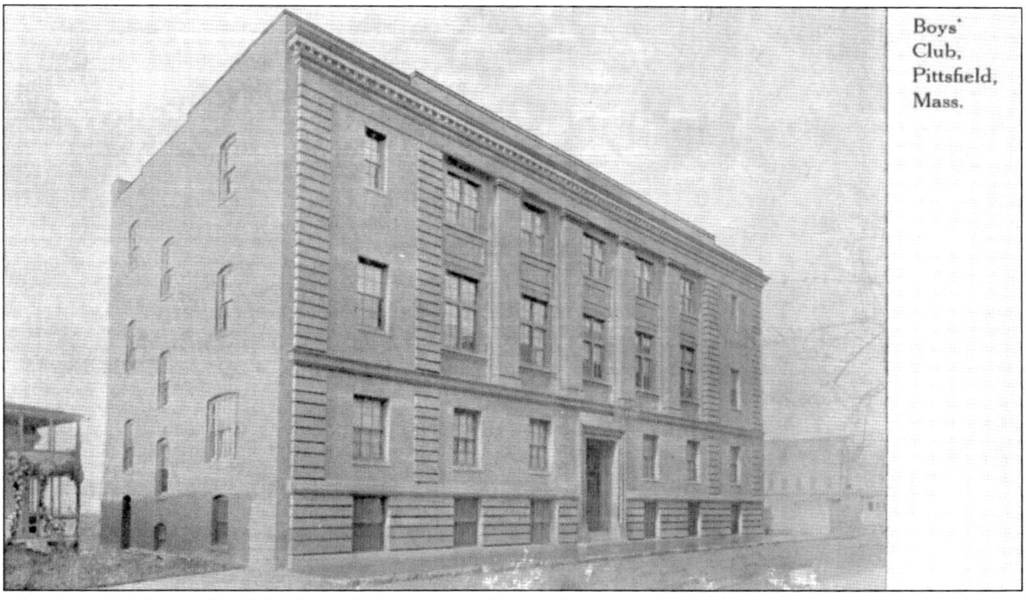

The Pittsfield Boys' Club, founded in 1900, focused on vocational training. In 1906, this new building was erected on Melville Street, funded by Zenas Crane on the condition that boys from Dalton be able to use the auditorium, bowling alleys, library, and classrooms. Over the years, a swimming pool and ice-skating rink were added. Today, the Boys' and Girls' Club has over 5,000 members.

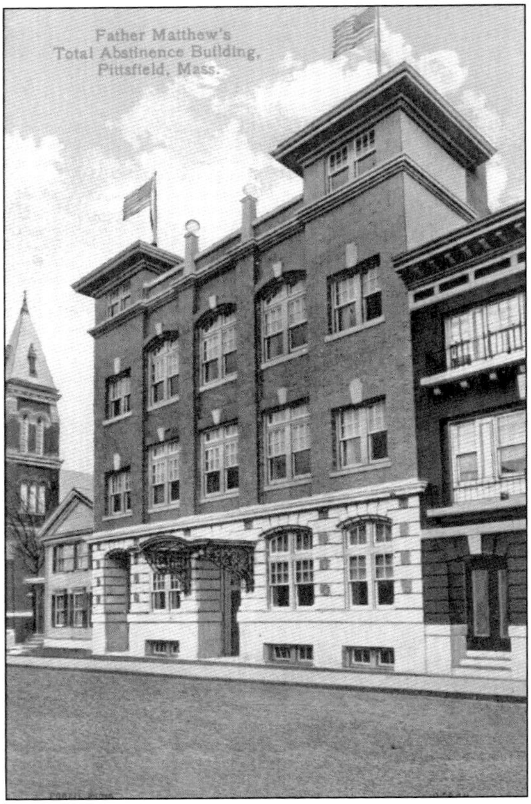

The Father Matthew Total Abstinence and Benevolent Society established its permanent headquarters on Melville Street in 1913. The building housed the Ladies' Aid Society, as well as religious, educational, social, and athletic facilities. In later years, the building housed the Catholic Youth Center, which merged with the Brigham Center in 2013. In 2015, the FMTA building was purchased by the adjoining Boys and Girls Club.

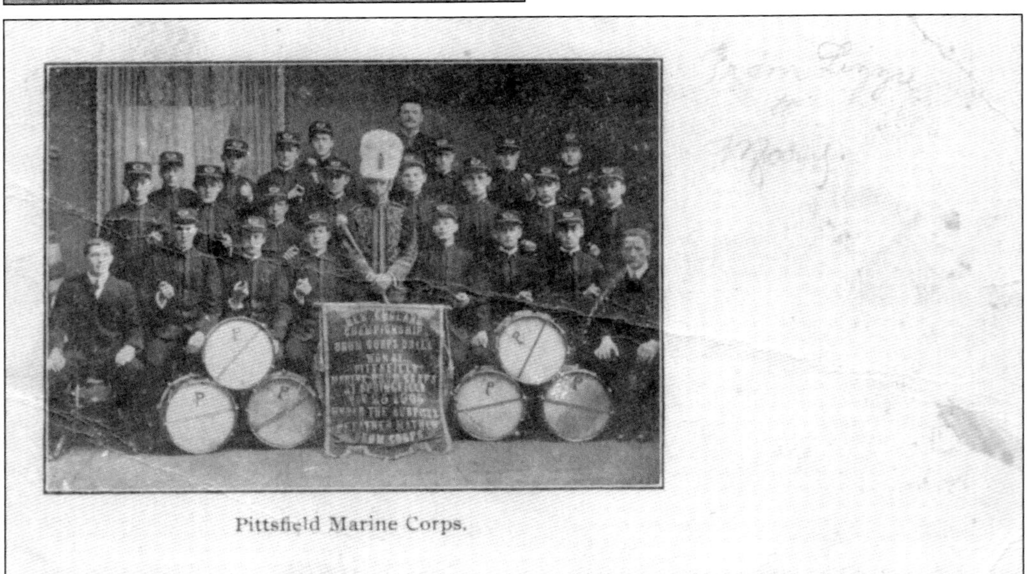

Members of the Pittsfield Marine Corps proudly displayed the banner they won at the New England Champion Drum Corps Drill on November 26, 1905. The Cathedral Drum Corps of Springfield extended the invitation to the Pittsfield Corps, which participated under the auspices of Father Matthew.

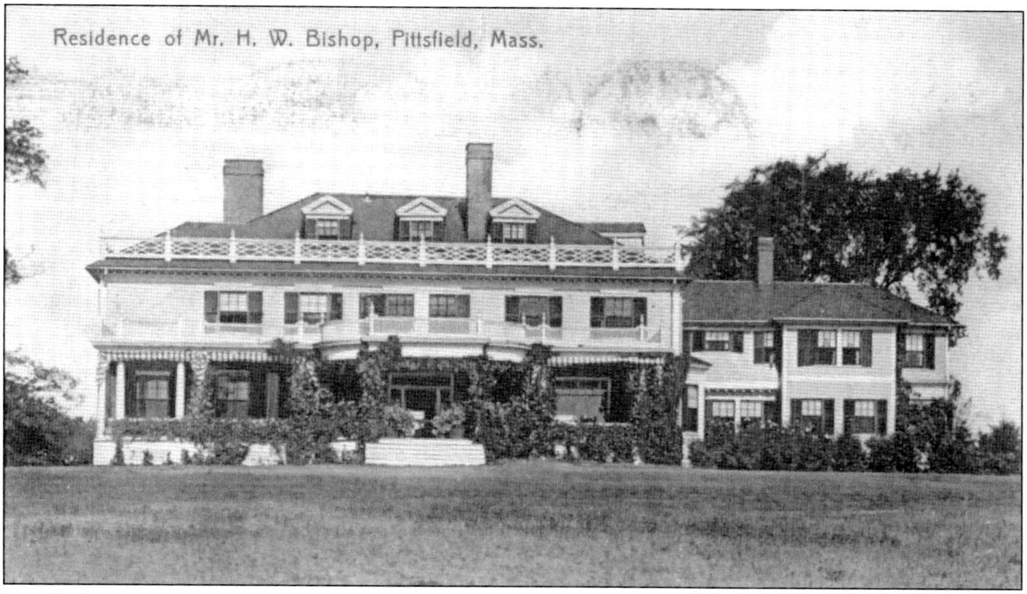

In 1897, this property was the site of the original Pittsfield Country Club. The nine-hole golf course was bordered by Dawes Avenue, Williams Street, Arlington Avenue, and Holmes Road. Two years later, the club moved, and the property was sold to Henry Bishop. He named his new estate Wiaka. Today, with Bishop's land subdivided, this area is often referred to as the Parkways.

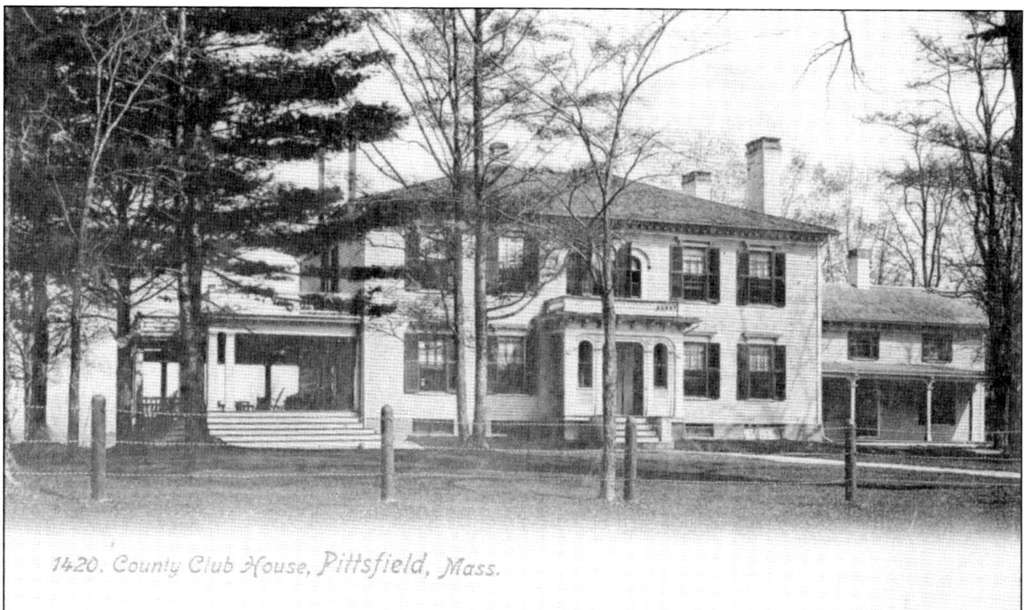

In 1899, the Pittsfield Country Club purchased Broadhall, a 230-acre farm on South Street. The golf course was expanded to 18 holes in 1917 and tennis courts built. The 18th-century house has been modified and expanded many times. Development of club facilities around Morewood Lake provided activities for both summer and winter sports enthusiasts. Members continue to enjoy the club's amenities today.

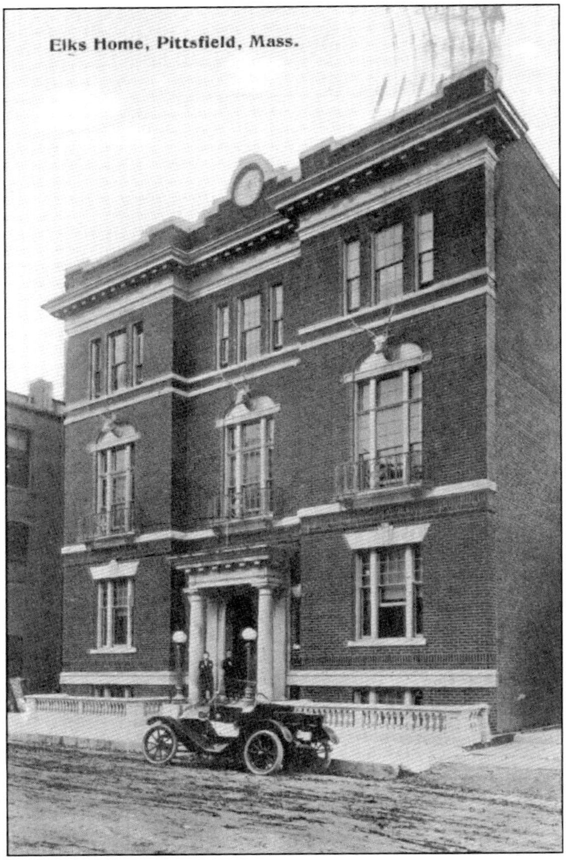

The Benevolent and Protective Order of Elks No. 272 was established in 1894. They built a lodge in 1910 at 27 Union Street and continue today as an active branch of the BPOE. Lodge members sometimes joke that their acronym means "Best People on Earth." Pittsfield, like many communities, once hosted many such fraternal organizations. Just a few survive today.

Pittsfield was the center of Masonic organizations in the region, and this elaborate building at 116 South Street served several lodges. Dedicated on May 4, 1914, the temple has a large ceremonial room on the second floor, a large public assembly hall, committee rooms, and a kitchen. In 1917, ten lodges used this temple, including the Mystic Lodge and Crescent Lodge. In 2014, the building was put up for sale.

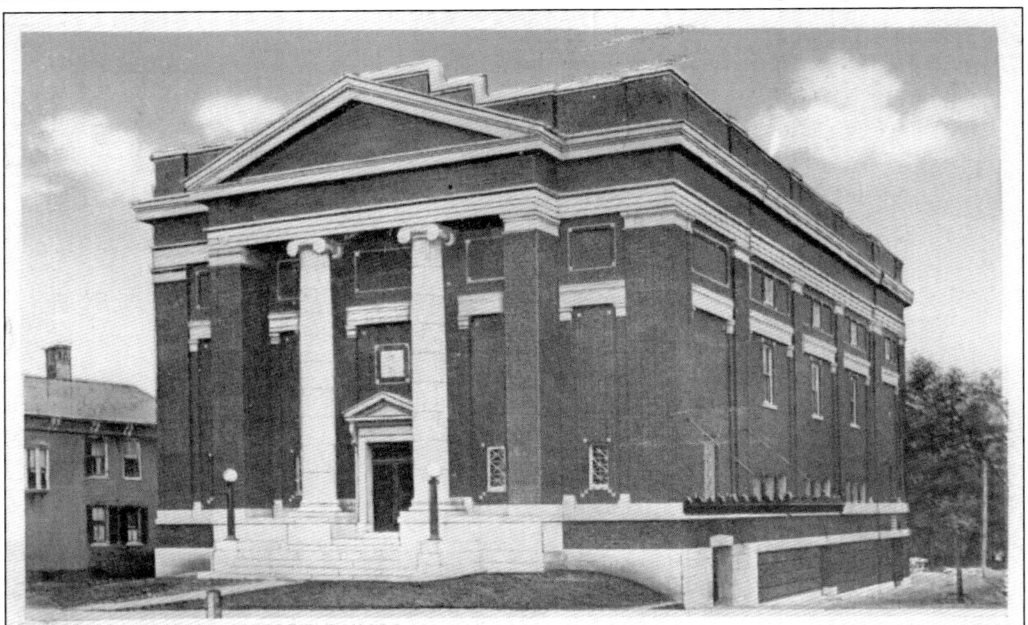

Eight

Restaurants and Lodging

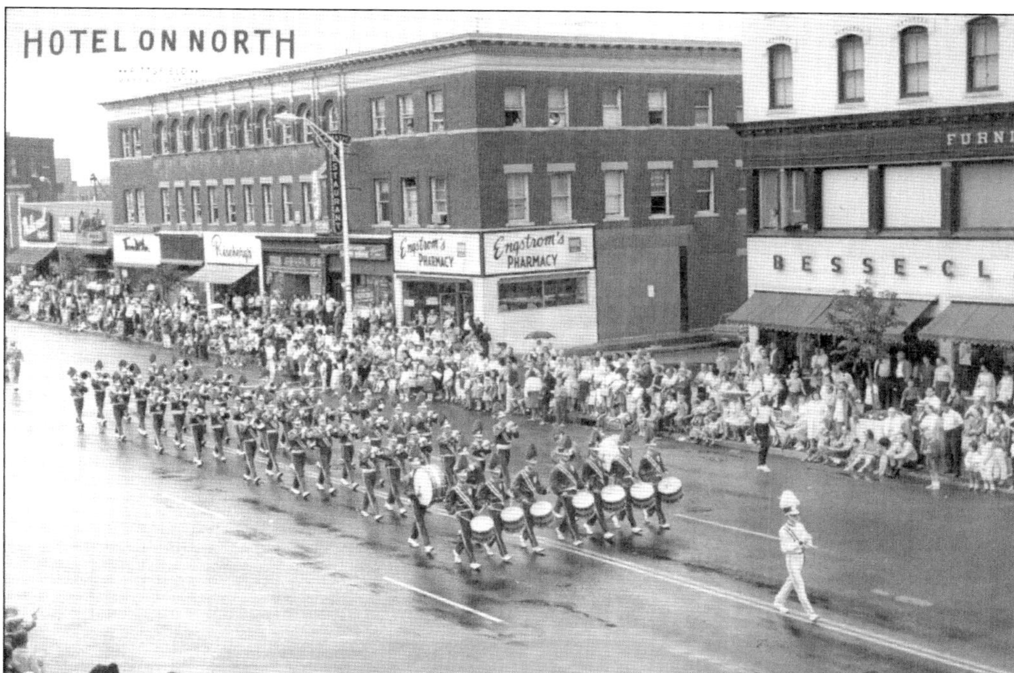

Pittsfield has long been a center of fine hotels and popular eateries. Hotel on North, a new 45-room boutique hotel, used this Fourth of July parade photograph from the 1960s for a postcard advertising their "rich blend of Berkshire roots and cosmopolitan style." The hotel at 297 North Street is a combination of two historic buildings, including the Besse-Clarke department store seen in the background.

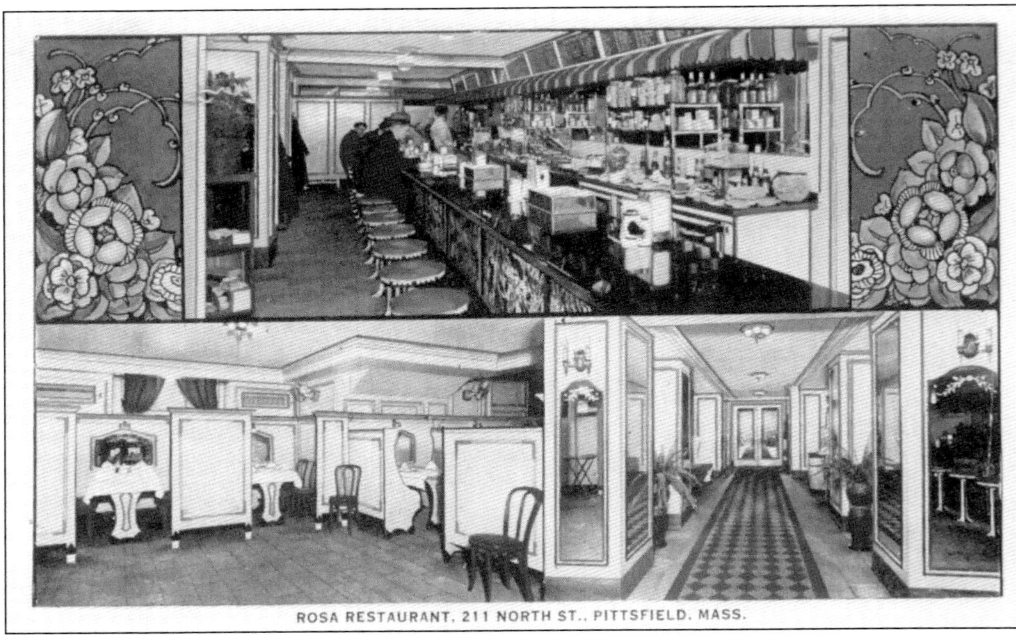

The stylish Rosa Restaurant first appeared in the 1936 Pittsfield City Directory and was located in the American Hotel at 211 North Street on the corner of Columbus Avenue.

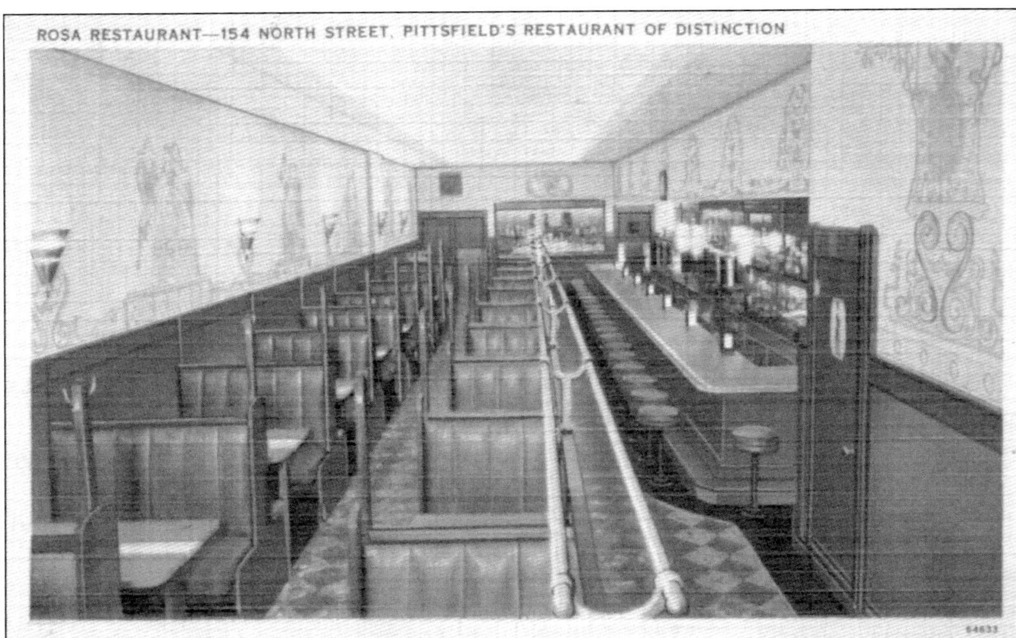

In 1941, when the American Hotel no longer existed, the Rosa Restaurant moved to 154 North Street to occupy space previously used by the New Berkshire Lunch and later by the Waldorf Lunch. By 2015, the eatery listed near 154 North Street is Pancho's Mexican Restaurant.

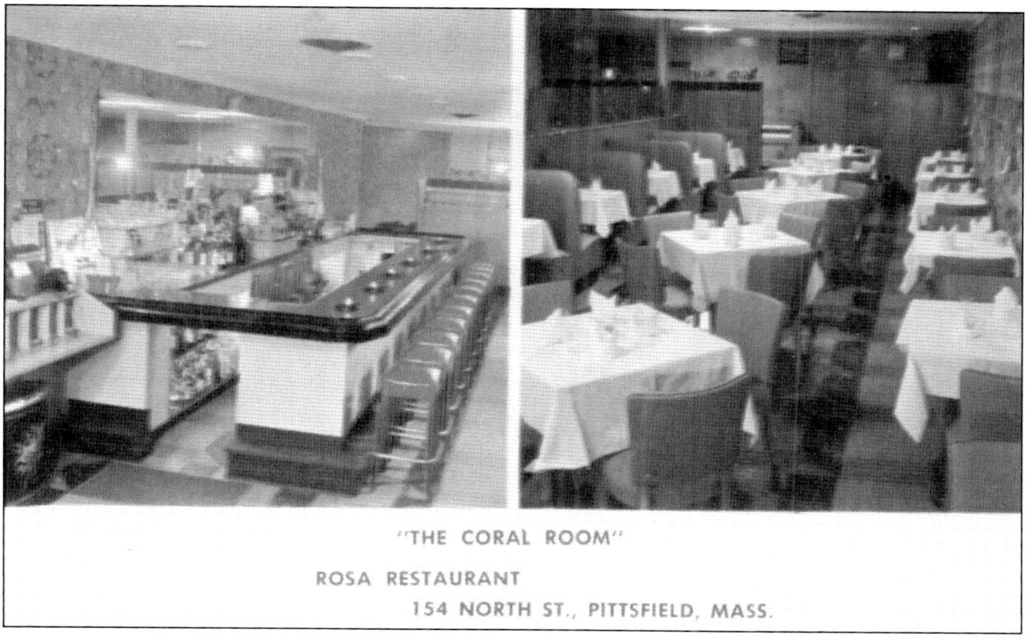

The Rosa Restaurant continued operating into the 1960s, adding the Coral Room dining area. The owners expressed their philosophy on the reverse side of the postcard: "Eating and drinking should always mean more to us than the mere satisfying of physical needs. We hope you have found here that warmth of welcome . . . which makes for a fuller life."

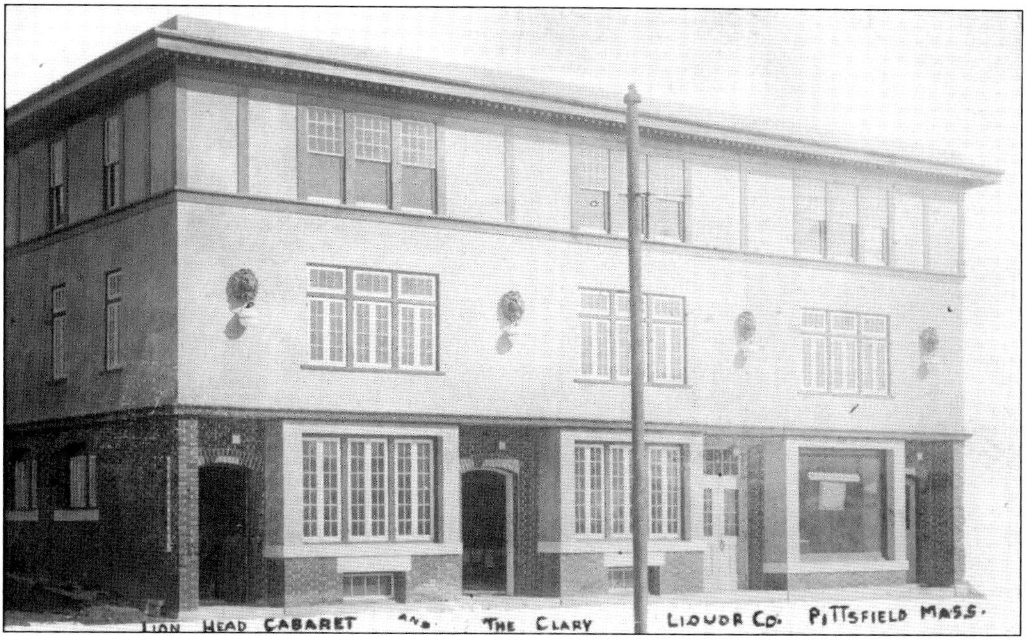

The Clary Liquor Company at 198–204 West Street was open for about 15 years in the early 1900s. They advertised "Family Wines, Liquors, Cordials, Ales and Lagers at the lowest price." Alongside the package store was the Lion Head Cabaret, whose proprietor, R.E. Clary, touted his closeness to Union Station as being convenient "for a beer and a bite."

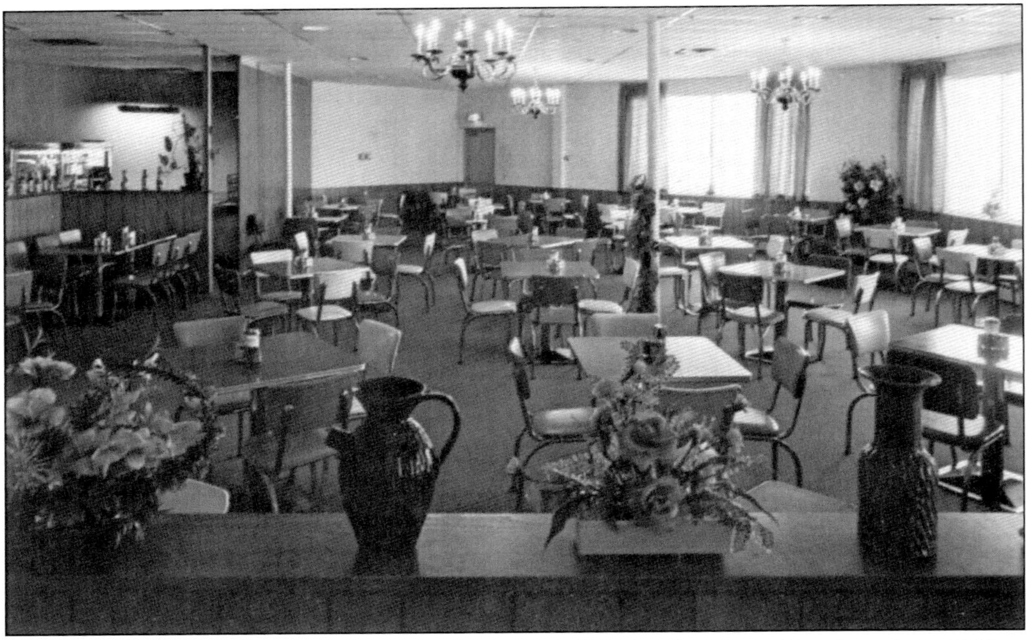

The Busy Bee Restaurant on West Street was operated by the Gamberoni brothers from 1927 to 1960. This popular family restaurant featured Italian food. A new proprietor, John Dobrustsky, took over the business, eventually moving the restaurant to the Allendale Shopping Center in Coltsville in 1967 (pictured here).

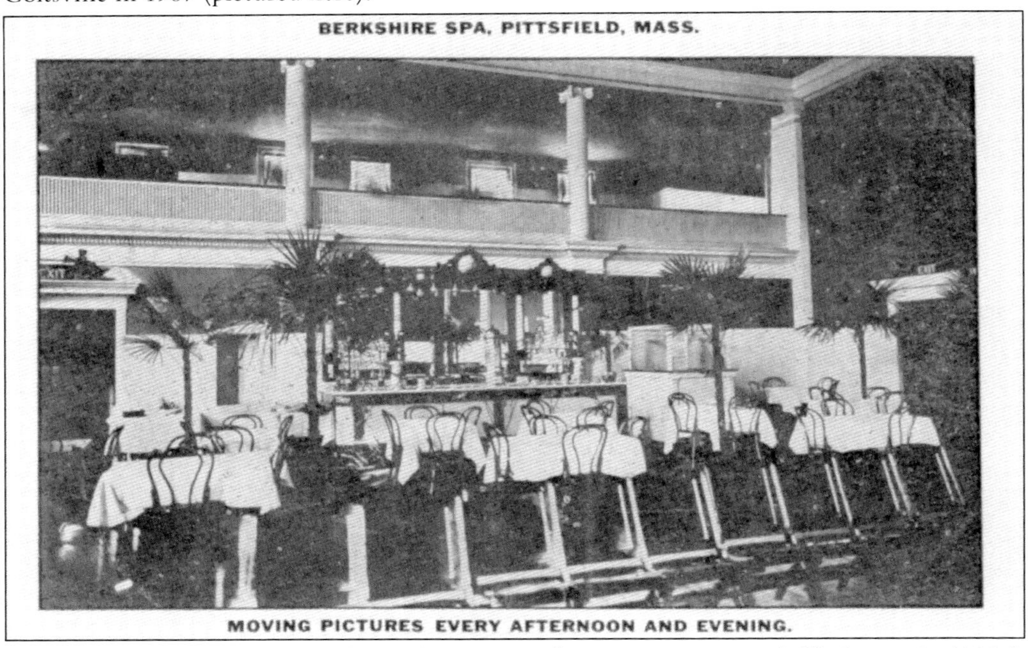

The Berkshire Spa Theater was located at 311 North Street opposite Melville Street. In 1916, it advertised afternoon and evening shows with "Picture Projection that is perfect." The cost for a matinee was 5¢ and an evening show 10¢. Patrons sat at cloth-covered tables among potted palm trees while enjoying refreshments.

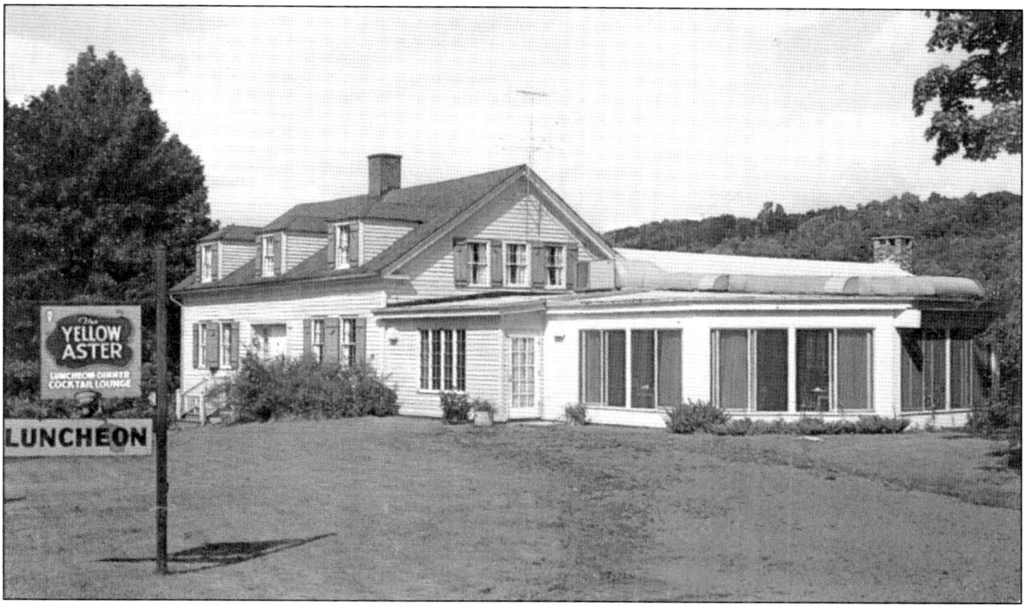

The Yellow Aster, a 1780 restored farmhouse at 1015 South Street, was first owned by Katherine Smith. In 1927, she added a restaurant at the rear of her home, running the Yellow Aster Tea Room until 1944. In 1955, restaurateur Nicholas Makes bought the business, managing the Yellow Aster with his wife, Marion, until 1984. The South Mountain Grill, the Asters, and Mazzeo's have operated at that same location.

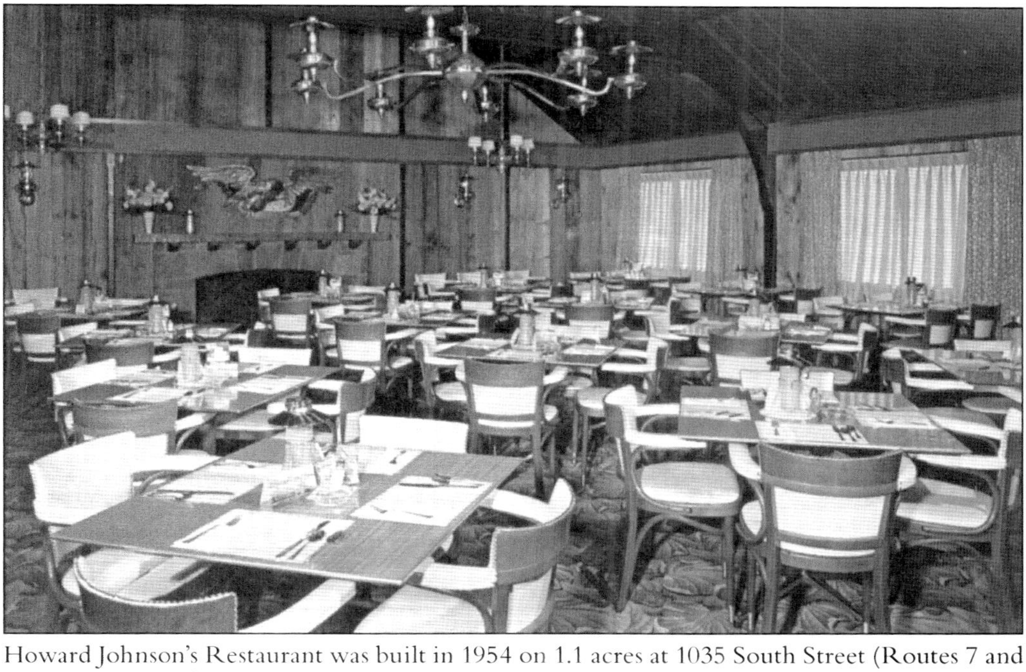

Howard Johnson's Restaurant was built in 1954 on 1.1 acres at 1035 South Street (Routes 7 and 20). It was part of the largest restaurant chain in the United States in the 1960s and 1970s. The buildings were known for their orange roofs and cupolas. This restaurant became the Dakota in 1984 until it closed in 2013. It is now the Enso Asian Bistro.

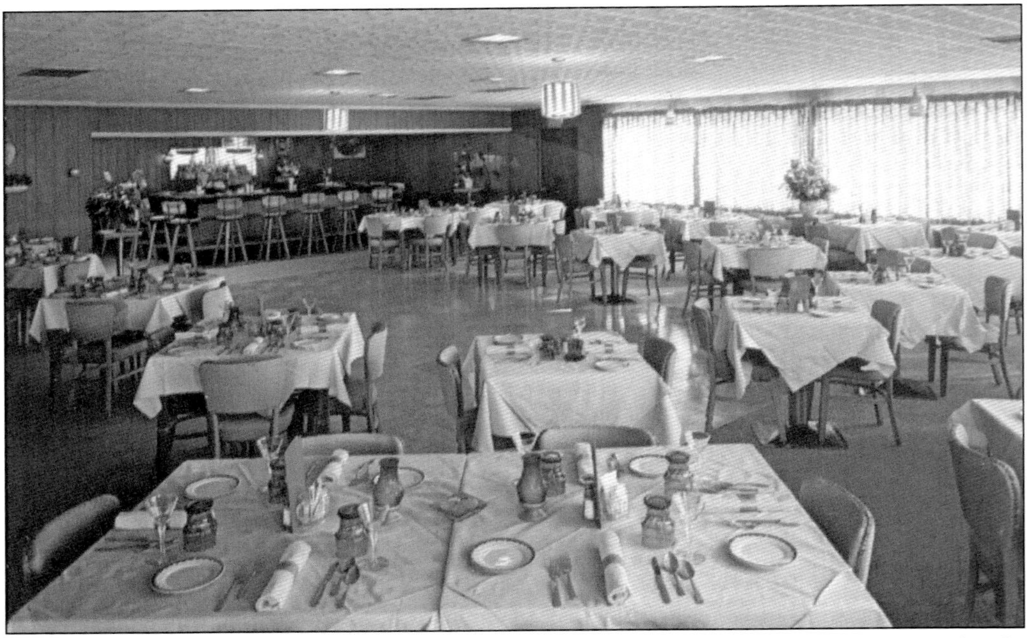

The Holly K Restaurant on West Housatonic Street was purchased in 1971 by Paul and Sally Bock. They renamed it the Coach Lite, and it became a very popular 250-seat gourmet restaurant. Paul Bock was an accomplished chef who was known for his elaborate ice carvings, artistic pulled-sugar creations, and miniature chocolate pianos. The Coach Lite was sold in 1987 and is now home to Fontaine's Auction Gallery.

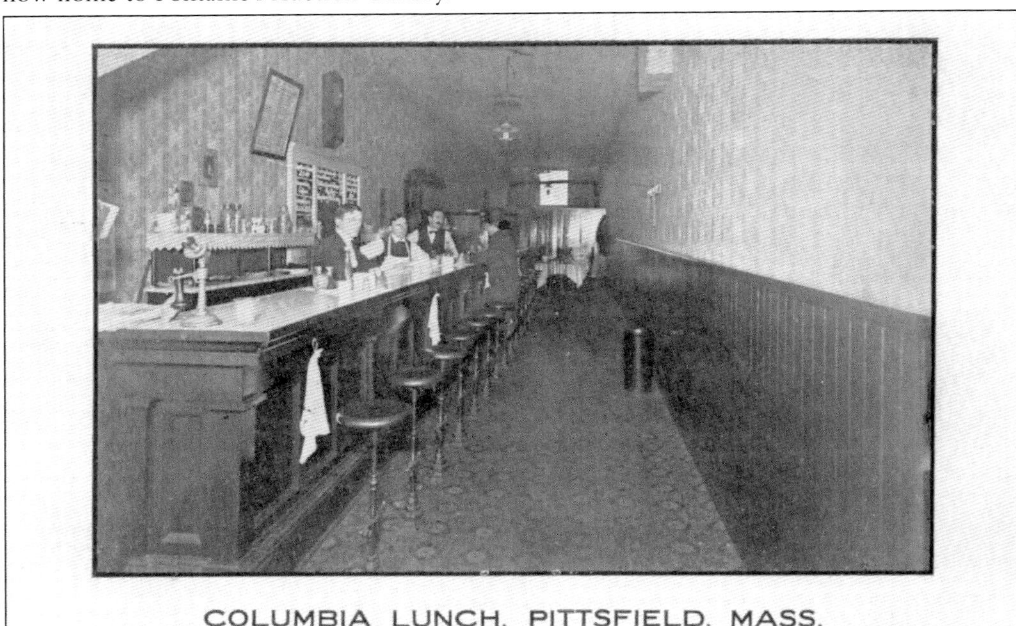

The Columbia Lunch opened for service in 1905 at 44 North Street. In 1915, it moved to 237 North Street and finally to 644 North Street in 1925. Proprietor Joseph H. Kessler used this postcard to commemorate the Columbia Lunch's fifth anniversary in 1910.

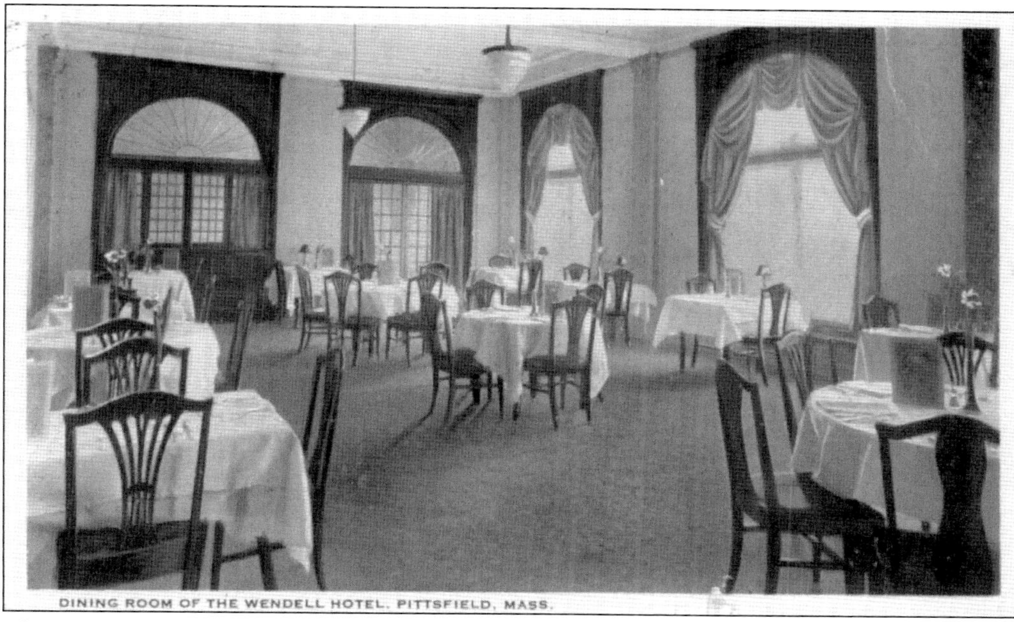

The restaurant at the Wendell was the scene of the hotel's lavish opening night celebration. It was attended by hundreds of dignitaries, who were served consommé, oysters, lamb chops, lobster salad, wine, lemonade, and coffee, all of which were listed in French on the menu. The opening night event was a benefit for both the Pittsfield Kindergarten Association and the Berkshire Home for Aged Women.

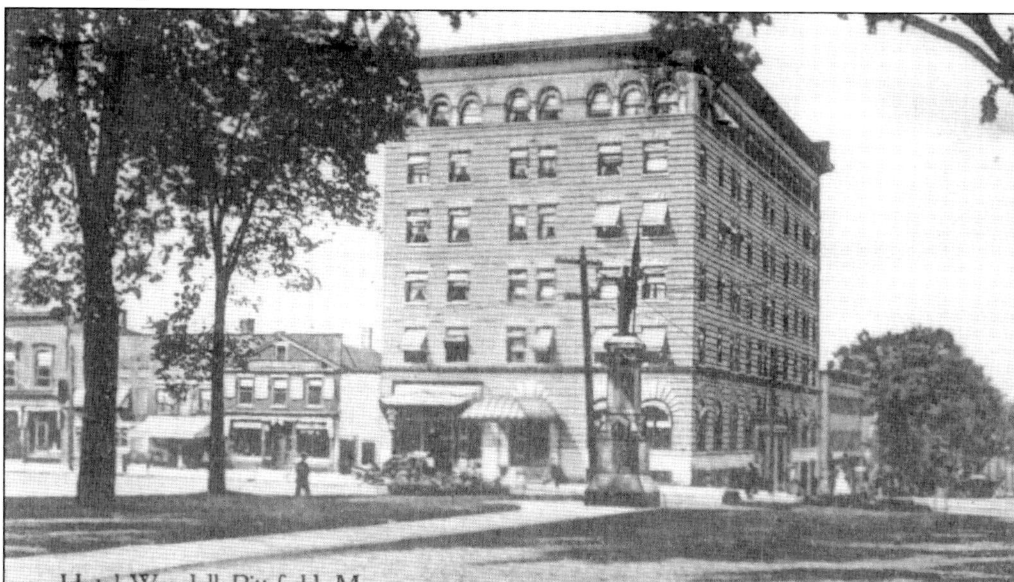

The Hotel Wendell was built in 1897 on the site of the United States Hotel, at the corner of West and South Streets. It was named in honor of Jacob Wendell for his role in founding Pittsfield in the 18th century. The cost to build and furnish the yellow brick and limestone building, seen here, was $125,000. In 1929, the owners added 160 rooms, including a ballroom, cafeteria, solarium, and five shops.

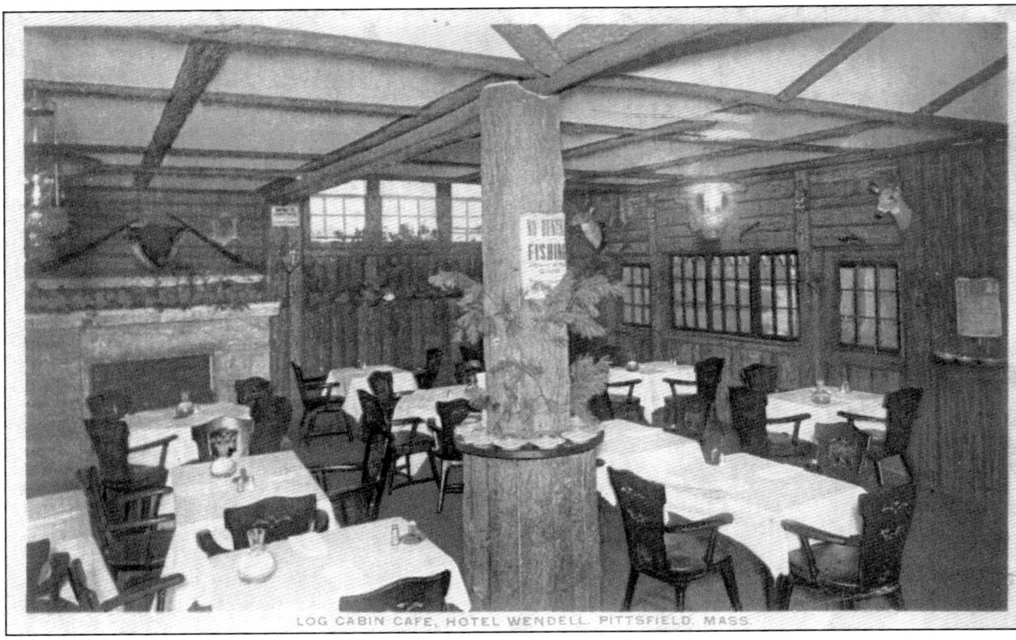

The Hotel Wendell was the site of many special community gatherings. One such banquet, in 1916, involved the bankers of Berkshire County who gathered to participate in the first transcontinental telephone call. The first question was reported to be, "How is the weather out there in San Francisco?" Listeners in Pittsfield insisted they could hear the ocean.

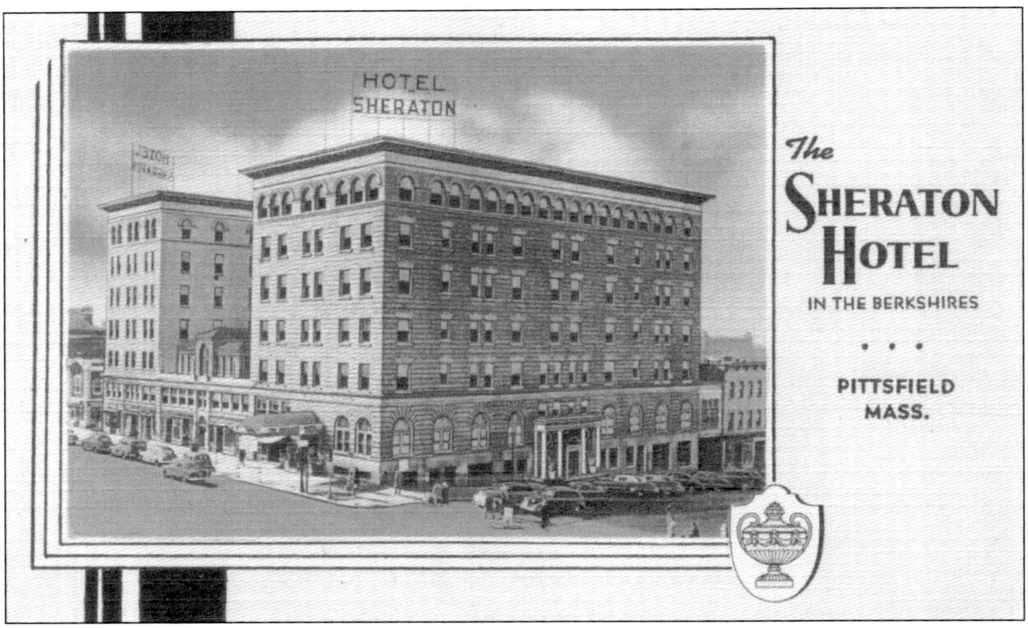

In 1944, the Hotel Wendell was sold to the Sheraton Hotel Corporation, briefly becoming the Wendell-Sheraton. In 1954, it was sold to the Sherwood Hotel Corporation for $1 million. Again known as the Wendell, it had almost 300 guest rooms. In 1965, this historic landmark was demolished to make room for the Berkshire Commons and the Colonial Hilton Inn.

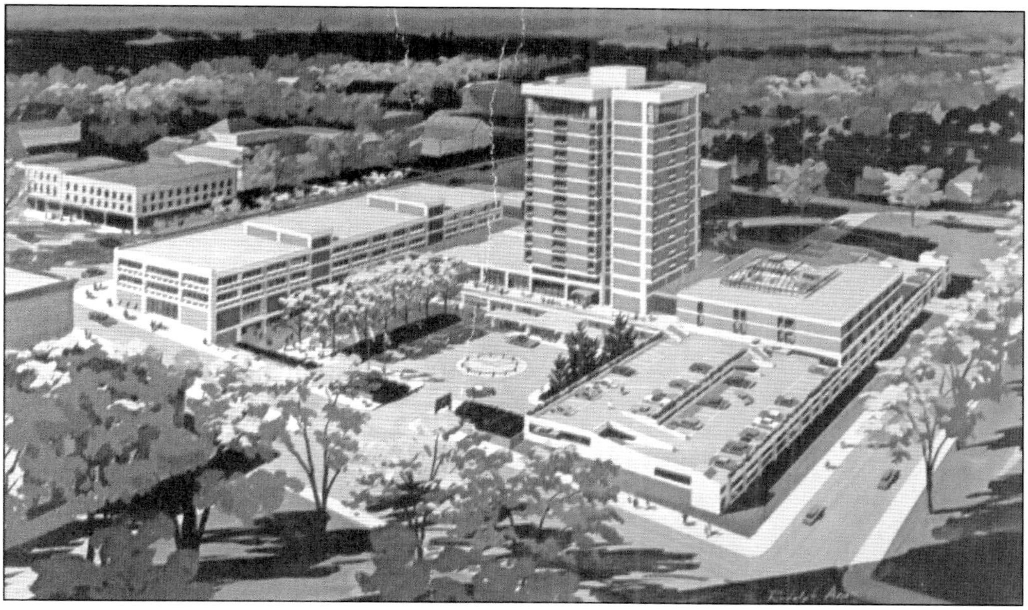

The Colonial Hilton Inn opened in 1971, part of the new Berkshire Commons on the corner of West and South Streets. The hotel featured 14 stories, 176 rooms, a top-floor cocktail lounge, restaurants, banquet facilities, a large parking garage, and a glass-domed swimming pool. It is now the Crowne Plaza Hotel-Berkshires. The Berkshire Commons also includes offices and retail shops.

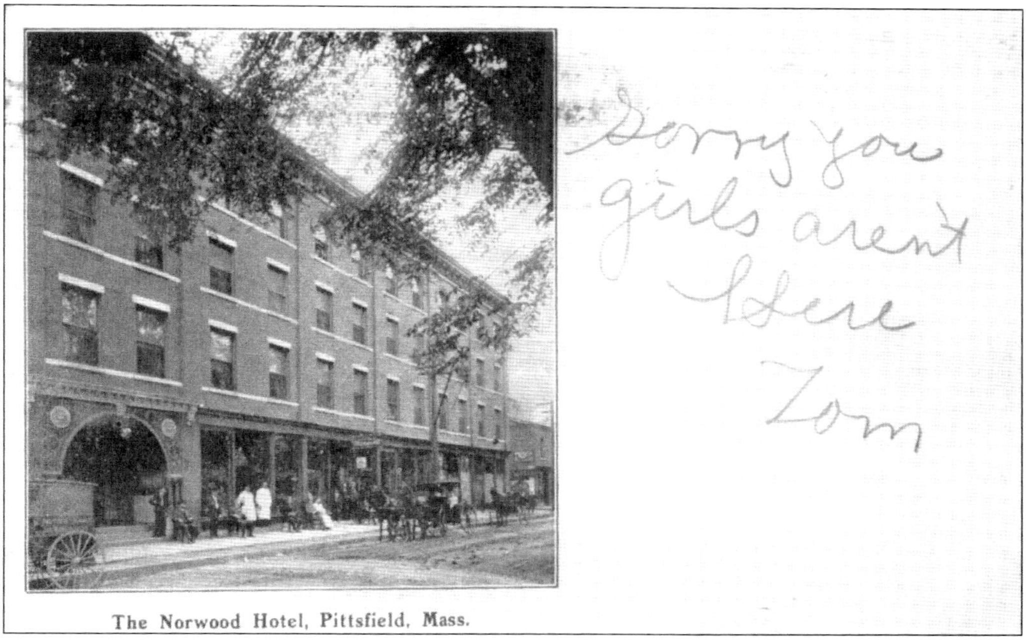

In 1902, the Norwood Hotel took the place of the New Burbank Hotel at 50 Summer Street. The Norwood offered newly renovated spacious rooms with steam heat and electric lights. It also offered a "superior table, moderate prices and special rates to permanent guests." The site is now a parking lot.

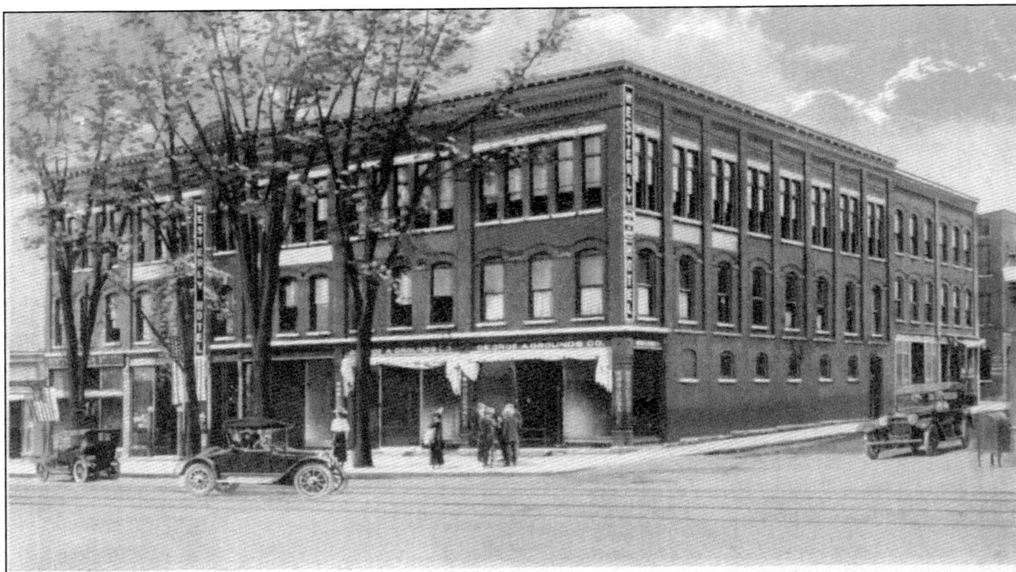

WESTERLY HOTEL, PITTSFIELD, MASS.

Located at 108 West Street, the Westerly Hotel delighted visitors for just $1 a room, with modern amenities such as "Shower Baths." Visitors were near the local theaters and shopping district. The Westerly prided itself on being only "Sixty-nine Seconds from Union Station." The Westerly became the Hotel Pittsfield in 1938 and the Pickwick Hotel in 1940; the area is now lawn near the headquarters of Greylock Credit Union.

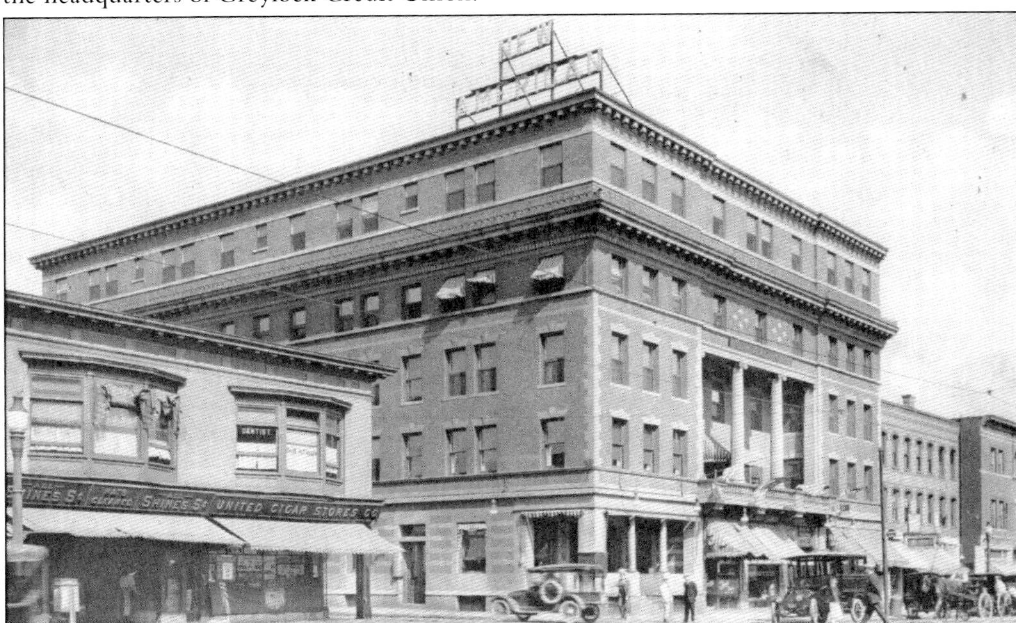

THE NEW AMERICAN HOUSE. PITTSFIELD, MASS.

The New American House, on the corner of North Street and Columbus Avenue, went through several changes since it opened in 1865. It was enlarged in 1888, then partially rebuilt in brick and limestone. In 1911, the hotel added a fifth story and more modern conveniences. The large hotel was demolished in 1937 to make way for retail stores. This card dates to the 1920s.

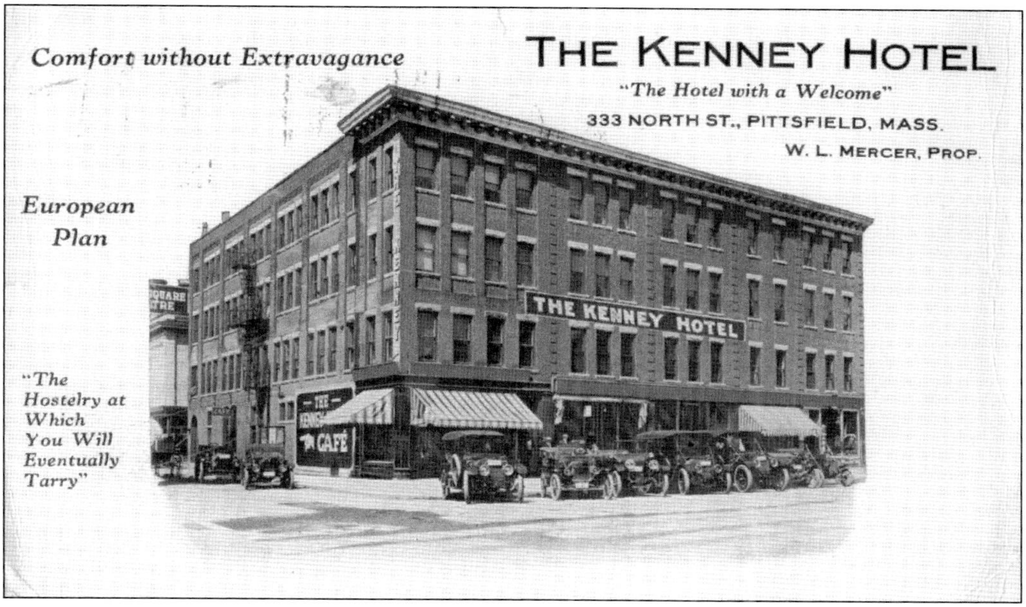

The Kenny Hotel opened in 1905 at 333–335 North Street. It was owned by Walter Mercer and grew out of a modest restaurant called the Arlington. In 1915, an advertisement proclaimed it the "Hotel with a Welcome," boasted of being "First-Class Café Connected" and "Comfort without extravagance." It is now apartments.

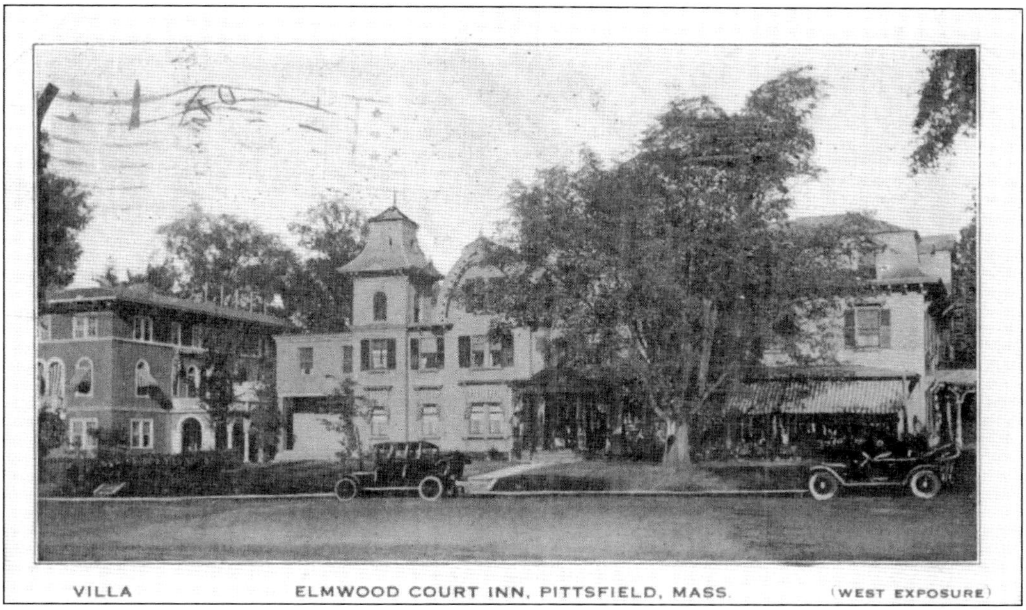

Built in 1853, this inn was originally the home of Edward and Caroline Learned and their 12 children. Following Edward's death in 1882, the estate was divided. Part was rented to Miss Hall's School. Eventually, Florence Learned opened the mansion as Elmwood Court Inn, with "a table well known for its excellence." The inn was divided into apartments in the 1920s and burned in 2011, leaving only a vacant lot.

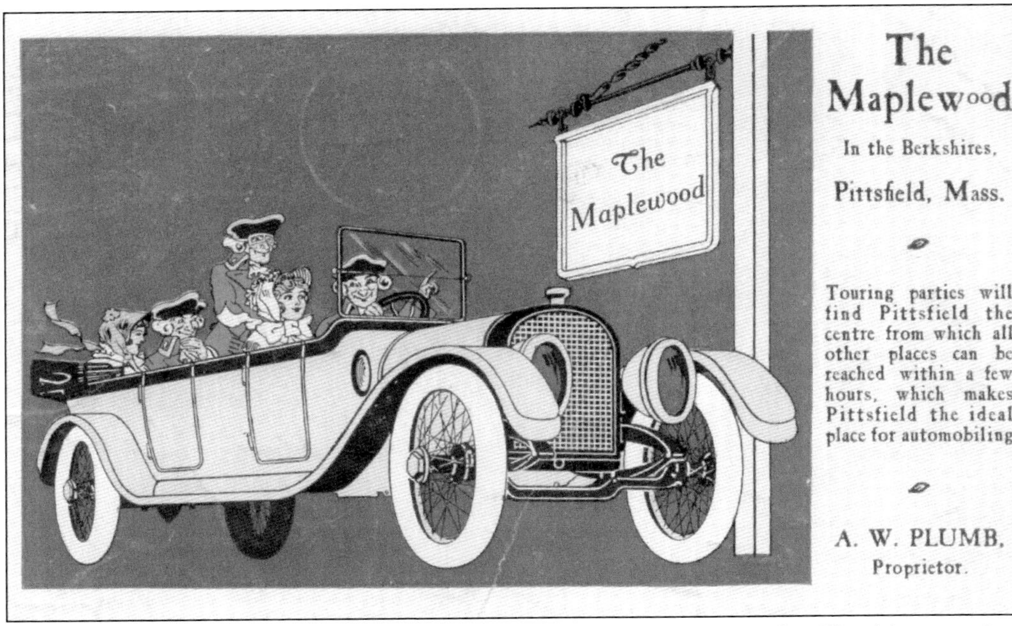

The Maplewood Hotel was established in 1886 to serve summer visitors. Arthur Plumb's renovations and additions to the former Maplewood School complex created "a delightful summer hotel with a fastidious clientele, a homelike atmosphere, and an unsurpassed table." In 1916, Plumb advertised that new horse cars provided transportation between the railroad station and the hotel. The Maplewood closed in 1931. Soon after, much of the complex was razed.

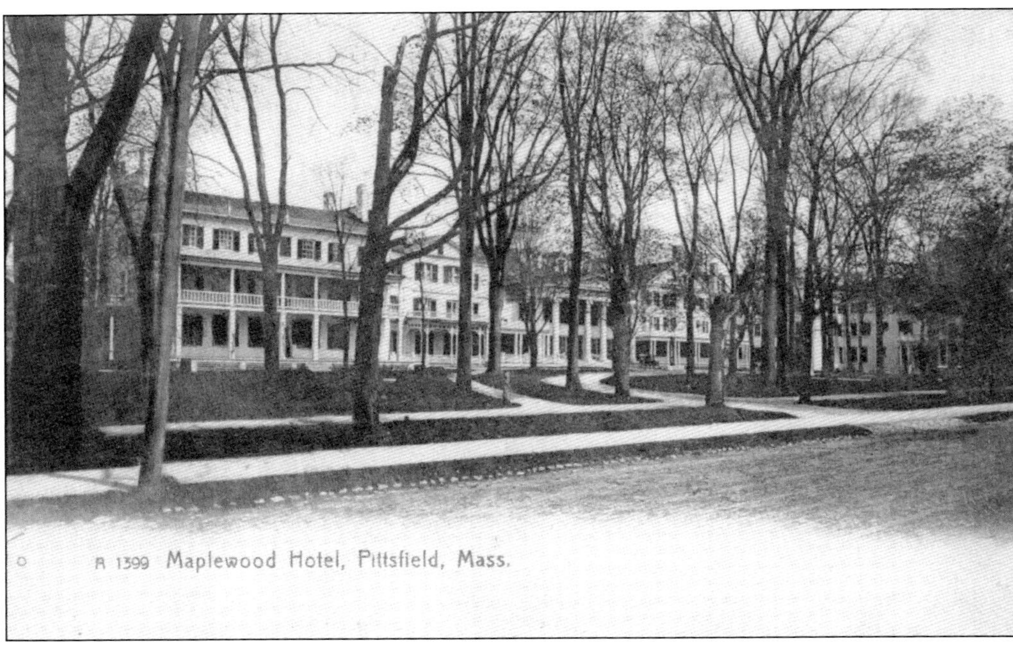

The Maplewood Hotel is seen here in its heyday around 1900. The surviving section of the complex, seen to the right in this view, has been converted into condominiums. The remainder of the site is now home to modern office buildings.

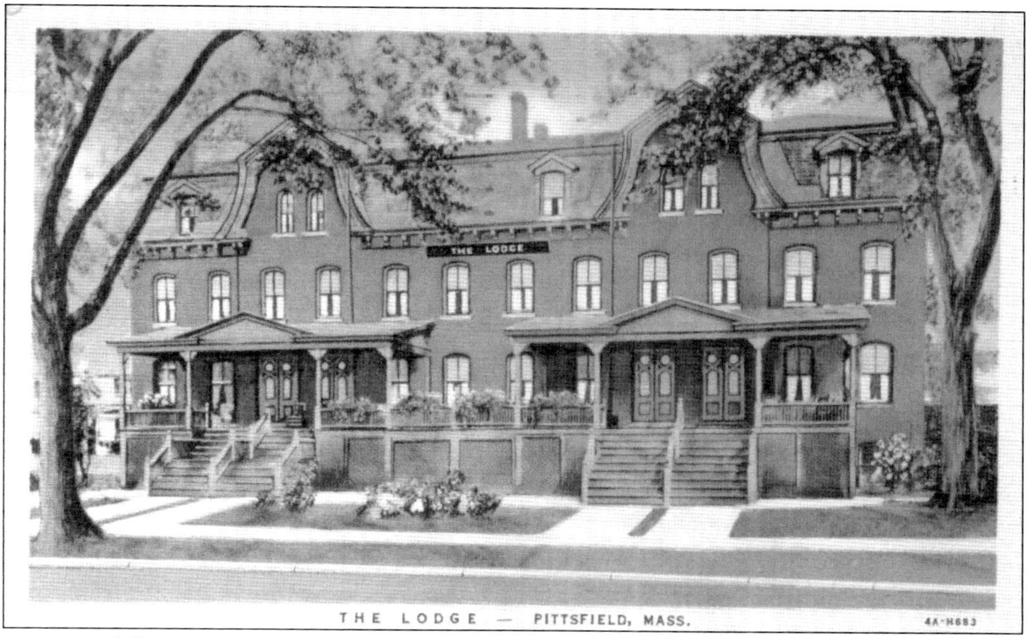

The Wendell Avenue Lodge, owned by Cora P. Savage in 1930, was located at 102 Wendell Avenue. She advertised her inn as "a home away from home on a quiet elm-shaded residential street. Near churches, theatres, library and art Museum . . . Elevation 1200 feet." Savage catered to permanent and transient guests. The lodge is now an apartment building.

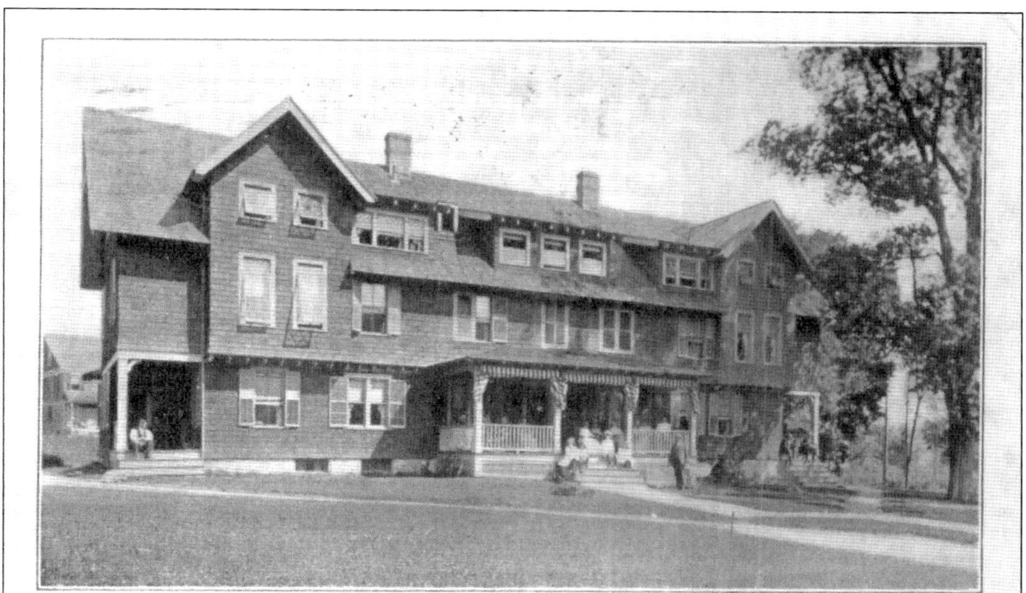

Woodlawn Inn, at 162 Woodlawn Avenue, was operated by Emma Carson from 1904 to 1929. The building, without its front porch, still stands. It is now apartments.

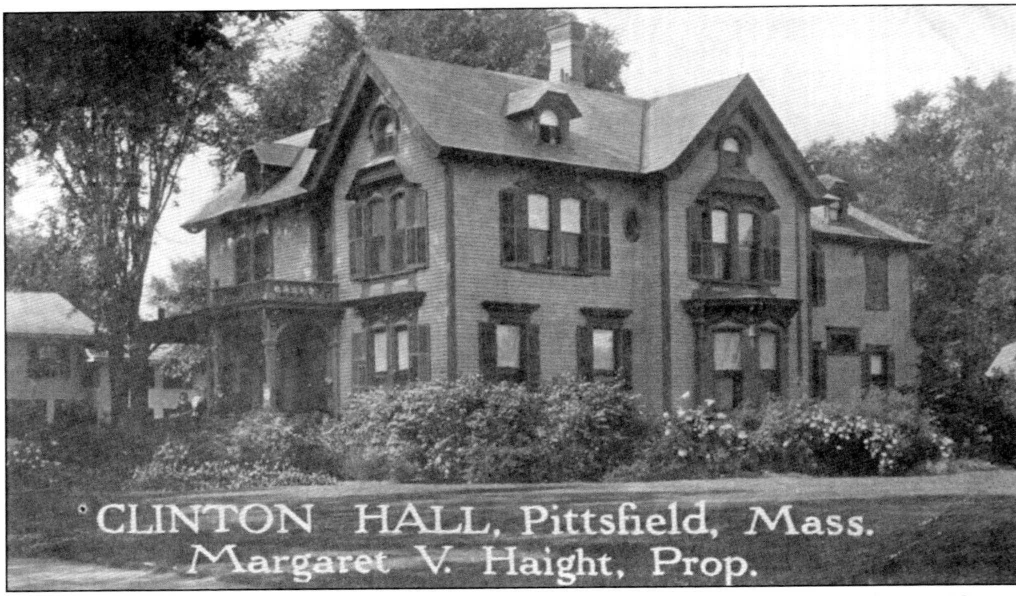

Another example of the small inns and hotels that dotted Pittsfield's neighborhoods was Clinton Hall, located at 192 South Street, at the corner of Clinton Avenue. It was operated by Margaret V. Haight from 1921 to 1937. That location is now the site of several retail shops and offices.

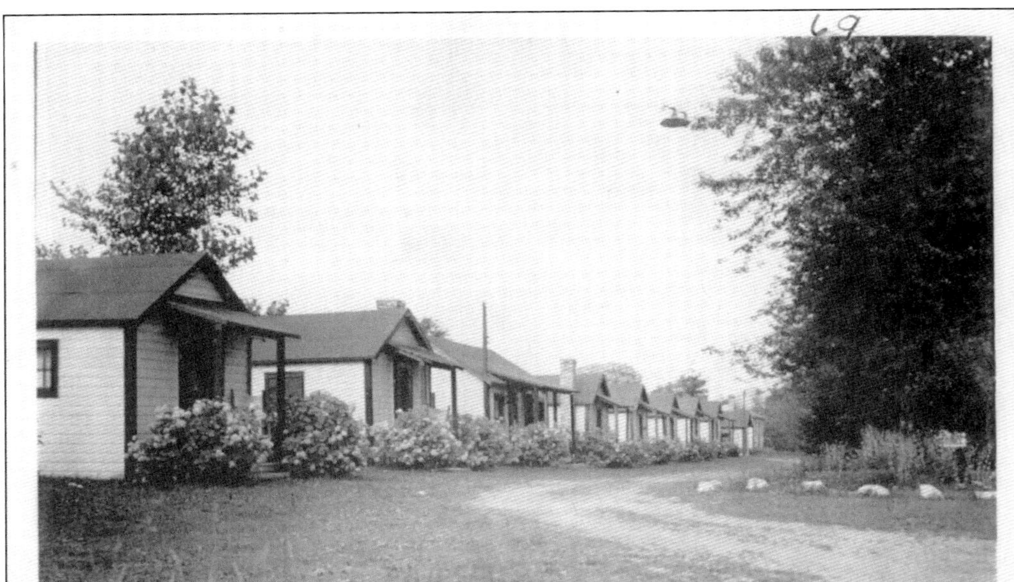

These tourist cabins were purchased by Major and Catherine Fitch in the mid-1940s as part of a complex of travel services on West Housatonic Street. The Fitchs operated a garage, the Miss Pittsfield Diner, and the 11 cabins, which were replaced by a new motel in 1961. The historic diner, the original gas station, and the motel have since been replaced by a mini-mall and modern gas station.

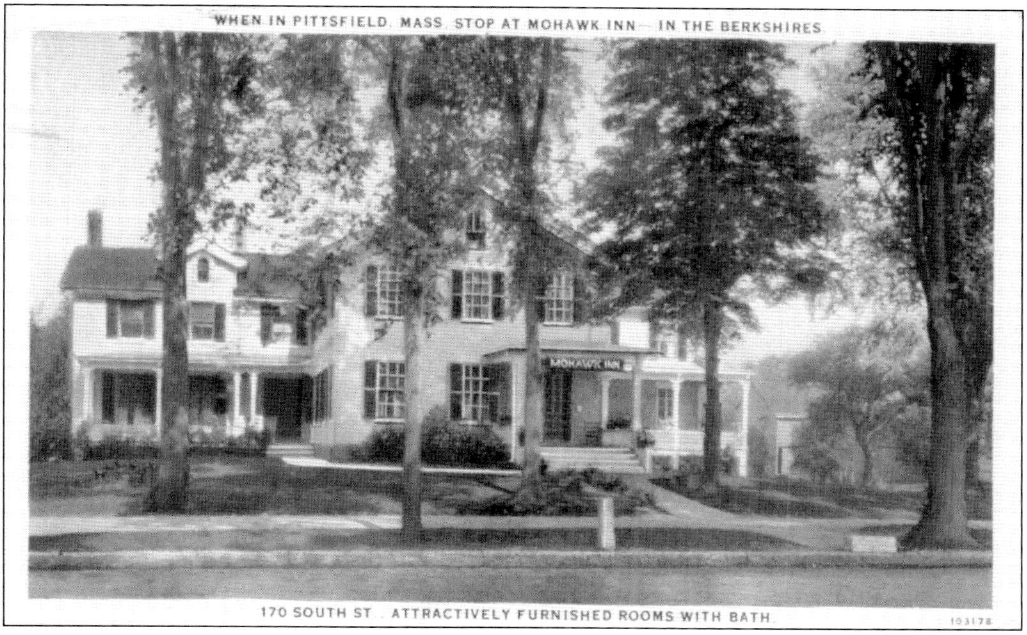

The Mohawk Inn was located at 170 South Street. In 1928, it was owned by Edwin and Abigail Killian, who resided there with their three children. Edwin worked at General Electric, so it was likely that Abigail ran the guesthouse. In this 1930 postcard, the Killians advertised attractively furnished rooms with baths. The site is now a parking lot next to an automotive tire store.

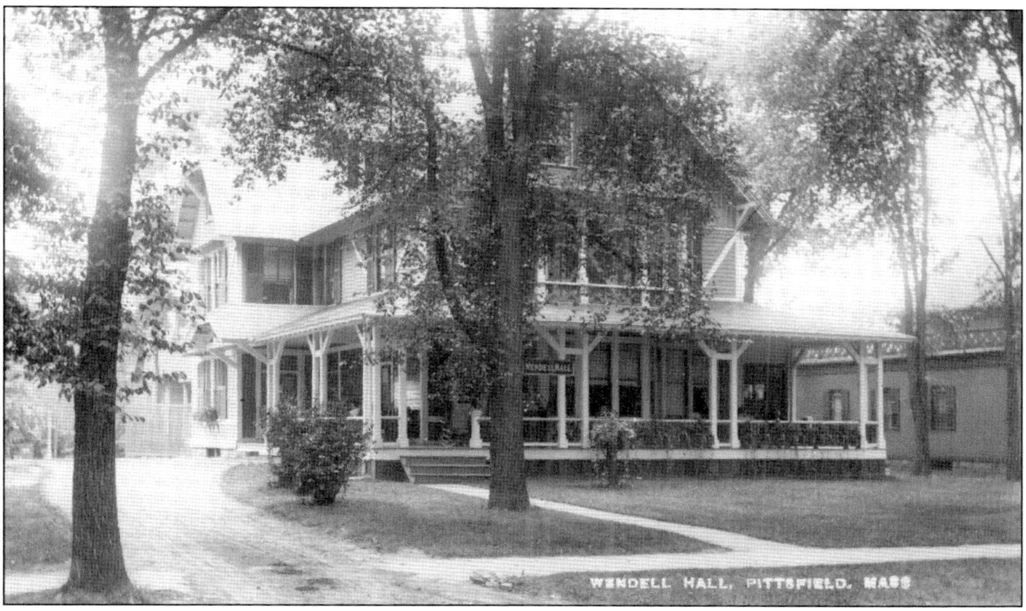

Boardinghouses were another type of accommodations available in Pittsfield. Located at 31 Wendell Avenue, Wendell Hall advertised itself as having "all the latest modern improvements" and as being "the largest and finest boarding house to be found in the city." Prices varied over years, but at one point, a stay cost $1.50 a day or $6 to $10 per week. In 1925, the proprietor was Morgan Mapley.

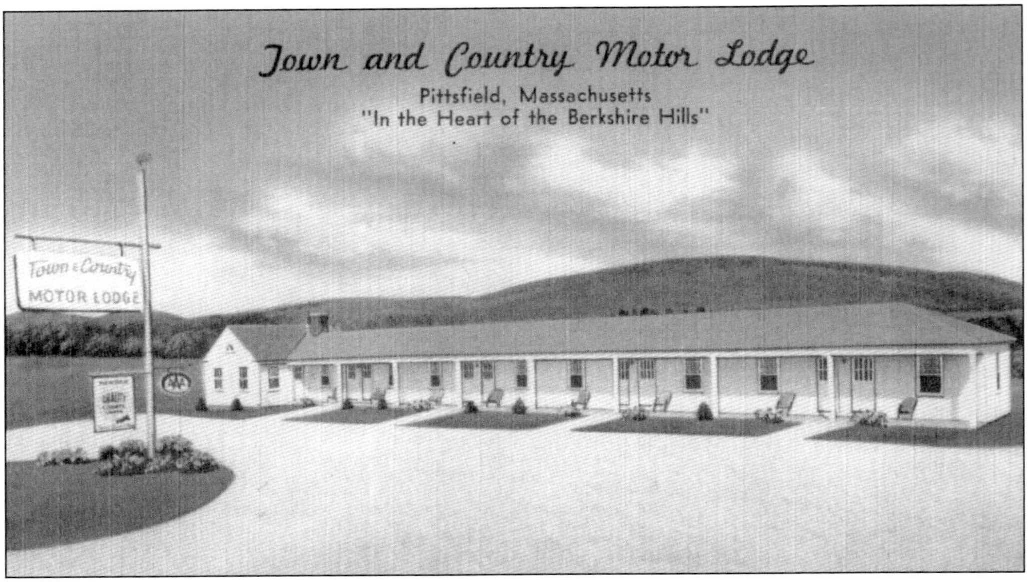

The motor lodge, pictured here around 1952, was located at 1350 West Housatonic Street (Route 20) and advertised that it was three miles west of the business district. Visitors slept on Beautyrest mattresses and found restaurants nearby. Owners George E. and Doris E. Burleigh later expanded the motel to two single-story wings. By the time the motel was razed in 2001, it was known as the Huntsman.

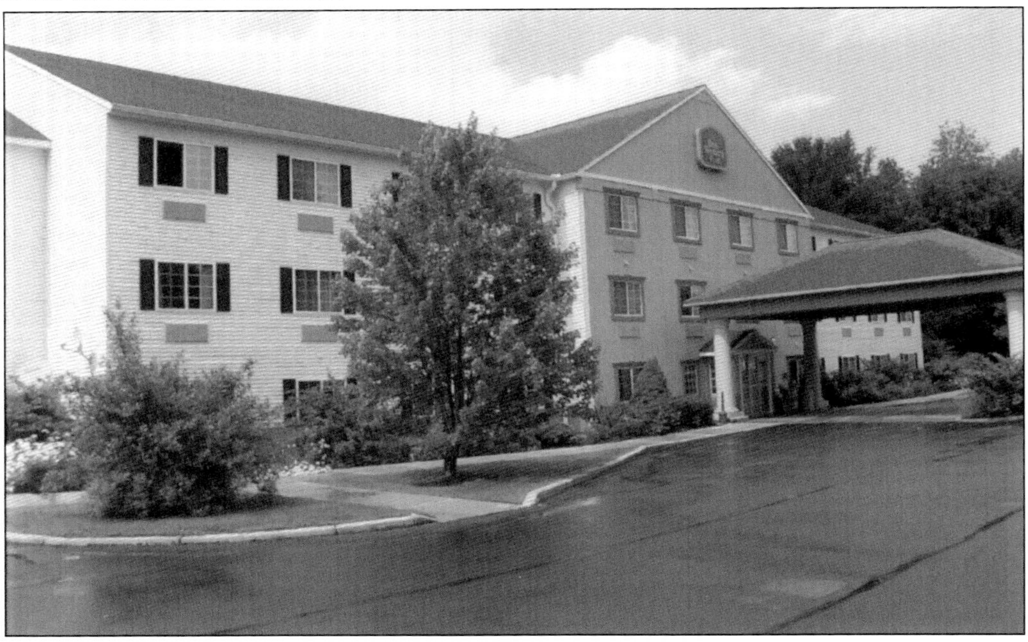

When the Huntsman was demolished in 2001, a new three-story Ramada Inn was constructed on the site. Ramada managed the hotel until December 2011, when Best Western assumed ownership. The renovated structure was renamed BW Berkshire Hills Inn and Suites. Now, guests at 1350 West Housatonic Street are served a complementary hot breakfast and no longer have to find restaurants nearby.

Nine

Disruptions and Disasters

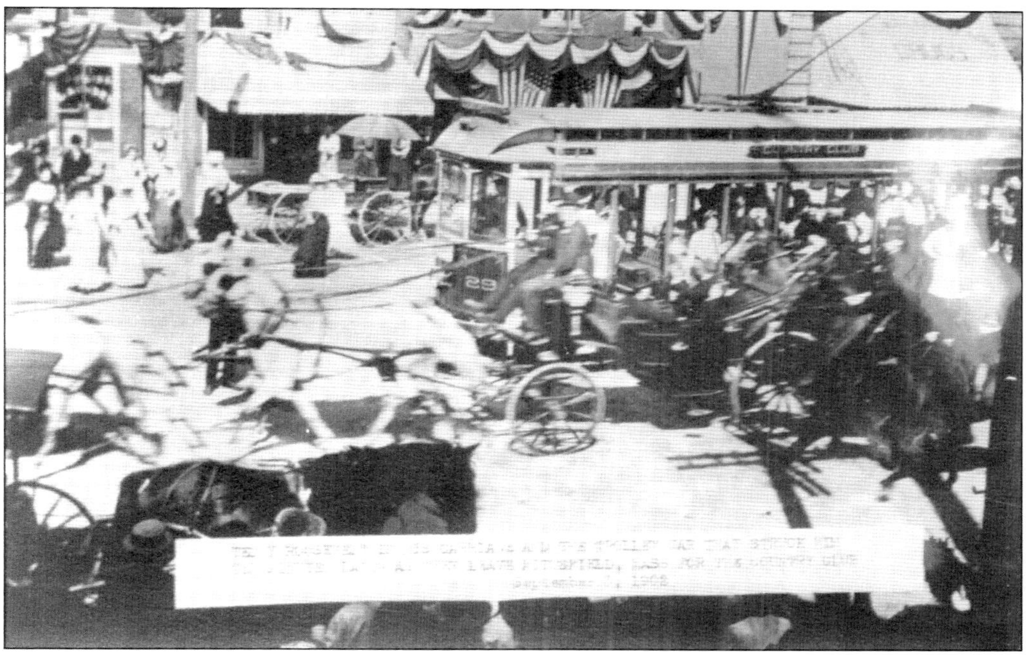

Events occurred during the beginning of the 20th century that disrupted the idyllic nature of Berkshire's county seat. Pres. Theodore Roosevelt, following a September 3, 1902, speech in downtown Pittsfield, was injured when Trolley No. 29 struck his horse-drawn carriage as both raced along South Street. Secret Service agent William Craig died, Roosevelt was injured, and a horse was killed. The Rough Rider, bloody and swollen, continued on his speaking tour.

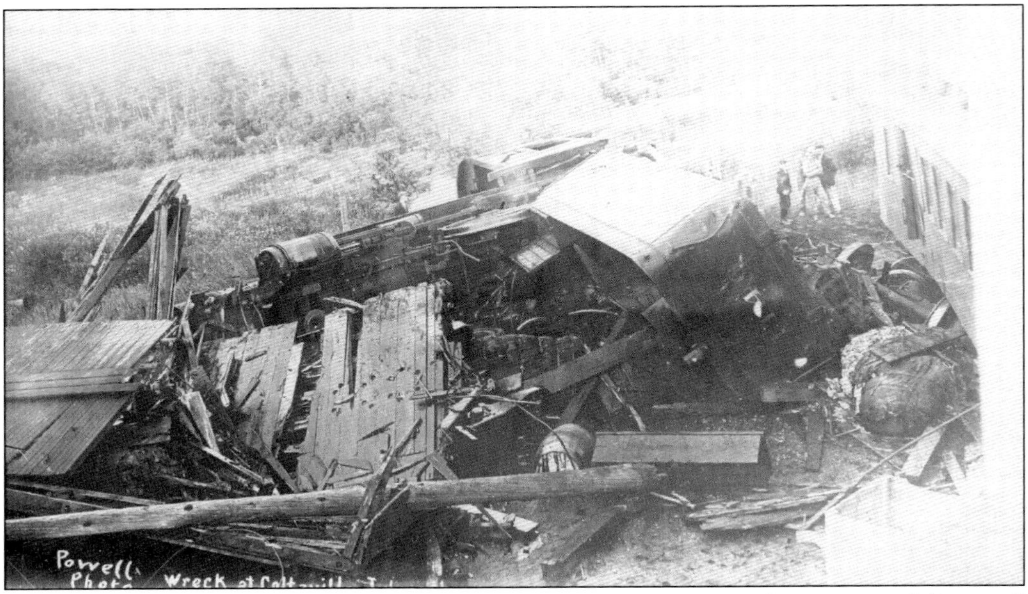

Pittsfield photographer Matthew H. Powell (1869–1922) recorded other "disruptions and disasters." Powell described himself as an "Out Door Photographer in all its Branches" and a preservationist of Pittsfield's history. On July 6, 1910, he took this photograph of a train derailment in Coltsville, in east Pittsfield. The photograph does not identify the train, but the Boston & Albany Railroad served Pittsfield and had tracks in this area.

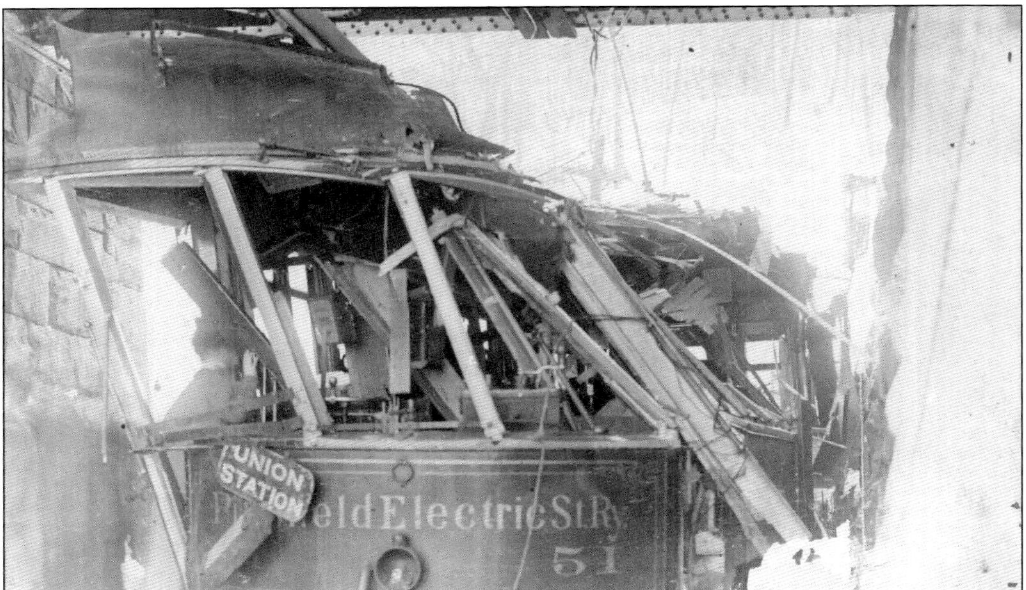

On February 9, 1910, Pittsfield Electric Street Railway car No. 51 was damaged beyond repair. The crash occurred on the 6:15 a.m. trip on East Street in Dalton during the Hinsdale to Pittsfield run and was known as the Gaffney Bridge Wreck. At an estimated speed of 50 miles per hour, the trolley failed to make a curve and left the track. Most of the 70 passengers were seriously injured, and one died.

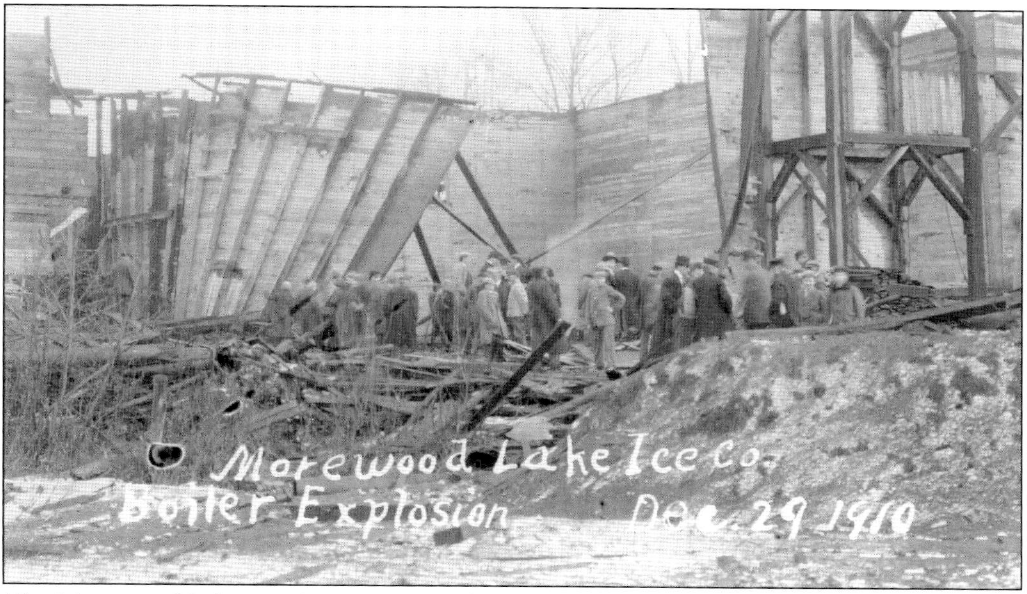

The Morewood Lake Ice Company was first certified to cut, sell, and store ice in January 1901. The $10,000 operation, with a separate boiler room and icehouses, was built on the lake's northeast shore. The boiler furnished the power to haul ice cakes up the incline to the storage houses. Morewood Lake, part of Sara Morewood's 230-acre estate, Broadhall, was sold to the Pittsfield Country Club in 1899.

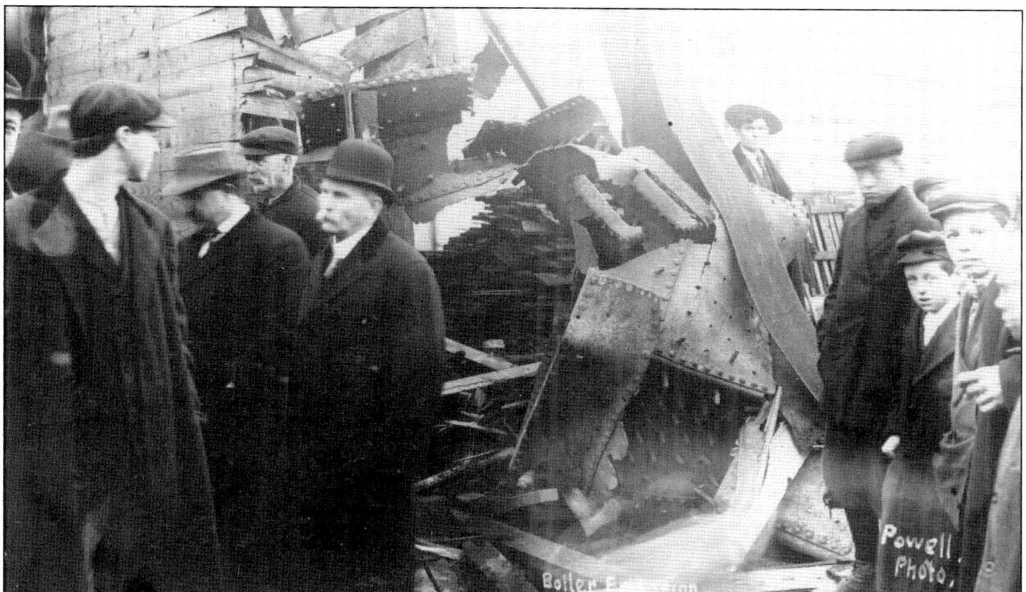

On the morning of December 29, 1910, as 125 men responded to the Morewood Ice Company's advertisement for day workers, a boiler exploded in the power house. Fourteen men died instantly, 3 died later of their injuries, and 20 men were seriously injured. The accident was described as one of the worst disasters in Pittsfield's history. A relief fund of $10,000 was established to help the victims and their families.

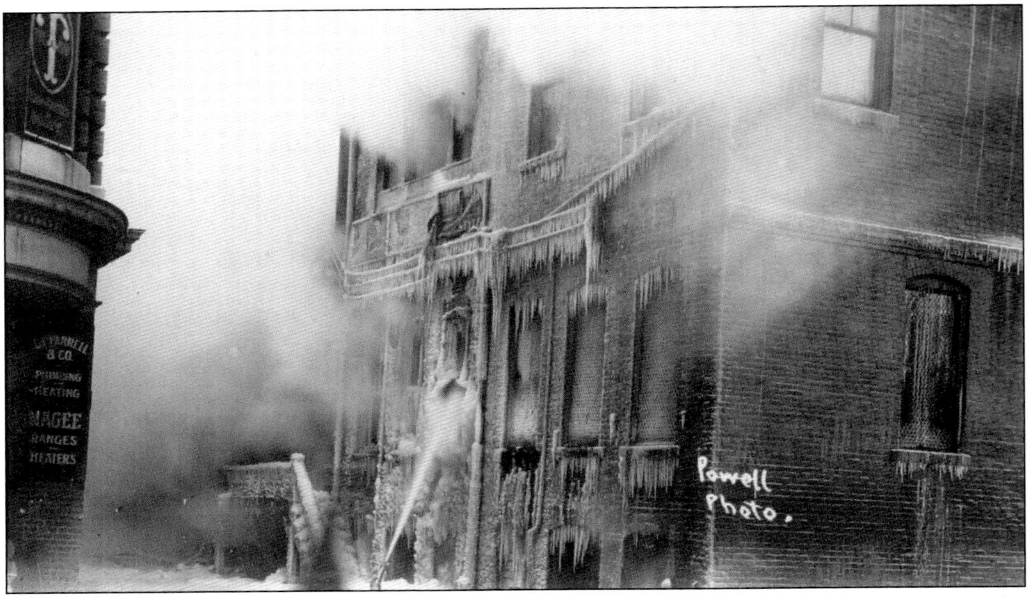

Firemen worked to prevent a serious conflagration from spreading to the businesses across the street. In 1914, Charles Lawton, a tea and coffee merchant, was at 30 Eagle Street, and D.F. Farrell's plumbing and heating firm was at 20 Eagle Street. Pittsfield's largest ever number of fire alarms, according to historian Edward Boltwood, numbered 219 in 1914 due to the work of a local "incendiary," who was finally arrested.

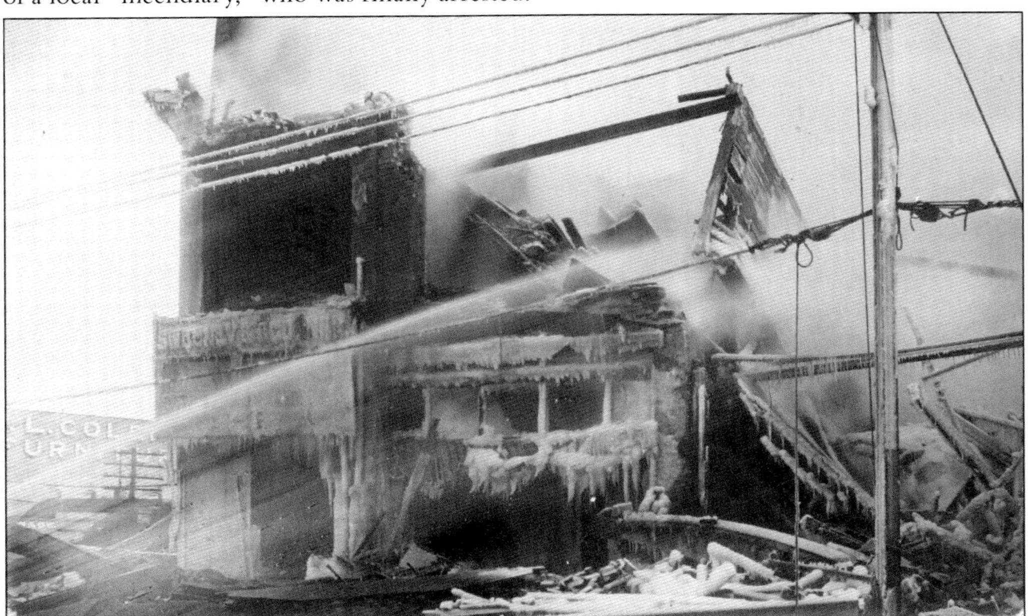

Once again, Matthew Powell, whose photographic supplies and framing business was located at 184 North Street, was on the scene. This time, he witnessed the fiery destruction of Sweeney & O'Connor's clothing business at 194–196 North Street. The W.L. Coleman furniture store at 242 North Street can be seen in the background. There were a series of disastrous fires on North Street in 1912.

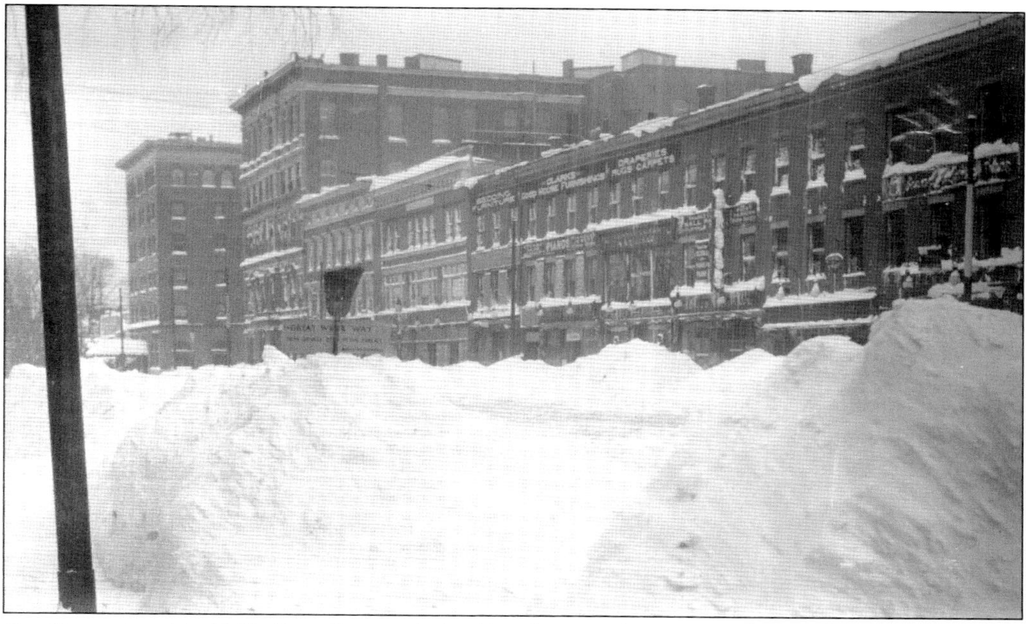

On December 14, 1915, Powell recorded a bit of winter humor by photographing this broom handle pushed into the snowbank, with this notice attached to it: "The Great White Way, Now Officially Open to the Public." It was signed "Bored of Pittsfield." Conducting business was definitely a challenge for anyone trying to reach Clark's Home Furnishings, Berkshire Life, or the Hotel Wendell.

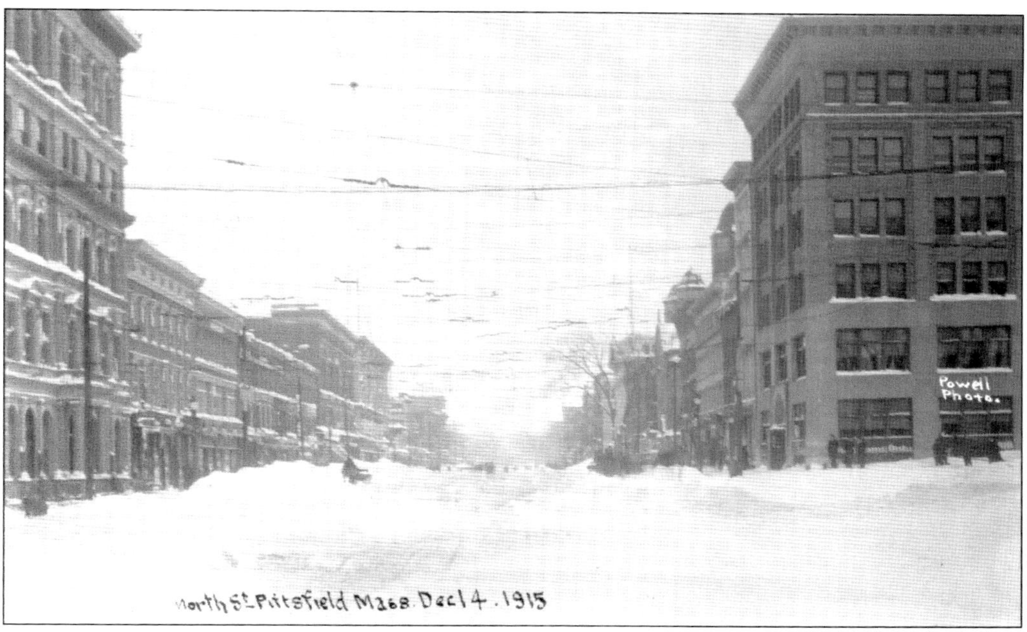

A major winter storm, captured by Matthew Powell on December 14, 1915, shows a snowbound North Street. Often, teams of men were hired to remove the snow by hand. The trolley wires are visible, with a trolley car barely visible in the distance, well beyond England Brothers (left) and the Agricultural Bank (right).

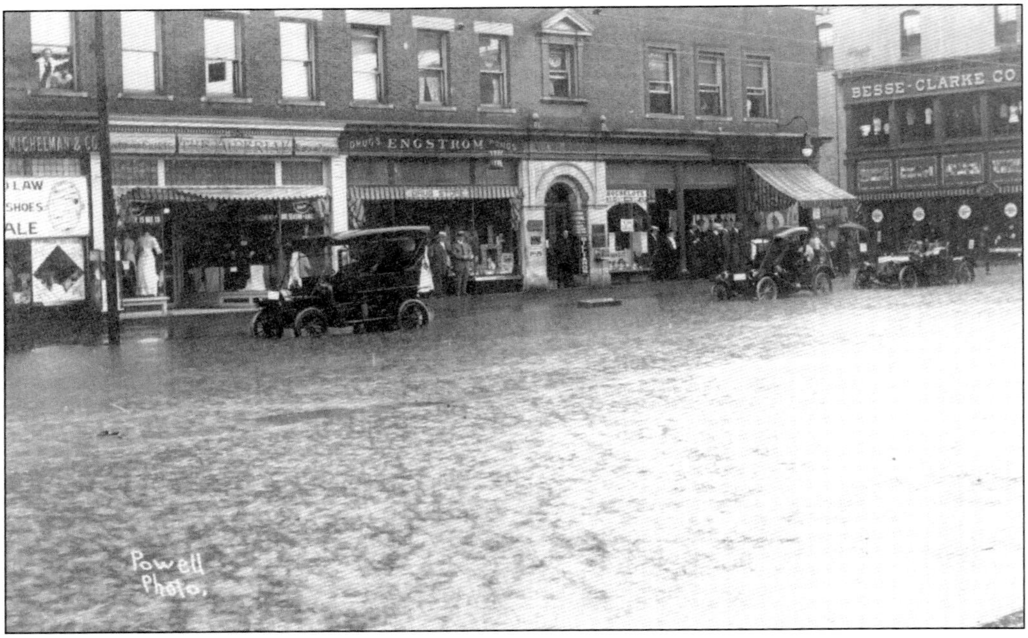

On July 29, 1914, Pittsfield had a tremendous rain and hailstorm. Mike, the sender of this postcard, wrote, "This was the condition of North Street Wednesday noon. The water was up to some of the stores' front doors . . . North Street looked like an ocean." This Powell postcard is looking northwest toward Besse-Clarke Co. at the corner of North and Summer Streets.

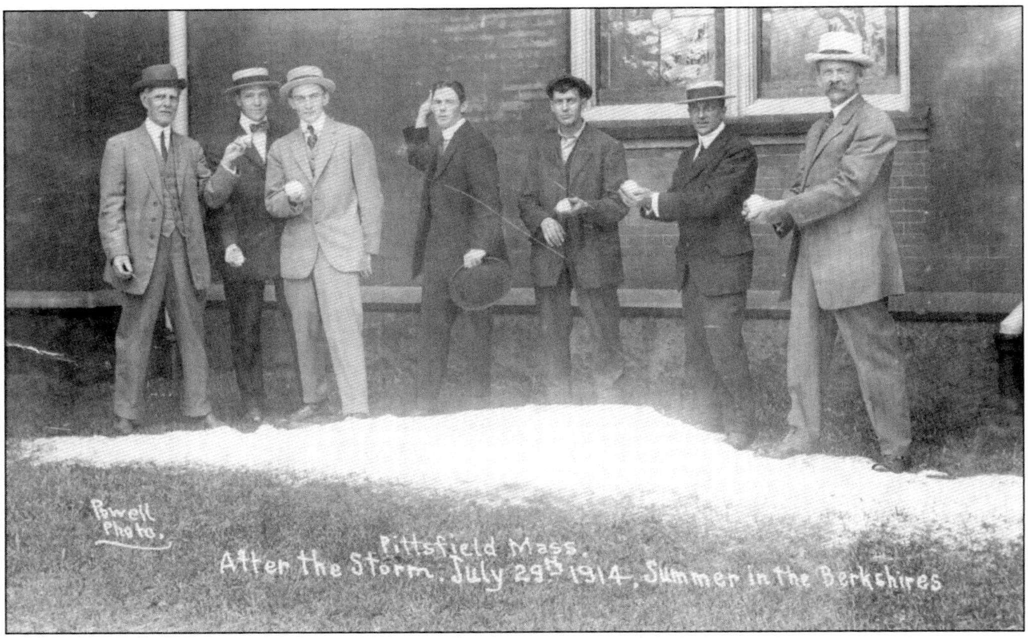

These seven gentlemen, some with straw hats and summer suits, were enjoying the remnants of the July 29, 1914, hailstorm. One Pittsfield citizen wrote, "The ground was white with hailstones this morning. It was very cold." Photographer Powell captured what looked like a "hail ball" rather than a snowball fight. The exact location of this photograph is unknown.

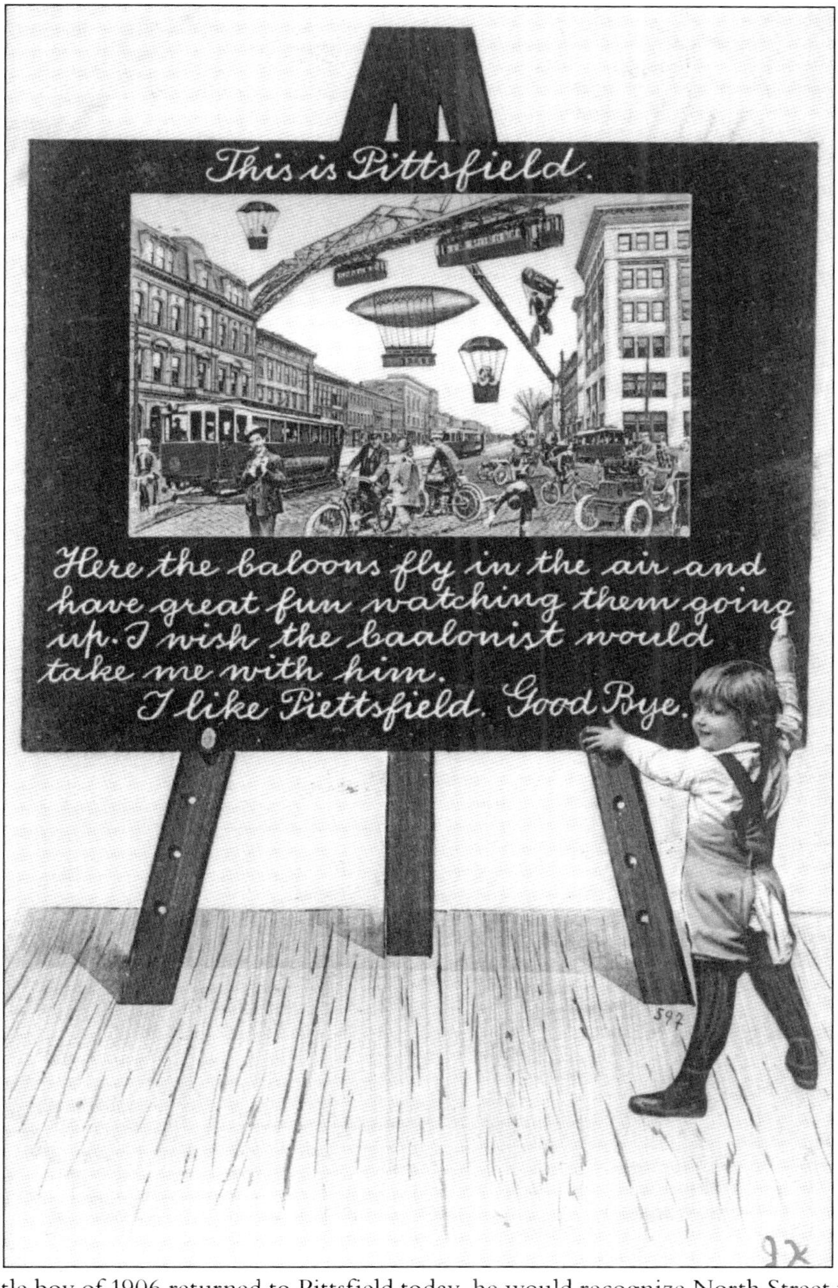

If this little boy of 1906 returned to Pittsfield today, he would recognize North Street with the old Berkshire Life Building (left) and the Berkshire Bank Building (right). And although the trolleys are gone, buses, modern cars, and motorbikes still circle Park Square. Airplanes use the newly expanded Pittsfield Airport, and passenger trains stop at the new station on Columbus Avenue. On the east side of the city, Aero Park is now the Mark Belanger Youth Athletic Facility, where baseballs fly instead of hot-air balloons. The vast area once occupied by General Electric factories is slowly refilling with new industries. As Pittsfield moves into the future, it retains those historic characteristics that gave it the name Gem City of the Berkshires.